T0301011

ROUTLEDGE LIBRARY EDITIONS: URBAN AND REGIONAL ECONOMICS

Volume 3

REGIONAL DEVELOPMENT

REGIONAL DEVELOPMENT

Problems and Policies in Eastern and Western Europe

Edited by
GEORGE DEMKO

Routledge
Taylor & Francis Group

LONDON AND NEW YORK

First published in 1984 by Croom Helm

This edition first published in 2018
by Routledge
2 Park Square, Milton Park, Abingdon, Oxon OX14 4RN

and by Routledge
605 Third Avenue, New York, NY 10017

Routledge is an imprint of the Taylor & Francis Group, an informa business

© 1984 George J. Demko

British Library Cataloguing in Publication Data
A catalogue record for this book is available from the British Library

ISBN: 978-1-138-09590-8 (Set)
ISBN: 978-1-315-10306-8 (Set) (ebk)
ISBN: 978-1-138-10193-7 (Volume 3) (hbk)
ISBN: 978-1-315-10328-0 (Volume 3) (ebk)

Publisher's Note
The publisher has gone to great lengths to ensure the quality of this reprint but points out that some imperfections in the original copies may be apparent.

Disclaimer
The publisher has made every effort to trace copyright holders and would welcome correspondence from those they have been unable to trace.

REGIONAL DEVELOPMENT
PROBLEMS AND POLICIES IN
EASTERN AND WESTERN
EUROPE

Edited by
GEORGE DEMKO

CROOM HELM
London & Sydney

© 1984 George J. Demko
Croom Helm Ltd, Provident House, Burrell Row,
Beckenham, Kent BR3 1AT
Croom Helm Australia Pty Ltd, First Floor, 139 King Street,
Sydney, NSW 2001, Australia

British Library Cataloguing in Publication Data

Regional development problems and policies in
Eastern and Western Europe.
   1. Regional planning—Europe—History
   2. Europe—Economic policy
   I. Demko, George
   330.94'055   HC240

   ISBN 0-7099-0851-2

This volume is a result of a conference sponsored and supported
by the Joint Committee on Eastern Europe of the American Council
of Learned Societies and the Social Science Research Council, with
funds provided by the Ford Foundation and the National Endowment
for the Humanities; the conference took place at the Bellagio
Conference and Study Center (Lake Como, Italy), which was made
available by the Rockefeller Foundation.

Printed and bound in Great Britain
by Billing & Sons Limited, Worcester.

CONTENTS

PART IV: National Case Studies in Regional Development

PART V: Summary and Conclusion

TABLES

Tables

FIGURES

PREFACE

     This volume is the result of a conference held in 1982
at the Rockefeller Center in Bellagio, Italy. The
conference was generously funded by the American Council of
Learned Societies with additional support from the
International Research and Exchanges Board and the
Rockefeller Foundation. The idea for a meeting of
specialists on the theme of European regional development
issues originated in the Joint Committee on Eastern Europe
of the ACLS.
     The conference was focused on problems of regional
development in Eastern and Western Europe (1) including
regional economic and social inequalities, lagging and
backward regions, and biased and constricted flows of labor
and capital to name a few. The issue of regional policies
and their effectiveness in addressing the problems was
included within the purview of the conference. Among the
basic assumptions of the conference organizers was that
these issues were and are of some significance in both
Europes, that the area contains a wide array of examples of
regional development problems, and that such problems are,
in large measure, independent of ideology and socio-
political system.
     The overarching goal of the conference was to bring
together leading specialists in the regional development
field from both West and East with specially prepared papers
on themes common to both Europes which would provoke
comparisons, analyses, discussion and identification of
important research questions of mutual interest and benefit.
The basic design of the conference included five sections:
theoretical aspects of regional development, identifying and
measuring variations in levels of regional development,
specific policy instruments and measures adopted to
intervene in regional development processes, current trends
and directions in regional development in Europe, and,
finally, a set of European case studies reflecting the range
of issues in regional development.

Whether the conference was a success or not is a very difficult and complicated judgement. If the intensity of the discussions and excitement generated by the papers are the criteria used, it was a great success. If one uses new contacts established, additional research and publications stimulated, and spin-off activities generated, then it again may be favorably rated. Further judgements will be made as many of these related activites are completed and as this volume is utilized.

The conference organizer and editor owes many people a debt of gratitude for help and encouragement rendered. Dr. Jason Parker of ACLS was always helpful and patient over the entire period of organization and implementation. Dr. Gordon Turner, former Vice President of ACLS, must be acknowledged for his original decision to turn the conference idea over to me. I hope I have confirmed his judgements.

Roland Fuchs, my collaborator and friend of more than twenty years and originally my co-organizer, is owed a great debt for all his help in the original planning of the conference. Dr. Sam Natoli of the Association of American Geographers and Dr. Ayse Gedik were invaluable as co-coordinators during the conference and contributed greatly to the success of the proceedings. I am particularly grateful to all the participants who entered into the spirit of the conference with zest and enthusiasm and thereby created a most stimulating set of sessions both intellectually and personal. Thanks are extended to Michelle Tufford who was essentially the unpaid secretary to the conference during the entire organizational period and underpaid manuscript preparer in the post-conference stage. Her contribution was enormous, unflagging and professional.

Finally, to my wife Jeanette I owe both thanks and apologies. Her lot has ever been to support, encourage, endure the work but rarely share the rewards and pleasures of such endeavors as these. May her time to share arrive soon and be worth the wait.

George J. Demko
Washington, D.C.

NOTES

1. The Soviet Union was not included explicitly in the coverage of the conference. Although this was an arbitrary decision it may be justified in part in that it is difficult if not impossible to obtain a commitment from a specific Soviet scholar to participate and thus pre-planning would be difficult at best. In addition, the scale of the USSR

renders it relatively incomparable with most East and West European nations. Nevertheless, the USSR's problems, trends and policies were frequently a part of the discussions and even some of the papers.

LIST OF PARTICIPANTS

Dr. Brian ASHCROFT
Department of Economics
University of Strathclyde
Glasgow, Scotland

Dr. Ellen BRENNAN
Population Affairs Division
United Nations
New York, New York
U.S.A.

Dr. Attilio CELANT
Faculty of Economics and Commerce
University of Rome
Rome, Italy

Professor John W. COLE
Department of Anthropology
University of Massachusetts
U.S.A.

Dr. George J. DEMKO
Director in the Office of the Geographer,
US Department of State,
Washington D.C.

Dr. György ENYEDI
Institute of Geography
Hungarian Academy of Sciences
Hungary

Dr. H. FOLMER
State University, Geographical Institute
Groningen
The Netherlands

Dr. Ayse GEDIK
Department of City and Regional Planning
The Ohio State University
U.S.A.

Professor Niles HANSEN
Department of Economics
The University of Texas
U.S.A.

Dr. Michael HECHTER
Department of Sociology
University of Washington
U.S.A.

Professor George W. HOFFMAN
Department of Geography
University of Texas at Austin
U.S.A.

Dr. L. LACKO
Deputy Director
Department of Physical Planning and Regional Development
Ministry of Building and Urban Development
Hungary

Dr. Jose R. LASUEN
Autonomous University of Madrid
Madrid, Spain

Dr. Sam NATOLI
Association of American Geographers
Washington, D.C.
U.S.A.

Dr. A. PEPEONIK
Greografiske Zavod
Zagreb, Yugoslavia

Dr. Harry RICHARDSON
State University of New York, Albany
and University of Southern California
U.S.A.

Dr. Allan RODGERS
Department of Geography
Pennsylvania State University
U.S.A.

Dr. Michel SAVY
Ministre D'etat
Ministre Du Plan et de l'Amenagement du Territoire
Paris, France

Dr. Walter STOHR
Interdisciplinary Institute for Urban and Regional Studies
University of Economics
Vienna, Austria

Dr. Andrzej WROBEL
Institute of Geographical and Spatial Organization
Polish Academy of Sciences
Warsaw, Poland

Dr. Henry ZIMON
Geography and Computer Science Department
West Point Academy
West Point, New York
U.S.A.

To Megan Elizabeth and Kerstin Sinnika – my greatest
   problems and pleasures in development.

PART I: THEORETICAL ASPECTS OF REGIONAL DEVELOPMENT

INTRODUCTION

George J. Demko

The original plan for this volume included sets of paired papers, one for Eastern Europe and one for Western Europe, on each theme included in the original conference at Bellagio. In most cases this was accomplished with one major exception. The paper on theoretical aspects of regional development in the Eastern European socialist context could not be arranged. A limited review-type discussion on this topic is attempted at the end of this introduction.

The volume is made up of five parts. Western regional development theory is discussed at some length by Harry Richardson at the outset. Part II addresses the issue of regional development trends in both Europes. General trends and concerns in Western Europe and Eastern Europe are reviewed by George Hoffman, and Gyorgy Enyedi reviews the issues of the quality and numbers of development indicators utilized to measure regional disparities in Europe. The section is concluded with a paper by Niles Hansen on recent development in economic integration and the new regionalism in Europe.

The third part of the volume focuses upon the policy measures and instruments employed in Europe to ameliorate regional disparities and the question of success. G. Demko and R. Fuchs describe and compare the wide array of particular measures which have been adopted by governments in Eastern and Western Europe. Brian Ashcroft's paper carefully assesses the effectiveness of regional policies in Western Europe and L. Lacko addresses this issue in Eastern Europe. The final paper of the section by W. Stohr and F. Todtling centers on the types of variables used in evaluating regional development policies and the complexity of this problem.

The fourth part of the volume contains a set of national case studies of regional development problems and policies. The situation in Italy is reviewed by A. Rodgers, Poland by A. Wrobel and France by M. Savy. An historical-political analysis of the Spanish case is offered by J. R. Lasuen as the final study of the section. It should be noted that the case studies were intended to be representative rather than exhaustive.

The final section of the volume, Part V, is designed to bring some issues together and to look ahead. The paper by Harry Richardson focused on regional policy in a slow growth situation is the result of discussions at the Bellagio Conference. The probability of slow growth economies in the near future led the discussions time and again to the question of regional policy's fate under such conditions. Stimulated by these deliberations and provoked by the editor, Professor Richardson produced an appropriate final paper.

As noted above, the only major _lacuna_ in terms of the original plan for this volume is that of regional development theory from an Eastern European perspective. Thus a general perspective is offered here as a background for the Eastern European case.

The goals of regional policy put forth in the socialist nations of Europe are tied closely to appropriate statements of Marx, Engels or Lenin. Most of the general goals are broadly stated, sometimes contradictory statements. The goal of regional economic equality is stated in terms of the development of a uniform distribution of productive forces. Further, such equality is described as equilizing levels of economic well-being at all scales, regional, urban-rural, etc. Marx's admonition regarding the "idiocy of rural life" is frequently cited in the latter case.

Other goals or general principles include the minimization of transport costs with regard to raw materials, markets and other factors and the promotion of regional specialization where resources permit.

Such a loosely structured regional development framework has been of little practical utility and hence, recently, refinements and modifications have been promulgated. The equality goal in regional levels of development has been altered to read "more equitable." There have been elucidated specific prohibitions on the location of industry which require large quantities of labor or other limited resources in regions of their deficit. The locational attraction of energy, markets or raw materials are now being distinguished by industry type.

However, even as regional and national location theory evolves toward a more specific and applicable body of tenets there continues the dominance of _sectoral planning_ which is dedicated to economic _efficiency_ rather than _equity_. Further compounding this problem is the difficulty or in many cases, the lack of coordination among the many economic planning and implementing bodies of these highly complex, centrally planned systems. Unfortunately, interesting and

2

potentially useful notions in regional development such as the territorial production complex used in the USSR have been poorly assessed and have not spread to Eastern Europe.

With this general view of the theoretical aspects of regional development in the East, attention should now be turned to the West.

APPROACHES TO REGIONAL DEVELOPMENT THEORY IN WESTERN-MARKET
ECONOMIES

Harry W. Richardson

An Empirical Frame for Theory

It is not possible to give a comprehensive review of
all regional development theories relevant to market
economies in one paper. The major criterion for selection
adopted here is that each theory discussed should be capable
of shedding some light on long-term interregional development trends in Western European countries. This does not
mean that the predictions of each model should be exactly
satisfied. Such a requirement would be impossible because
the experiences in Western Europe are quite varied. Nor
does it mean that there should necessarily be a close
correspondence between the key predictions of the mainline
model and observed regional development trends (e.g. the
"naive" neoclassical model predicts interregional per capita
income convergence which has indeed occurred in Western
Europe). Many of the theories to be discussed can generate
different predictions by varying some of the assumptions or
as a result of changes in parametric variables. For
instance a revised neoclassical model can produce interregional income divergence while a cumulative causation
model can, if the coefficients of the models fulfill certain
conditions, result in convergence. In other cases, the
basic theory can be expanded to produce results that are
different from those implied by the most simple version of a
model. An illustration of this is where the core-periphery
polarization associated with primitive versions of the
cumulative causation model will break down if a shift in the
locus of cumulative causation forces from the core to the
periphery takes place, and can be explained.

Since this paper is not concerned with the empirical
testing of alternative hypotheses implied by different
models, the selection criterion is simply that each theory
discussed should be generally helpful in understanding some
aspect of interregional development trends in Western Europe
or be relevant to an interpretation of trends in some
particular country. To make a judgment on this point it is

4

necessary to summarize some of the conclusions of recent
empirical research. Also, much of the research refers to a
period ending in 1970 (in a few cases 1975), and there are
some grounds for suspicion that, as in the United States,
major shifts or at least marked changes in pace may have
taken place in the 1970s. Furthermore, the geographical
scope of different studies varies. While some are national
in scope, others refer to the European Economic Community
countries (at different dates) and yet others deal with
Western Europe as a whole or with a particular subset.
Hence, to summarize the research results in a few paragraphs
is far from easy.

The following generalizations, however, appear
reasonable:

1) There is a wide variation in experience among
countries so that any generalization in terms of experience
in Western Europe as a whole has to be expressed very
cautiously.

2) The process of population concentration continued
within most West European countries between 1950 and 1970,
but there was a slight reduction in population density
disparities across EEC countries (1).

3) After 1970, on the other hand, population became
more dispersed in most European countries. The evidence for
this is largely based on a sharp decline in net internal
migration to an overbounded core region in each country; in
many cases net migration became negative (2).

4) Between 1950 and 1970 there was a marked decrease
in regional per capita income disparities both within and
between EEC countries (3). However, this convergence has
little to do with the integration process of the EEC itself
since "the creation of a customs and also the formation of a
monetary union may well lead to increased regional disparities (4)." Instead, the main convergence force within
countries was the shift of population from low-to-high
income regions while between countries it was the fact that
lower income countries tended to experience higher rates of
per capita growth GDP (5). However, regional growth rates
tended to cluster in national blocs rather than be explained
in terms of an EEC-wide core-periphery pattern. This
suggests the dominance of national influences over the
concept of the EEC as a system of regions.

5) Since 1970, on the other hand (more specifically,
over the period 1970-77) disparities among EEC regions have
increased, though convergence among regions within countries
has continued (6). These variations in experiences reinforce the hypothesis that national influences predominate.

6) In spite of these convergence forces, per capita
income differentials between regions within each country and
across countries remained wide. For example, in Italy in
1970 the per capita gross value added ratio of the highest

5

(Liguria) to the lowest (Calabria) region was 2.63, in the United Kingdom it was 1.43, in West Germany 2.62, France 2.09, Belgium 1.66, the Netherlands 1.56, Ireland 1.60 and in Denmark 1.45 (7). Across countries, the extremes were even wider. For instance, GNP per capita in Portugal, Greece, Spain and Ireland in 1978 was only 16.4 percent, 26.9 percent, 28.7 percent and 28.7 percent respectively of the level in Switzerland. Within the EEC, GNP per capita in Greece was 32.8 percent, Ireland 35.0 percent, and Italy 38.8 percent of Denmark's (8). These data imply that convergence forces work slowly, even within countries with policies in operation to narrow regional income differences. This evidence should be kept in mind when extolling the predictive accuracy of regional convergence theories.

7) Considering the national space economy as a system of urban regions, the timing of decentralization of population from metropolitan cores to rings observed in European countries since 1960 has varied from one case to another. The United Kingdom led the way with Scandinavia following after a lag of about a decade. While decentralization was apparent in Belgium and the Netherlands by 1970, in France the cores continued to grow faster than the rings even into the 1970s (on the other hand, non-metropolitan areas in France simultaneously experienced acceleration in their growth). By the 1960s both jobs and people were decentralizing in Switzerland and Austria, but in Germany jobs continued to centralize. Finally, metropolitan concentration continued in Spain, Portugal and Italy throughout the period 1950-1975 though by the 1970s the core areas' growth slowed relative to the rings. This confusing picture is difficult to generalize. In the words of Hall and Hay (9):

> from 1950 to 1975 the European urban system was failing to operate like that in the United States. The tendency was still for population to move from rural to urban areas, not the reverse. The industrial heartland was still strong, and the remoter rural areas were still losing. There was a drift to the sunbelt, but for reasons quite different from those obtaining in the United States. Even the movement from central urban core to suburban ring was more tardy than in North America, with Atlantic Europe in the vanguard and southern Europe in the rear of the process (10).

8) As the preceding quotation suggests, the experience of the United States is relevant to any assessment of regional development trends in Western market economies, partly as the first country to enter the "post-industrial age," partly because of the continued dominance of an

ideological commitment to the efficiency of market forces
and a distaste for explicit spatial intervention. It is
widely believed that, with certain qualifications, the
United States experience today is a harbinger of what might
happen in Western Europe tomorrow. For these reasons it may
be helpful to discuss the United States experience in more
detail.

Spatial changes in the United States are taking the
following paths: down the urban hierarchy from larger to
smaller urban areas; outwards within metropolitan areas from
cores to rings; outwards from metropolitan to non-metropolitan areas; and across the country from the older regions
of the Northeast and the Midwest dominated by manufacturing
cities to the newly industrializing and urbanizing regions
of the South and West, the cities of which have a stronger
service orientation (11). Of these trends, the last (the
so-called Frostbelt-Sunbelt shift) is the most important in
this context. The population shifts, paralleled by
differential rates of job growth, from the Northeast and
Midwest to the South and West are of long duration (they
have been evident in the data for more than fifty years),
though they have accelerated in the 1970s. The four census
regions of the Northeast and Midwest accounted for 59.2
percent of U.S. population in 1930; by 1970 this share had
declined to 51.9 percent, and in 1980 it was down to 47.7
percent. In the last decade, two States have lost
population, New York (-3.8 percent) and Rhode Island (-0.3
percent) (12). There was net outmigration between 1970 and
1980 from three census regions (the Middle Atlantic, East
North Central and West North Central), while net inmigration
contributed 55-68 percent of the population of four of the
five regions of the South and West (the exception was the
East South Central region where the migration share was only
45 percent).

The shifts in regional income shares and the associated
interregional income convergence were more dramatic than
those of population. The Northeast and Midwest share of
personal income fell from 71.5 percent of the U.S. total in
1930 to 55.2 percent in 1970 and again to 49.4 percent in
1980. As a result, there was a marked convergence in
regional per capita incomes. As shown in Table 1.1, per
capita income levels in New England, Middle Atlantic and, to
a lesser extent, East North Central converged downwards
towards the national average, whereas incomes in the South
Atlantic, East and West South Central and Mountain regions
converged upwards. The West North Central region is a
frostbelt region with below-average income levels that have
converged slowly upwards, while the Pacific region has
consistently been a high-income region that converged
downwards between 1930 and 1970, but enjoyed a minor
reversal in the 1970s. The gap between the poorest and the

7

Table 1.1: Personal Income Per Capita in U.S. Census
Regions as a Percent of the U.S. Average, 1930, 1970 and
1980

Region	1930	1970	1980
New England	129.2	109.2	106.1
Middle Atlantic	147.6	113.1	106.4
East North Central	108.1	103.5	102.7
West North Central	85.0	94.7	98.1
South Atlantic	64.0	91.4	92.0
East South Central	43.2	74.8	78.1
West South Central	58.0	84.7	95.4
Mountain	83.7	91.6	94.5
Pacific	124.4	111.4	112.6
U.S.	100.0	100.0	100.0
Lowest/Highest Ratio	.393	.661	.694

Source: 1930 - U.S. Department of Commerce, Regional Trends
in the United States Economy; 1970, 1980 - Survey of Current
Business, July 1981.

most prosperous region narrowed rapidly, especially before 1970. The U.S. data indicate a clear-cut pattern of inter-regional population dispersion combined with a marked degree of interregional population dispersion combined with a marked degree of interregional per capita income convergence to be contrasted with the somewhat blurred and certainly more heterogeneous picture suggested by Western European data.

This brief discussion of regional development trends in Western market economies provides a backcloth of casual empiricism for the analysis of relevant regional development theories (13).

Mixed not Market Economies

Although the title of this paper refers to "market economies," it is obvious that there are no such entities in the real world. All Western economies are to varying degrees "mixed," characterized by both explicit and implicit spatial intervention. Income and welfare differences among regions are narrowed by the operation of automatic fiscal stabilizers and by public investment policies that tend to allocate infrastructure among areas according to criteria that stress "fair shares" (e.g. equal expenditures per capita). Moreover, most Western European governments have implemented explicit regional policies to aid lagging regions. Although the policy mix varies from one country to another, common ingredients include fiscal incentives to induce the private sector to move to or start up in lagging regions:

> ranging from capital grants to interest-subsidized loans, from accelerated-depreciation allowances to direct tax concessions, from employment premia to rent subsidies, from concessions on electricity prices to labor-training aids, and from removal-cost assistance to transport subsidies (14),"

locational discrimination in infrastructure, public enterprise activities in backward regions, and the use of direct controls on, or disincentives to, development in the more prosperous regions. Furthermore, even in countries without a consistent regional development policy (e.g. the United States), there exist a variety of place-oriented policies while national government expenditures (e.g. on defense) are not only sizeable but have markedly uneven regional impacts.

Given the range and scale of government intervention in the process of interregional development, it is not foolish to question the relevance of market models to explanations of this process. However, apart from the fact that it is very difficult to model the government sector, there are at least two justifications for perseverance with market models. First, many observers doubt that explicit regional policies have had much effect. "Much of what has been considered a success of regional development policies in the past decades may in reality have been due mainly to the market mechanism, which in periods of recent economic expansion has produced 'spillovers' from congested to less developed areas." Moreover, "traditional regional policy instruments recently practiced in most market trends but not attacked the basic parameters underlying spatial inequalities in living levels (15)." Second, the changes in the international and national economic environments since the early 1970s, and their most obvious consequence - the slowing down in national economic growth rates - have weakened the resolve of governments to promote regional development so that in some cases policy instruments have been abandoned while in others policies have been applied half-heartedly. In EEC countries this has been aggravated by the hostility of the European Commission's Competition Directorate (DG IV) to national policy measures that do not conform to its harmonization objectives and by the substitution of the diluted aid of the Regional Policy Directorate (DG XVI) for national assistance in some countries.

The Neoclassical Model

Given the dominance of neoclassical ideology in Western economies, it is hardly surprising that neoclassical models of regional development have received most attention in the literature on regional growth theory. A major appeal of the neoclassical model is that its simplest and most naive version predicts interregional per capita income convergence. If the following assumptions are made (full employment, perfect competition, a single homogeneous commodity, zero transport costs, identical production functions exhibiting constant returns to scale in all regions, a fixed labor supply, and zero technical progress), this model shows that the marginal product of labor (wage rate) and the marginal product of capital (rate of return to capital) are direct and inverse functions respectively of the capital-labor ratio. Labor will flow from low-to-high-wage regions and capital will flow in the opposite direction (since low (high) wages are associated with high (low) returns to capital) until factor returns are equalized in each region. Thus, the regional growth process is associated with a convergence in regional per capita incomes (16).

A more flexible variant of the model would allow for regional differences in production functions. From a regional production function of the type

$$Y_i = K_i{}^{a_i} L_i{}^{1-a_i} T_i \qquad \qquad -1-$$

10

where Y = output, K = capital, L = labor, T is a residual,
reflecting technical progress and similar considerations,
a = a parameter (o<a<1), and subscript i represents region
i, it is possible to drive the growth equation

$$y = a_i k_i + (1-a) l_i + t_i \qquad -2-$$

where y, k, l and t are the growth rates in output, capital,
labor and technical progress respectively. Furthermore,
since net investment is the sum of local savings and net
capital inflow minus depreciation,

$$k_i = s_i v_i^{-1} + \sum_j b_{ji} (a_i v_i^{-1} - a_j v_j^{-1}) - d_i \qquad -3-$$

where s = savings/output ratio, v = capital-output ratio,
b_{ji} = a parameter for converting the differential in the
marginal product of capital (a/v) between region i and
region j into a net capital import rate (k_{ji}) and d = annual
depreciation rate. Similarly, labor supply is the sum of
natural increase plus net inmigration so that

$$l_i = n_i + \sum_j c_{ji} (W_i - W_j) \qquad -4-$$

where n = rate of natural increase and c_{ji} = a parameter for
converting the differential in the regional wage (W) into a
net migration rate.

To achieve equilibrium growth in the interregional
system a mechanism is needed for equating investment with
full-employment savings. The national rate of interest r is
such a mechanism if a perfect capital market is assumed.
Thus, an equilibrium condition is that $r = a_i/v_i$ in each
region. Hence steady growth requires

$$r = a_i v_i^{-1} = a_i Y_i/K_i \qquad -5-$$

If r is given, output and capital must grow at the same rate
if a_i is to remain constant. Thus, $y_i = k_i$. Substituting
for k_i in equation 1:

$$y_i = k_i = t_i/(1 + a_i) + l_i \qquad -6-$$

In the special case of zero technical progess ($t_i = 0$),
output, capital and labor must all grow at the same rate to
achieve steady growth. However, the equilibrium growth rate
does <u>not</u> have to be the same in <u>all</u> regions. Borts and
Stein (17) showed that equilibrium growth rates in output
could vary among regions because of differential growth
rates in labor supply, if the demand for labor is perfectly
elastic. This result is compatible with equalized rates of
return to capital and labor in all regions, because demand
adjustment to a faster rate of increase in labor supply

11

implies that a faster rate of growth in output will not lead
to higher wages. Growth is clearly supply-determined in
this model. The requirements for equilibrium growth become
more complicated if the zero technical progress assumption
is dropped. Moreover y_i and k_i may be permitted to diverge
if the capital-output ratio (v_i^i) is variable. Also, it is
possible to introduce variable returns to scale (18). But
these refinements need not be considered here.

A Cumulative Causation Model

The main rival to the neoclassical model is the class
of theories known as cumulative causation (CC) models. The
simplest versions of these models predict regional income
divergence, though this prediction is by no means an
inevitable consequence of adopting this model. The major
difference between the "naive" versions of the CC and
neoclassical models is that the CC approach requires
increasing returns to scale rather than assuming constant
returns. As a result, both capital and labor flow in the
same direction rather than in opposite directions. Not only
may growth rate differentials persist over time they _may_
become wider as long as the increasing returns to scale
effect continues. The attraction of CC models is not so
much their predictions as the fact that they are compatible
with the existence of agglomeration economies that many
regional economists consider to be an important determinant
of regional growth performance.

There are many variants of the CC model. The first but
loose conception was by Myrdal (19) who argued that regional
inequality will tend to increase over time as a few leading
regions exploit initial advantages that become self-sustaining. Linkages between the growing and lagging regions will
be both favorable (spread effects) and unfavorable (backwash
effects), but the latter will tend to predominate. Dixon
and Thirlwall (20) developed a CC model in which growth was
export-led so that regional growth is a function of demand
for its exports. Although this is consistent with another
mainstream regional development model, the so-called export
base model, other growth triggers besides exports could be
allowed in a more general CC model.

Perhaps the simplest version of a CC model is based on
the idea that the rate of productivity growth is a function
of the growth rate in regional output (the so-called
Verdoorn effect). This relationship could reflect the
importance of agglomeration economies and increasing returns
to scale in regional development. Ignoring subscripts, we
may write

$$t = e + f y \qquad \qquad \text{-7-}$$

where f is the Verdoorn coefficient. Efficiency wages are

12

obtained by deflating an index of money wages with an index of productivity. The rate of growth in efficiency wages (w) will therefore be inversely related to the rate of technical progress

$$w = g - ht \qquad -8-$$

But, low efficiency wages will stimulate output growth if markets are competitive. Hence, the lower the rate of growth of efficiency wages the faster output grows:

$$y = m - pw \qquad -9-$$

Substituting equations 7 and 8 into 9, and introducing a time term, yields

$$y_{t+1} = m + p \ (eh - g) + fhpy_t \qquad -10-$$

or $\qquad y_{t+1} = x + zy_t \qquad -11-$

where $x = m + p$ (eh - g) and $z = fhp$, where $z < 0$ (by assumption). To find the equilibrium growth rate (y^*), we set $y^* = y_t = y_{t+1}$ in equation 11 and solve for y^* to obtain

$$y^* = x/(1-z) = [m+p \ (eh-g)] \ (1-fhp)^{-1} \qquad -12-$$

The general solution to the first-order linear equation 11 is

$$y_t = (y^0 - y^*) \ z^t + y^0 \qquad -13-$$

where y^0 is the initial rate. It is important to note that this model generates cumulative growth <u>only</u> if the coefficients of the model have particular values. The conditions for cumulative growth are that $z > 1$ (implying $x < 0$) and that $y^0 > y^*$. Interestingly, the only test of this particular model (21) showed that in Canada $z < 1$ so that the interregional growth process was convergent rather that cumulative. On the other hand, the signs of the regression coefficients of equations 7 - 9 were all correct, i.e. $f > 0$, $h < 0$, and $p < 0$. Moreover, since the values of the f coefficient varied widely among Canadian provinces, the test suggested that interregional growth differentials might persist even in equilibrium.

A Post-Keynesian Model

A version of a post-Keynesian demand model (22) of interregional growth may start with the concept of a probabilistic interregional savings-flow matrix

$$P = \sum_i \sum_j S_{ij} \qquad -14-$$

13

where S_{ij} = flow of savings from region i to region j.
Dividing each element of this matrix by its corresponding
sum we obtain a transitional probability matrix P* with
elements $p_{ij} = S_{ij}/S_i$. This matrix P* can be partitioned
into

$$P* = \left(\begin{array}{c|c} Q & R \\ \hline 0 & I \end{array} \right) \qquad -15-$$

where the Q matrix represents transient states and R is a
matrix of absorbing states. There is a matrix T with the
same dimensions as R such that

$$T = (I - Q)^{-1} R \qquad -16-$$

This contains the probabilities of inputs to the system
(i.e. savings) getting from each transient state (e.g. a
short-term savings institution in one on the regions) to
each absorbing state (fixed investment in one of the
regions). Eventually an equilibrium will be reached where
all savings are absorbed into investment in one or another
of the regions of the system.
Given an initial vector of regional savings (S^o) and a
diagonal matrix ($\hat{R}$) of intraregional absorption coefficients
we can derive an equilibrium distribution vector of capital
stock increments ($\Delta K*$), assuming that total system savings
= total investment,

$$\Delta K* = S^o (I - Q)^{-1} \hat{R} \qquad -17-$$

The system of regions can grow endogenously if a savings-
income and an output-capital stock relation are introduced
on Harrodian lines.

$$S = \hat{S}Y \qquad -18-$$

and

$$Y = \hat{V}^{-1} K \qquad -19-$$

where y + a vector of regional incomes, $\hat{S}$ = diagonal matrix
of regional propensities to save, and $\hat{V}$ = diagonal matrix of
regional capital-output ratios. Combining equations 18 and
19 and substituting $\hat{S}\hat{V}^{-1} K^o$ for S^o and ΔK^1 for $\Delta K*$ in
equation 17:

$$\Delta K^1 = \hat{S}\hat{V}^{-1} K^o (I - Q)^{-1} \hat{R} \qquad -20-$$

Since $K^1 = K^o + \Delta K^1$ $\qquad -21-$

$$K^1 = K^o + \hat{S}\hat{V}^{-1} K^o (I - Q)^{-1} \hat{R} \qquad -22-$$

By matrix multiplication, let

$$Z = \hat{S}\hat{V}^{-1} (I - Q)^{-1} \hat{R} \qquad -23-$$

$$\therefore K^1 = K^0 + K^0 Z \qquad -24-$$

$$= K^0 (I + Z) \qquad -25-$$

and by expansion

$$K^n = K^0 (I + Z)^n \qquad -26-$$

Thus, regional growth depends upon capital investment, and in particular the future interregional distribution of the capital stock depends upon its initial distribution and on the structural parameters of the system (propensities to save, capital-output ratios, the interregional savings flow matrix, and intraregional investment (absorbing) coefficients). The model allows the comparative static conditions of savings-investment equilibrium (i.e. total system savings = total system investment at the end of each period) to be satisfied within a framework of continuous growth (capital→ income → savings → additions to capital).

The important feature of this model is that there is no steady-state growth path (except as a result of flukes in coefficient values). Each region will grow at a different rate from its closed-economy growth path. Whether the growth paths converge or not depends upon the coefficients of the interregional savings flow matrix. However, if there are built-in polarization flows in favor of the higher-income regions (23), regional incomes will diverge over time. Also, by changing the coefficients the model can accommodate divergence in some phases of development and convergence in others; for example, it could be made compatible with Williamson's inverted-U curve measuring changes in an index of regional disparities over time (24).

Uneven Regional Development

A quite different approach from the more formal models discussed earlier is called "uneven regional development." In effect, this involves the application of neo-Marxist or other radical analyses to interpretations of interregional economic trends (25). Although the work tends to be theoretical or at least conceptual, it pays much more attention to institutional forces. Also, some of the research has an empirical component usually in the form of case studies illustrating the theory rather than in the form of hypothesis testing.

It is very difficult to summarize these theories in a few paragraphs because the literature reflects wide variations in points of view. For example, there is a debate as to whether analogues to imperialism, such as the internal colonialism model, are useful for explaining the persistent backwardness of lagging regions. The current tendency is to discredit this type of model, mainly because it ignores or at best underestimates, the significance of the class struggle. For instance, Lovering (26) argues that it is wrong to treat the Welsh experience as the subordination of a distinct society to a central elite (the English ruling class) with separatism seen as the solution. Instead, economic development in Wales is best understood as an example of capitalist uneven development.

A central proposition of the uneven regional development theorists is that regional growth differentials do not reflect the net result of the operation of abstract and impersonal market forces but the purposive actions of the capitalist class. Moreover, as long as capitalism survives, intervention to correct regional inequalities will be ineffectual because the State is merely the coercive instrument of capitalist class interests. In the spatial context capitalism manifests itself in several ways. First, there is the antagonism between the city and the countryside. The rural sector is exploited so as to extract its surplus for the benefit of urban capitalists. Cheap food allows the capitalists to keep down industrial wages while rural savings are diverted to the cities to fuel capital accumulation there (27). Second, the spatial concentration of production is not the result of market orientation (i.e. minimization of transport costs) or the uneven spatial distribution of raw materials but is explained by the centralization of capital into large production units, especially in manufacturing. Third, and related to the preceding point, the spatial penetration of capital is very uneven. Since capitalist decisions are motivated only by the pursuit of private profit rather than social benefit, there may be vast areas of a country that are chronically deprived of investment (a "permanent reserve of stagnant places") (28). These areas may be found at all spatial levels - interregionally (core-periphery), intraregionally (growth pole-hinterland) and within cities (ghetto-suburb). Fourth, capital is highly mobile, and this mobility offers many opportunities for exploitation. Examples include the shift of industry to the Southern United States to exploit nonunionized labor (29) and the development of ephemeral boomtowns as a response to the world energy crisis (30). Fifth, regional policies will have only marginal impacts in improving welfare because "the 'regional' element of policy is completely subsidiary" and a smokescreen for giving "a large subsidy to industrial capital to enable it to survive the profits squeeze (31)." To sum up, uneven regional development is an inevitable manifestation of the built-in crises and instability of capitalism, and "capitalist expansion and change produce regional inequality insofar as it is necessarily a by-product of personal inequality, the basis of capital accumulation (32)."

Of these influences, the mobility of capital is probably the most important, since sudden and dramatic shifts in the location of capital accumulation can have devastating impacts on area economic development (e.g. plant shutdowns in company towns). The extent of these shifts is intensified by the increasing internationalization of capital and the associate behavior of the multinational corporations. Advances in communications technologies have facilitated spatial separation between corporate head-quarters and production plants. As a result, head offices are heavily concentrated in a few world metropolises (Manhattan, London, Frankfurt, Zurich, Tokyo) while pro-duction operations are becoming more dispersed. According to Goldsmith (33), this is the overwhelmingly predominant trend in Western Europe. However, the decentralization of production plants into peripheral regions is not primarily to achieve real productivity gains but to raise profits by direct reductions in wage bills permitted by the social conditions (unemployment, weak unions, etc.) found in labor reserve regions (34). At the same time, in certain sectors (e.g. marine-related industries, petrochemical complexes) locational concentration into large "territorial production complexes" is necessary for survival. It is unclear whether or not the centralization forces dominate the dispersal tendencies.

Even where dispersal of economic activity and apparent convergency occur, the benefits are negligible. First, the penetration of peripheral regions in the developed countries is very unstable because capital may easily relocate if it becomes more profitable to exploit lower wages in the developing countries. Second, the rapidity of the shifts from the heartland to the periphery (especially in the United States) have exacerbated the problems of regional decline and stagnation in the heartland (Northeast and Midwest); capital has been scrapped sooner than necessary, a tendency aggravated by investment and tax policies. Third, the spatial penetration of lagging regions have been very uneven creating wide gaps in the rate of development <u>within</u> regions. Finally, the dispersal in economic activity has not been accompanied by improvements in the distribution of income because dispersal has taken place to raise profits and hold down wages rather than to raise general levels of welfare. Hence, interregional convergence in average incomes per capita has been associated with a worsening income distribution in leading and lagging regions alike.

<u>Regional Imbalance and Meso-Economic Power</u>
Holland (35) has developed a theory of regional

development that shares some affinity with the "uneven regional development" school in its emphasis on regional imbalance and the role of the capitalist industrial sector in generating and maintaining this imbalance. Holland also directly acknowledges the contributions of Marx: "there is a wealth of virtually unmined regional source material in Marx whose relevance to regional problems in contemporary capitalist economies is compelling (36)." However, the uneven regional development theorists repudiate Holland as an apologist for State capitalism.

Holland's text is, nevertheless, "as extension of imbalance or disequilibrium theory, and an attempt to demonstrate that the trend to regional inequality is intrinsic to capitalist economic growth (37)." He combines Marx's analysis of the concentration of capital (and long-term substitution of capital for labor) with Myrdal's principle on cumulative causation and Perroux's emphasis on unbalanced growth and polarization (38). His own specific contribution is to analyze the role in this process of two major trends in modern capitalism: the rise of meso-economic power in national economies and the spread of multi-national operations by very large firms. Holland argues the need for a new branch of economics, meso-economics, intermediate between macroeconomic theory and policy and the micro level of the small competitive firm. Meso-economics is concerned with the analysis of the behavior of the very large firms in the economy, the meso-economic sector. They dominate the economy (in Britain the top 100 manufacturing firms' control of net output rose from one-fifth in 1950 to one-half in 1970; it may reach two thirds by 1985), eliminating many of the small dependent satellites that provide them with inputs. From the point of view of spatial inequality these large firms and their satellites tend overwhelmingly to locate in the more developed regions. The result is a pattern of spatial dualism with the modern meso-economic firms concentrated in the developed regions and the small-scale, low productivity microeconomic firms concentrated in the lagging regions.

The situation has been aggravated by the rapid expansion of meso-economic firms into multinational operations. The regional incentives available for locating in the problem regions of developed countries are swamped by the profitability of using cheap labor in developing countries and the greater ease of extracting profits from these locations to tax havens abroad. As a result, when multinational meso-economic firms decentralize out of the core regions or establish branch plants they are likely to leapfrog the peripheral regions of the developed countries and choose profitable sites in developing countries.

In other words, regional meso-economics is concerned with the analysis of how the locational strategies and tactics pursued by large corporations distort the pattern of development reinforcing regional imbalances and counter-acting the spatial redistribution policies of national governments. The policy implications of this theory are the harnessing of meso-economic power by direct controls, large by conditional subsidies to priority growth sectors in lagging regions, "planning agreements" on location between the State and monopoly corporations, and above all by new public enterprise - direct State participation in production in growth industries.

Autonomous Growth Centers and the Life-Cycle Theory of Agglomeration Economies

As pointed out above, a feature of interregional development trends in the United States has been a redistribution of population from the metropolitan areas of the older industrial regions of the Northeast and Midwest to those of more recently developed regions of the South and West. The evidence of a similar trend in Western Europe is very sparse, in some cases because the major lagging regions in many Western European countries were stagnant industrial rather than newly developing areas, and elsewhere perhaps because of the European lag behind United States trends. However, on both sub-continents spatial development is more comprehensible in terms of the differential growth of nodal regions than of homogeneous regions. The expansion of urban (later metropolitan) areas has been the hub of regional growth, and these areas have grown because cities offered agglomeration economies to both firms and households. The spatial unevenness of development within regions suggests the relevance of growth pole (or growth center) analysis.

The concept of the growth pole was originally aspatial, i.e. limited to economic space. The basic idea focused on a propulsive industry and its linked industries that grow faster than the rest of the economy because of modern technology and high rates of innovation, income-elastic demand for their output in national and/or international markets, and large multiplier effects. Subsequently, the concept was applied to geographical space by spatially clustering this set of dynamic industries in an urban area and by concentrating the spillover and multiplier effects not over the economy as a whole but in the surrounding hinterland. In even later versions the growth pole was generalized to mean the geographical clustering of economic activity as a whole rather than interdependent sectors. The policy implication of this broadened concept is that the spatial concentration of economic activity induces faster regional development than dispersal.

However, even in this diluted form the growth pole concept is not very helpful to explanations of interregional trends in regional development, the focus of this paper.

There are two problems. First, the growth pole is almost
invariably conceived as an intraregional phenomenon functioning in the context of its hinterland. Second, the
growth pole or growth center is a link between theory and
regional policy much more than an obvious component of
regional development theory. However, these problems can be
resolved by conceptualizing a nationally dispersed system of
autonomous growth centers (AGCs) rather than a planned
growth pole within a single region (39).

These AGCs will grow at different rates at varying
points of time depending upon the strength of their
agglomeration economies and other locational advantages, and
there will be a high correlation between the growth rate of
an AGC and that of its surrounding region (40). An
interesting hypothesis to explain the southward and westward
shifts in the United States in the pace of metropolitan (and
hence regional) growth is that agglomeration economies
follow an inverted U-shape over the life-cycle of the city
(41). The older cities suffer from weakened agglomeration
economies which reduce their attractiveness for mobile
economic activities (and dampen the growth rates of existing
industries) while in the newer cities the opposite forces
are at work (42). The hypothesis remains theoretical,
because agglomeration economies are notoriously difficult to
measure (43).

It is worth noting that this hypothesis may be made
compatible with cumulative causation models if the shift in
the locus of cumulative advantages from the Northeast and
Midwest to the South and West can be explained
satisfactorily. The realization that the shifts in economic
activity and population have taken place rather slowly (and
go back more than 50 years) makes the life-cycle theory of
agglomeration economies a more convincing explanation since
they imply a relatively smooth movement up (in the
periphery) and down (in the core) the slopes of the
agglomeration economy function. At some point, however,
what begins as a gradual diffusion process quickens and
cumulative causation gets under way at the new locations
(the so-called "turnaround" or "clean break" of the 1970s in
the United States?).

Of course, the plausibility of this theory to explain
what is happening in the United States does not necessarily
imply its relevance for Western Europe. In addition to the
lag in spatial trends noted earlier, a major obstacle to its
adaptability is that such a model works best in a national
urban system composed of many large metropolitan areas. It
is much less likely to work in urban systems dominated by a
primate city where the agglomeration economies on the
downturn of the inverted U-function will probably nevertheless be much greater than those on the relevant range of
its upward slope for other cities in the system. There are

20

several primate city size distributions in Western Europe
including Portugal, Austria, Denmark, Ireland and Norway.
Such a model might be more relevant to West Germany, Italy,
the United Kingdom and possibly even France and the
Netherlands where there are many other urbanized regions
outside the core region.

Evaluation

The most obvious way of evaluating the alternative
theories of regional development and their relevance to
Western market economies might be to test them with data
drawm from such economies. However, there are two main
objections to this approach. First, each of the theories
has several variants and, by changing a few assumptions and
some of the parametric variables, the alternative models can
generate the same predictions. In principle, the way around
this problem would be to test sub-hypotheses embodied in
each theory, but this invokes a second problem. This is the
scarcity of data for some of the key variables, especially
those on interregional capital flows and yields. In view of
these constraints, this paper will be restricted to making
some general comments on the alternative theories and to a
very broad evaluation of their merits. The justification
for the theories discussed in this paper is as a resource
pool to be tapped as needed in any diagnosis of regional
problems or to provide a context for regional policies in
Western Europe.

A naive approach to evaluation would be to determine
whether regional development trends in Western Europe were
convergent or not and then to determine which of the
alternative theories best explained the observed trends.
Unfortunately, this approach will not work. First, although
there appears to be a tendency towards interregional per
capita income convergence in many Western European
countries, this tendency is far from universal, it varies in
intensity over time, and it has failed to equalize regional
ncome disparities by a wide margin. Second, although the
neoclassical model is widely regarded as the convergence
model __par excellence__, several other regional development
theories (certainly the post-Keynesian and life-cycle theory
of agglomeration ecomonies models and even in some
circumstances the cumulative causation model) can lead to
convergence under certain conditions, while a multisector
neoclassical model (or one with increasing returns to scale
or with heterogeneous regional production functions) can
generate divergence. Third, the spatial dispersion of
population (labor) and economic activity (capital) is not
identical with interregional per capita income convergence;
both may be important aspects of subnational development,
yet both may not be predicted by the same model. Certainly,
the simple neoclassical model described above would not

21

predict population dispersal <u>unless</u> the low-income regions also had the highest population densities.

   If there were better data on interregional factor flows (especially elusive capital flow data), a sounder test of the robustness of the alternative theories might be whether their predictions of the direction of capital and labor flows were correct. The models discussed in the paper separate into two main groups on this point. The exception is the post-Keynesian model since whether capital flows in the same direction as labor depends on the coefficients of the interregional savings flow matrix (but other post-Keynesian models such as a two-region Harrod-Domar (44) model are more specific in their predictions). Neoclassical, neo-Marxist (uneven regional development) are Holland's regional imbalance theory (45) all predict that capital folws from high to low wage regions with the inference that profits and wages are inversely related (46). Conversely, both the cumulative causation and life-cycle theory predict that capital and labor flow in the same direction because of increasing returns and agglomeration economies. However, the only way of testing the directional hypotheses about factor flows is to assume that capital flows are embodied in fixed capital, and to use data on the establishment of new firms and on plant relocations as proxies for capital flows. This is far from satisfactory. Evidence from the United States suggests that capital and labor flow in the same direction. The Western European experience is mixed, even within the same country, partly because there are housing and other constraints on interregional labor mobility and partly because regional policy impacts may intervene. The internationalization of capital has undoubtedly resulted in the flow of capital from high to low wage countries with labor flowing in the other direction, to the limited extent permitted by national immigration laws. On the whole, a confusing picture!

   The two main rivals in regional development theory remain the neoclassical model and the cumulative causation model. Notwithstanding the versatility of both models with respect to convergence-divergence, the emergence of an interregional equilbrium in per capita incomes would powerfully strengthen support for the neoclassical position. Regional income gaps in Western Europe remain wide, but the convergence process is far advanced in the United States (see Table 1.1), especially after correction for regional cost-of-living differentials. In the relatively near future, an opportunity will develop to test the appropriateness of the neoclassical compared with the cumulative causation model. The key question is whether regional per capita income curves will stabilize close to equality (i.e. an approximation to neoclassical equilibrium) or whether they will cross over, with the four lower income regions

(South Atlantic, East South Central, West South Central and Mountain) then becoming progressively richer than the four regions of the Northeast and Midwest (47). The latter development would be more consistent with the cumulative causation model. The competing hypotheses of interregional income equilibrium and the "cross over" is the most intriguing question in contemporary regional economics.

An important criterion for evaluating alternative regional development theories is in terms of the usefulness of their policy implications. The theories discussed in this paper imply quite different policy prescriptions. The neoclassical models suggest the need to eliminate barriers to the mobility of both labor and capital and the use of taxes and subsidies to change the relative prices of inputs among regions, especially in the presence of externalities (48). The cumulative causation theories are consistent with strategies to promote agglomeration economies in lagging regions (e.g. growth center policies), measures to reduce efficiency wages (e.g. wage subsidies to labor in backward regions), and capital incentives to boost productivity growth (by raising the Verdoorn coefficient, f, in equation 7). The policy implications of post-Keynesian regional growth models vary with the specifications of each model. In the model discussed in the text, much depends on the structure of the interregional savings flow matrix. This could be changed to favor low-income regions via the provision of incentives to place savings in development banks or other institutions that invest in lagging regions. The growth-rule model, on the other hand, implies the promotion of regional export growth, particularly by measures to shift the region's economic structure in favor of export products with a high income elasticity of demand.

The policy implications of the uneven regional development theories are no different from those of other neo-Marxist models. They posit that state intervention is useless as long as control of the means of production remains in the hands of the capitalist class. Social democratic versions of regional imbalance theories, on the other hand, could imply a wide range of policies from controls on the internationalization of capital and taxes and/or direct controls on the sudden relocation of capital, to measures that equalize levels of investment within and between regions (perhaps by using State enterprises to compensate for the unevenness of private sector investment), to support unionization and to design regional policy incentives that maximize the benefits to target groups. Holland's version of these models calls for harnessing meso-economic power by direct controls and public sector participation in production. Finally, the life-cycle theory of the agglomeration economies model is, like some versions of the sumulative causation model, compatible with growth-center stragegies, at least in the sense that it implies reinforcing the advantages of spontaneously growing urban centers by helping them to move up the agglomeration fundtion more rapidly. The policy problem may be acute, however, if the lagging regions lack autonomous Growth Centers or if the city size distribution is heavily primate. In such situations regional policies will probably fail. The least damage will be done by avoiding "worst-first" regional strategies at all costs.

Questions for Future Research

Deductive economic theories are not produced in a vacuum. They implicitly assume a specific environment that is usually based on stylized facts. The regional development theories reviewed here not only assume a particular place (Western market economies) but also a particular time and background (the growth and technology of the present and recent past). There may be emerging trends and changes in the future environment that will make current theories obsolete and require new theories. A state-of-the-art review cannot be expected to resolve this problem, but it may be helpful for future research to point to some of these changes.

One of the more interesting ideas of recent years is that there are complex interactions among five bell-shaped curves, relating to economic growth, income inequality, regional inequality, geographic concentration and dispersion, and demographic change (49). Although much is known about what happens on the left-hand side and inflection point of these curves, at least with respect to first-order interactions, "the right-hand side has been left largely dangling and unexamined (50)." Obviously, the industrialized countries are well on the right-hand side of most of these curves. Better understanding of the interactions among the curves in this range might demand revision of regional development theory. For instance, what are the implications of the slowing down in national economic growth for regional development? It is well known that concern for national growth has diverted attention for regional policies. But slower growth may impact upon regional development trends. In such an environment interregional factor flows will tend to be dampened. Conceivably, the main source of interregional economic change might be differential rates of decline (in terms of plant closures and layoffs) rather than of growth (51). Would this phenomenon lead to a new process of regional income divergence or would it be spatially random? Although there have been a few case studies of economic stagnation and decline in individual regions, there is no general theory of regional economic decline. Yet there is no sound reason for expecting economic growth and decline to be symmetric.

24

Similar questions are raised by the possibility that the demographic curve might become negative in the near future (52). What are the implications of such a development for interurban and interregional migration? The impact of the decline in the population size of urban areas on regional development has barely been examined at the theoretical level.

Another problem posed for regional development theory is the current significance of agglomeration economies. These have played a critical role in many models of regional development. Many observers believe that agglomeration economies are becoming less important (53). A major reason is that rapid changes in telecommunications and computer technology are reducing the need for face-to-face contacts and eroding the benefits gained from minimizing communication costs. If spatial proximity is no longer a major efficiency factor for firms in interdependent industries and for departments within the same company, not only are agllomeration economies weakened but locational constraints are substantially relaxed. When this is combined with the fact that in most Western European countries almost all regions are sufficiently well endowed with infrastructure and skilled labor pools to be considered feasible locations for all economic activities other than resource-based industries, existing location theories have not much to contribute to the theory of regional development. The determinants of location and of regional growth differentials in developed countries may be coming increasingly non-economic, such as the pull of amenities on migrants and the loactional preferences of managers. My own work of some years ago (54) identified agglomeration economies and locational preferences as the key variables in regional growth theory, but suggested that the former was the more important. Perhaps it should be the other way around.

A third important set of questions revolves around the importance of natural resource constraints on regional development, a problem that has become of increasing concern since the oil embargo of 1973-74 and its aftermath. This problem has several dimensions, some of which have theoretical significance (55). The gap between energy-rich and energy-poor adds a new twist to the convergence-divergence debate, espeically since in many countries evergy and other natural resources are concentrated in the periphery. Energy-poor regions suffer in at least two ways: production costs are increased for evergy-intensive industries and the internal terms of trade shift unfavorably against them. The theory of regional development needs modification when applied to resource frontier regions (e.g. Northeast Scotland) since rates of economic development pick up much faster than when regional growth is based upon industrial-

ization, a much more gradual process. Another consideration
is that natural resource expoitation may generate fast rates
of development only for a relatively short time. This
creates a need for relatively disposable infrastructure,
which raises not only critical technological and policy
issues but also some interesting theoretical questions such
as those posed by the theory of boomtowns (56). As for the
debate on agglomeration economies, an unresolved question is
whether or not lower communication costs will be offset by
rising transport (= energy) costs. The more general
question is how important access to cheap energy resources
is as a determinant of regional development. It is not
doincidental that the six fastest-growing states in the
United States in the 1970s, in terms of per capita income,
were Wyoming, Louisiana, Oklahoma, North Dakota, Alaska and
Texas, nor that the population of West Virginia grew faster
than the national average after two decades of population
decline.

Conclusion
        This paper has reviewed some of the major current
theories of regional development. Selection was based in
part upon their importance in the literature but mainly upon
their relevance for explanations of interregional development trends in market (de facto mixed) economies (more
specifically Western Europe) and for providing guidelines
for regional policy. Three of the theories analyzed (neoclassical, cumulative causation and post-Keynesian) are very
formal. Their assumptions are quite restrictive and they
treat space only implicitly. However, their level of
abstraction is not considered a major drawback. Many of
their assumptions can be relaxed without changing the
generality of their results, whereas changes in coefficient
values give them a flexibility that enables them to
accommodate a variety of different circumstances (e.g.
convergent or divergent regional income trends).
        The uneven regional development and the regional
imbalance/meso-economic theories share some similarities in
their emphasis on historical factors and on the behavior of
capitalist corporations. Also, neither offers much hope for
improving welfare in lagging regions under conditions of
unconstrained capitalism. They differ in ideological
underpinnings, however, and hence in their policy
implications (one stressing the otherthrow of capitalism,
the other the reinforcement of State capitalism). The
life-cycle theory of agglomeration economies hypothesis
provides a plausible explanation of current regional
development trends in the United States, but its
applicability to Western Europe may be limited by the
differences between the United States and European national
urban systems. If could possibly by more relevant if

26

applied to the Western European spatial system considered as a whole.

An effective screening of these models would be a test of whether they predict the direction of factor flows accurately: in particular, do capital and labor flow in the same or in the opposite direction? Unfortunately, the poverty of data on interregional capital flows rules out a satisfactory test on these lines. Impressionistic evidence from the United States, Western Europe and in the international economy yield contradictory results.

Undoubtedly, the two dominant theories of regional development are the noeclassical and cumulative causation models. The advanced convergency among United States regions will offer an opportunity for evaluating these models in the Near future depending upon whether regional income paths are equalized or whether they cross over, with the four (out of five) lower-income Sunbelt regions surpassing those of the Frostbelt.

Changes in general economic conditions may demand major revisions in regional development theory, perhaps even new theories. For example, the slowing down of national economic growth rates may require the formulation of theories of regional economic decline, while the implications of zero or negative population growth for regional development have scarcely been explored. Moreover, locational preferences, amenities and other non-economic factors may be becoming more important than agglomeration economies in regional development, as technological advances in communications weaken the force of the latter. Finally, natural resource constraints may be a serious retarding influence on regional growth, especially in core regions. On the other hand, some peripheral regions are being stimulated by access to abundant and lower-cost energy resources. These changes may give a boost to the revival of supply-led models of regional development.

NOTES

1.   W. Molle, B. Van Holst and H. Smit, _Regional Disparity and Economic Development in the European Community_ (Saxon House, Farnborough, 1980), pp. 70-78.

2.   D. Vining, R. Pallone and D. Plane, "Recent Migration Patterns in the Developed World: A Clarification of Some Differences Between our and IIASA's Findings," _Environment and Planning A_, 13, pp. 243-250.

3.   Molle, _et al_, op. cit., pp. 78-92.

4.   N. Vanhove and L. H. Klaassen, _Regional Policy: A European Approach_ (Saxon House, Farnborough, 1980), p. 250.

5.   Molle, _et al_, op. cit., pp. 85.

6. R. Camagni and R. Cappellin, "Scenarios of Economic Change in the European Regions," paper presented at the Regional Studies Association International Conference on "The Changing EEC Context for Regional Development," King's College, University of London, April 15-16, 1982.

7. Vanhove, et al, op. cit., pp. 70-71.

8. World Bank, World Development Report (World Bank, Washington, D.C., 1980); of course, Ireland and Greece are relatively new members, and in the case of Greece there are constraints on the mobility of labor for an intermediate period of seven years.

9. P. Hall and D. Hay, Growth Centers in the European Urban System (University of California Press, Berkeley, 1980), p. 228.

10. In the United States, population movements towards the Sunbelt reflect both changes in locational preferences (affecting both retirees and workers) and the response of urban dwellers to differences in interregional rates of job growth. In Europe, they are explained primarily by migration from rural areas to the cities in search of job opportunities and higher real wages.

11. Hall, et al, op. cit., p. 224.

12. However, as a warning against over-generalization, three "Frostbelt" states grew faster than the U.S. average in the 1970s, New Hampshire (24.8 percent compared with the U.S. average of 11.4 percent), Vermont (15.0 percent) and Maine (13.2 percent). They may have been the beneficiaries of the shifts in locational preferences favoring life in non-metropolitan areas.

13. Comprehensiveness would require some mention of the cases of Canada, Australia and Japan. Analysis of the Canadian and Australian situations is complicated by the huge significance of immigration from abroad relative to internal migration in both countries, the self-contained spatial systems of French and English-speaking Canada and the inertia of the heavily primate city-size distribution that exists in Australia. In both countries, the largest cities may be expanding their sphere of influence since many of the fastest-growing small cities were located relatively close to the large metropolises. In Canada, there has been a major shift in favor of the West, largely in response to exploitation of highly favorable resource endowments, but there has been little convergence upwards in the Maritime provinces or the less-developed parts of Quebec (L. S. Bourne and M. I. Logan, "Changing Urbanization Processes at the Margin: The Examples of Australia and Canada," in B. J. L. Berry (ed.), Urbanization and Counter-Urbanization (Sage, Beverly Hills, 1976), pp. 111-143). In Japan, the degree of population concentration towards major urban regions such as the Tokyo agglomeration continued to increase though there was some decentralization within these regions (N. J.

Glickman, <u>The Growth and Management of the Japanese Urban System</u> (Academic Press, New York, 1978). However, there has been a recent deceleration in the rates of growth of the larger urban regions (T. Kawashima, <u>Changes in the Spatial Population Structure of Japan</u> (International Institute for Applied Systems Analysis, Laxenburg, 1977), perhpas suggesting that Japan does not offer an experience contrary to other developed countries but merely one that is later. Even Japan conforms to the pattern of dramatic decline in net migration to core regions in the 1970s mentioned above.

14. D. Yuill, K. Allen and C. Hull (eds.), <u>Regional Policy in the European Commuity: The Role of Regional Incentives</u> (St. Martin's Press, New York, 1980), p. 14.

15. W. Stohr and F. todtling, "An Evaluation of Regional Policies - Experiences in Market and Mixed Economies," in N. M. Hansen (ed.), <u>Human Settlement Systems: International Perspectives on Structure, Change and Public Policy</u> (Ballinger, Cambridge, 1978), p. 86.

16. D. M. Smith, "Neoclassical Growth Models and Regional Growth in the United States," <u>Journal of Regional Science</u>, 15, pp. 165-181.

17. G. H. Borts and J. L. Stein, <u>Economic Growth in a Free Market</u> (Columbia University Press, New York, 1964), pp. 167-169.

18. P. S. Lande and Pl Gordon, "Regional Growth in the United States: A Re-examination of the Neoclassical Model," <u>Journal of Regional Science</u>, 17, pp. 61-69.

19. G. Myrdal, <u>Rich Lands and Poor</u> (Harper and Row, New York, 1957).

20. R. Dixon and A. P. Thirlwall, "A Model of Regional Growth Rate Differences on Kaldorian Lines," <u>Oxford Economic Papers</u>, 27, pp. 201-214.

21. L. M. Kumar-Misir, "Regional Economic Growth in Canada: An Urban-Rural Functional Area Analysis," M. A. Thesis, University of Ottawa, 1974.

22. There are many post-Keynesian regional growth models, all of them relatively similar (e.g. Hartman and Seckler, "Towards the Application of Dynamic Growth Theory to Regions," <u>Journal of Regional Science</u>, 7, 1967, pp. 167-173; Richardson, <u>Regional Economics: Location Theory, Urban Structure and Regional Change</u> (Praeger, New York, 1969), pp. 323-331; Bolton, <u>Defense Purchases and Regional Growth</u> (Brookings Institution, Washington, D.C.,1966); Guccione and Gillen, "A Metzler-Type Model for the Canadian Region," <u>Journal of Regional Science</u>, 14, 1974, pp. 173-189.). A particularly interesting version (Thirwall, "Regional Problems are 'Balance-of-Payments' Problems," <u>Regional Studies</u>, 14, 1980, pp. 419-425) derives a simple growth rule

$$y = X / \pi$$

where y = growth rate of income, X = growth rate of exports and π = income elasticity of demand for imports as a dynamic version of the Harrod foreign trade multiplier. This is very similar to the export base model where regional growth depends upon regional export performance. It can also be comgined with the Verdoorn effect to obtain a CC model where regions producing goods with a high income elasticity of demand in export markets will be persistently favored because output (export) growth boosts productivity growth.

Thirwall's discussion of the model's policy implications is illuminating. Policymakers should aime at raising the rate of growth of regional exports and reducing the income elasticity of demand for imports. It has been pointed out elsewhere (Kaldor, "The Case for Regional Policies," *Scottish Journal of Political Economy*, 17, 1970, pp. 337-347) that regional labor sibsidies can be regarded as a regional equivalent to currency devaluation. But imposing such subsidies to make a regions' exports cheaper will not be effective in raising the growth rate of exports. Instead, policymakers should introduce measures to stimulate industries producing goods the demand for which is income elastic outside the regions. Obviously, it is very difficult for <u>regional</u> policymakers to intervene to reduce the income elasticity of demand for imports.

23. H. W. Richardson, "A Markov Chain Model of Interregional savings and Capital Growth," <u>Journal of Regional Science</u>, 13 (1973a), pp. 17-27.

24. J. G. Williamson, "Regional Inequalities and the Process of National Development," <u>Economic Development and Cultural Change</u>, 13 (1965), pp. 3-45.

25. <u>Review of Radical Political Economics</u>, 10, 3 (Fall 1978), Special issue on "Uneven Regional Development;" D. B. Massey and P. W. J. Batey (eds.), <u>Alternative Frameworks for Analysis</u> (Pion, London Papers in Regional Science 7, London, 1977); J. Carney, R. Hudson and J. Lewis (eds.), <u>Regions in Crisis: New Perspectives in European Regional Theory</u> (Croom Helm, London, 1980).

26. J. Lovering, "The Theory of the 'Internal Colony' and the Political Economy of Wales," <u>Review of Radical Political Economics</u>, 10, 3 (1978), pp. 55-67.

27. Whereas there is some empirical support for these views in developing countries (e.g. government pricing policies shift the internal terms of trade in favor of the urban sector), it is unconvincing in Western Europe (particularly within the EEc) where the agricultural sector is heavily subsidized.

28. R. A. Walker, "Two Sources of Uneven Development Under Advanced Capitalism: Spatial Differentiation and Capital Mobility," <u>Review of Radical Political Economics</u>, 10, 3 (1978), p. 34.

29. E. Malizia, "Organizing to Overcome Uneven Development: The Case of the U.S. South," Review of Radical political Economics, 10, 3 (1978), pp. 87–94.

30. A. R. Markusen, "Class, Rent and Sectoral Conflict: Uneven Development in Western U.S. Boomtowns," Review of Radical Political Economics, 10, 3 (1978), pp. 117–129.

31. C. G. Pickvance, "Policies as Chameleons: An Interpretation of Regional Policy and Office Policy in Britain," in M. Dear and A. J. Scott (eds.), Urbanization and Urban Planning in Capitalist Society (Methuen, New York, 1981), p. 241.

32. W. W. Goldsmith, "Marxism and Regional Policy: An Introduction," Review of Radical Political Economics, 10, 3 (1978), p. 15.

33. Ibid, p. 13–17.

34. D. Lapple and P. van Hoogstraten, "Remarks on the Spatial Structure of Capitalist Development: The Case of the Netherlands," in Carney et al, op. cit., pp. 117–166.

35. S. Holland, Capital Versus the Regions (Macmillan, London, 1976).

36. Ibid, p. 36.

37. Ibid, p. 54.

38. F. Perroux, "Note sur la nation de pole de croissance," Economie Appliquee, 7 (1955), pp. 307–320; Holland, op. cit., pp. 49–50 overemphasizes the spatial aspects of polarization in Perroux's work. It should be recalled that Perroux considered geographical space as "banal."

39. The concept of an autonomous growth center is very similar to that of a "spontaneous growth center." "spontaneous growth centers are those that are growing without benefit of special assistance or at least without benefit of conscious or explicit policy. In a lively socioeconomic system, there will always be a number of these centers, whose growth derives from the dynamics of the system," (W. Alonso and E. Medrich, "Spontaneous Growth Centers in Twentieth-Century America Urbanization," in N. M. Hansen (ed.), Growth Centers in Regional Economic Development (The Free Press, New York, 1972), p. 230). The term AGC is used in preference to SCG merely to avoid commitment to the size class ranges and operational definitions used in Alonso and Medrich's paper.

40. For example, in the United States if the large SMSAs with above-average growth rates and their State are treated as proxies for the AGSc and their regions, inspection of their population growth rates over the decade 1970–1980 confirms this correlation. In many cases (e.g. Dallas, Phoenix, San Jose, New Orleans, Denver, Nashville, El Paso) the two growth rates were very similar.

41. M. S. Fogarty and G. Garofalo, "The Urban Capital

Stock and the Life-Cycle of Cities," paper presented at the
Eastern Economics Association meeting, Philadelphia, April
9-11, 1981.

42. Vining (Vining and Kontuly, "Increasing Returns to
City Size in the Face of an Impending Decline in the Size of
Large Cities: Which is the Bogus Fact?" Environment and
Planning A, 9 (1977), pp. 59-62; Vining et al, op. cit.)
subscribes to the first part of this typothesis ("the
disappearance of the agglomeration advantages of the core
regions") but prefers to explain the growth of cities in the
periphery in terms of the "site-specific natural endowments
of the periphery."

43. Carlino (G. A. Carlino, "The Role of Agglomeration
Economies in Metropolitan Decline," paper presented at the
Eastern Economics Association Meeting, Philadelphia, April
9-11, 1981) uses a returns-to-scale (RTS) parameter in
manufacutring as a measure of agglomeration economies and
found no significant difference between core and periphery
cities. Fogarty and Garofalo (M. S. Fogarty and G.
Garofalo, "The Urban Capital Stock and the Life-Cycle of
Cities," paper presented at the Eastern Economics
Association meeting, Philadelphia, April 9-11, 1981) suggest
that the type of RTS measure used by Carlino and others is
seriously biased. Their results provide evidence of the
declining efficiency of capital in older cities. They also
point out that the benefits of productivity growth may
easily be swamped by rising labor energy and other resource
costs.

44. Richardson (1969), op. cit., pp. 323-331; Holland,
op. cit., pp. 70-81.

45. However, in Holland's theory meso-economic firms
bypass the low wages of lagging regions of developed
countries to benefit from the far lower wages prevailing in
the developing countries (see especially Holland, op. cit.,
p. 57).

46. These theories may appear strange bedfellows until
it is remembered that Marx's economic theory drew heavily
upon the principles of the classical economists. The
process of spatial development is essentially similar in
both the neoclassical and the neo-Marxist models, even in
their contemporary versions. What differs is the language
("profit maximization" becomes the "werewolf hunger for
surplus value") and intent (are capitalists callously
indifferent to the social effects of capital shifts on
regions of origin as the neo-Marxists suggest?) However,
the outcomes of the spatial development process are also
perceived differently, equilibrating in the one case and
crisis-ridden and unstable in the other.

47. This question was also raised by Alonso (op. cit.,
p. 12): "Regional equalization of per capita incomes in the
United States has proceeded rapidly among the nation's

geographic regions and between metropolitan and non-metropolitan areas. Indeed, it is not unreasonable to consider the possibility that the per capita income curves of the Sunbelt and the Frostbelt will not merely stop at convergence, but may in fact cross over . . . Will the curve of regional inequality rise once more?"

48. For example, the imposition of pollution taxes equal to marginal damages would accelerate convergence by depressing wages and profits in the high-density, high-income regions where marginal damages are greated (H. Siebert, "Environment and Regional Growth," <u>Zietschrift fur Nationalokonomie</u>, 33 (1973), pp. 79-85.

49. Alonso, op. cit.

50. Ibid, p. 5.

51. This is much more likely in Western Europe where in many countries almost all regions, both leading and lagging, are economically mature.

52. Of Western European countries, in only two (Ireland and Spain) is the rate of growth of population higher than one percent and in only four (Ireland, Spain, Portugal and Greece) is the total fertility rate greater than 2.0 (World Bank, op. cit., Tables 17 and 18).

53. There is some evidence to the contrary, though it is not fully convincing. Carlino (op. cit.) found that agglomeration economies in manufacturing were still increasing even into the late 1970s, but as pointed out above there is some doubt that the returns-to-scale measure is an appropriate proxy for agglomeration economies.

54. H. W. Richardson, <u>Regional Growth Theory</u> (Macmillan, London, 1973b).

55. H. W. Richardson, "Natural Resources, Factor Mobility and Regional Economics," in B. Ohlin (ed.) <u>The International Allocation of Economic Activity</u> (Macmillan, London, 1977), pp. 115-123; W. H. Miernyk, "A Note on Recent Regional Growth Theories," <u>Journal of Regional Science</u>, 19 (1979), pp. 303-308.

56. R. G. Cummings and W. D. Schulze, "Optimal Investment Strategies for Boomtowns: A Theoretical Analysis," <u>American Economic Review</u>, 68 (1978), pp. 374-385.

PART II: TRENDS IN REGIONAL DEVELOPMENT IN EASTERN AND
WESTERN EUROPE

SPATIAL AND TEMPORAL TRENDS IN REGIONAL ECONOMIC DEVELOPMENT
IN EASTERN AND WESTERN EUROPE

George W. Hoffman

Introduction

Spatial imbalances having an impact on the integration
of the state are brought about by various spatial economic
activities of states, by historical or cultural developments, by physical deficiencies in the natural environment
and by a variety of regional or local grievances (1). Locational problems and contrasts in population density, e.g.,
core versus periphery (2), forced both Eastern and Western
European countries to seek solutions to their regional
inequalities.   The basic problem with regard to regional
development policies in both East and West is simply the
need to close the gap between their more developed and the
underdeveloped/backward regions by leveling regional disparities (3) or by aiming at regional equality (4).   To
obtain a more balanced spatial economy both East and West
often make use of similar regional development indicators
(5) and measures.   The regional problems in Eastern and
Western Europe often show great similarity, but the chief
objective of regional policies in Europe's two subregions
always has been the emphasis on reducing regional imbalances.   The real differences have occurred in the implementation of a regional policy.   In large part these differences are based on the type and ownership of the economy - a
planned economy with a collective ownership versus a market
economy, even though the latter is often partially government controlled.

Regional inequalities in the socialist countries are as
numerous and complex as in the countries of Western Europe,
but regional development decisions "pertain to all segments
of the economy made at the center and evaluated from the
national point of view. . . planning is basically normative
and not, as in many other countries indicative (6)."   It
also should be stressed that a distinction must be made
between regional policies in their national context and
policies for individual regions.   In the socialist countries
regional planning stressed from the beginning "an action-

34

oriented activity geared to tackling economic as well as spatial (physical) and social aspects of regional development more or less comprehensively (7)." All economic as well as the so-called social sectors are involved in regional planning in the Eastern European countries with economic and social planning complementing each other. Thus regional development planning encompasses an integral part of national planning processes. It embraces the whole national territory and provides a framework for the regional distribution of development funds (8). For the Western European countries, especially those of the European Community, it meant the introduction of specific regional but often also of national planning as the cornerstone of their economic and social policies with specific emphasis on economic incentives (fiscal and financial) and measures such as investments creating jobs, usually in problem areas and specifically at employing organizations such as the European Community's Regional Development Fund (9).

Regional Development Policies

The Socialist Countries of Eastern Europe. The determination of long term development policies in the socialist countries which form the basis for middle and short-term development plans is fundamental. Such a strategy reflects social goals of the country and ultimately aims to establish, in spatial terms, conditions which should reduce and eliminate regional inequalities in the various parts of the country. The central authorities make decisions on the basis of actual and potential performance of the economy and the need to maintain a fast rate of growth and on the natural and demographic potentials and constraints, including the scarcity of resources. A particular region may receive special attention in the overall development program of the country. The interplay of these various forces represents the conflict between equity, an equitable distribution of regional income and welfare and efficiency, the maximization of the national GNP.

Another criteria in the economic planning of the socialist countries which influences regional development policies is the so-called "sectoral matrix." Here the authorities must reach a decision as to the location of new or the expansion of existing production as far a capital and infrastructure investments are concerned. That these decisions have a regional impact is obvious, but they clearly are not regionally disaggregated development policies. The authorities must decide between sectoral and regional priorities, as well as between decentralized and centralized emphasis. Depending on the type of sectoral emphasis in a specific growth center the hinterland will be affected by the spread effects.

On the other hand, this sectoral emphasis on economic development can establish priority development regions if a concensus decision is made to funnel above average investments to a specifically designated region or area within a region. As a result of decisions at the central level in the socialist societies two basic development regions emerge, one that is oriented directly toward achieving long-term societal goals, and the other motivated by sectoral growth considerations (10). During various periods both motivations often influence the selection of specific development regions, but as a rule sectoral considerations dominate planning decisions in all centrally planned economies.

Centrally planned economies for some years have concentrated most developmental decisions in one <u>center of authority</u>. These decisions were expressed in the form of a central national development plan. Some degree of decentralization, which increases with complexity of their economies exists in all these countries and has recently appeared to be increasing. In addition, the various socialist countries show some variation in the scope of their centralized decisions. Obviously such an approach demands powerful planning machinery, comprising planning authorities at the central, regional and local levels. While the problem of spatial economic planning after the initial period of neglect now has been recognized, regional policies <u>per se</u> are considered "an integral part of the socioeconomic development as a whole and are considered only a part of the total societal goals in the socialist countries (11)." Slow growing and underdeveloped regions, regardless of their nationality, were singled out only in the later stages of their economic development. They received assistance in the form of special investments within the overall development plan. Bulgaria has recently issued a decree on developing backward regions (12). The aim of the decree is for specific regions "to come close to or to reach by 1985 the working and living conditions in systems of inhabited places." These were formally set up in 1977, dividing the country into 252 such systems which have the status of administrative units.

Emphasis on sectoral priority in the past, together with the absence of disaggregation of national plans, has not always accomplished the most desirable balance in national economic development. A greater realization of the need for regional and local participation expressed in the decentralization of ever-increasing planning indicators obviously is proof of the increased fluidity and flexibility in the existing planning system. The establishment of comprehensive and consistent policies for regional development, closely integrated with national sectoral priorities, including detailed locational studies, assumes

an important shift in priorities in the rapidly advancing
and technological economies of the countries of Eastern
Europe. Hungary offers here a good example, with its
increased emphasis since 1971 on optimal utilization of
local resources and its effort aim at equalizing "leveling"
the regional differences in living conditions within its
various regions (13).

Regional Development Policies - The West European
Countries. Regional planning in the Western European
countries are largely the result of historical processes
associated with economic development and grievances voiced
by individual regions having high unemployment or
agricultural surplus labor and low per capita income. These
processes are the result of structural problems within
individual countries and/or regions, such as the
availability of a large work force with a limited range of
employment and income opportunities, the absence of or an
insufficient infrastructure essential for the location of
industrial plants, and a stagnating or declining
manufacturing sector with lower than average growth
potentials.

In general, most Western European countries have broad
national plans giving special attention to their regional
problems, though their policy objectives are more limited
than those of the Eastern European countries. Regional
development planning has received special attention for the
countries of the European Community since the mid-1970s with
the creation of the Regional Development Fund emphasizing
regional investments, and a Regional Development Committee
as part of the Community's common regional policy. It is
also important to distinguish for planning purposes between
countries with a decentralized administrative structure at
the regional level (West Germany, most of the Northern
European countries, Austria and Switzerland) and countries
with centralized institutions. Regional policy decisions in
the Federal Republic of Germany and Austria for example are
characterized by "widely distributed aid, designed to create
jobs, especially industrial jobs in lagging regions . . .
they also try to lessen out-migration in order to slow
downward spirals in local economies and reduce urban agglomeration . . . (14)." Both countries in the past emphasized
investments in a large number of dispersed urban places.

Among all West European countries France has given
special emphasis to national and regional planning through
the creation of an interministerial national agency - The
DATAR (Delegation a l'Amenagement du Territoite et a
l'Action Regionale). In 1963 DATAR began to give attention
to three main targets in public policies, a balanced
development of Paris vs. its provinces, restructuring of the
production of agricultural and industrial regions, and a
modernization of obsolete industrial areas (15). Other

37

Western European countries that give increased attention to national and regional planning are Greece, the Netherlands, Portugal, Spain and the United Kingdom. Belgium, Italy and France have recently taken steps toward modifying their centralized institutions. Regional policies in Western Europe have undergone drastic postwar changes from a piecemeal approach to physical planning to comprehensive planning objectives. Today a broad spectrum of regional development policies are in use, together with numerous types of regional policy instruments either singly or in combination.

A recently published report by the European Community, The Regions of Europe assesses:

> the capabilities of regions to adapt their economies to changing circumstances and to develop their indigenous resources to the fullest extent possible. Improvement of social conditions in the regions is considered to be a consequence of economic development as well as resulting from other policies with social priorities. The Commission takes the view that however policy measures may attempt to solve regional problems by social income transfers from stronger to weaker regions, such policies can have no more than a temporary effect on the income-generating capacity of the weaker regions of the Community (European Community). These regions must also - aided by appropriate by national and Community policy measures - achieve in the foreseeable future levels of economic development at which they will be capable of producing goods and services which can be sold in a situation of ever increasing competition. This criterion is a necessary precondition for assuring self-sustained regional development (16).

The problem of international cooperation in the field of regional policies was first attempted by the European Community, though "the problem of who, on balance, is subsidizing whom is made even more difficult by the fact that national policies that were not designed specifically as regional policies may nonetheless have important differential regional consequences (17)." These countries finally agreed after many years of discussing an overall plan for a Community solution to its regional problems. A special Regional Development Fund was created in July 1973 although final agreement on its allocation was reached only in December 1974 and the Fund officially started operation January 1, 1975. Perhaps the decisive feature of the Community's regional policy concern is the right of the

Regional Policy Committee to examine national programs and targets (regional growth plans) and to decide whether they comply with Community aims. The European Community therefore has both a consulting and a decision-making function and is involved at all levels in formulating or at least influencing a Community regional policy. On the other hand, the greatest deficiency of this policy and its long-term impact is the lack of an all Community comprehensive economic plan emphasizing regional problems and policies and an insufficient budget to satisfy all the demands.

Changing Regional Economic Development Trends

Regional development policies in the postwar period in Western and Eastern Europe underwent a number of changes and differ in their planning approach, though these policies also have many common characteristics. Some of these differences were briefly pointed out earlier in this paper; a more detailed analysis follows. Regional problems have come to be seen, especially over the past years, by both parts of Europe as a long-term issue. Earlier discussions in the Eastern European countries emphasized a reconciling of the twin goals of rapid economic development with the decrease and ultimate elimination of regional inequalities and an emphasis on balance in economic growth, thus achieving "socialist equality" as the ultimate goal in the socioeconomic development of its society (18). Grievances from rural and older industrial regions having relatively low per capita income or high unemployment as well as areas with special problems were the determining factors in establishing regional policies in the Western European countries. The solution of these problems shifted from individual governments to the international political arena and was finally implemented by the nine members of the European Community. For the countries outside the Community of 280 million people regional policies are implemented by their domestic policies.

Eastern Europe. The history of spatial and temporal trends in regional economic development between the two regions of Europe followed a very different path. Already in the original (1946) spatial development plans of the individual socialist countries (19), regional plans were part of the national plans, but as stated earlier, while their decisions left a regional impact, they are not regionally disaggregated development policies. The broad structure of planning remained unchanged over the years, but details varied among different socialist countries. Over the past years it assumed two basic tasks, "to secure the most efficient location of all development activities, and to bring about an income distribution among inhabitants of all parts of the country which would create opportunities for equal sharing in the benefits of development (20)." In its implementation regional planning in the socialist system becomes an integral part of national planning. The long-term plans extending over a period of 10 to 20 years for all socialist countries outline the basic strategies. This is followed by the middle-term regional development plans of individual countries, usually for a period of five years and stating specific targets and programs. Their implementation is allocated to specific institutions and organizations. A short annual or biennial development closely tied to budgets and fiscal plans is responsible for resource allocations needed for implementing the plan.

Actual execution of the development plan is in the hands of central or regional/local bodies, referred to as national sectoral plans for each centrally controlled district and territorial plans whose implementation is regionally/locally supervised. The regional aspects of such development plans are prepared under the general guidance of central authorities by regional/local bodies which are to consider specifically local needs. These proposals are transmitted to the central planning authorities. Once the details have been approved they are returned as a binding parameter to the regional/local bodies for the preparation of their more specific development plans. It is not at all unusual if the plans originally submitted to the central planning authorities and those returned differ substan- tially. This is due simply to the varying priorities of the central planning authorities (21).

Socialist countries of Eastern Europe believe that the comprehensive nature of their plans is sufficient to coordinate various regional programs such as income distribution, growth processes, location activities, population distribution, e.g. migration to urban centers, etc. The reduction of spatial imbalances in the economies of Eastern Europe such as the growth of less developed regions is given increased importance, though as emphasized by Mihailovic (22), Hoffman (23) and later by Gruchman (24), the chronic difficulties of a structural nature are not easily eliminated.

Between the mid-1960s and the mid-1970s all the countries of Eastern Europe frantically searched for new or improved ways to update their outmoded planning and management systems. These reforms basically emphasized the transfer of economic decision-making power and for the delegation of important micro-decisions to lower eschelons. The basic hypothesis of earlier years - that economic planning had to be carried out at the top only - was quietly dropped. A partial decentralization of the decision-making structure at least on the micro-level as well as reorgan- ization of the incentive structure, served as guiding principles for all reforms of the 1960s and 1970s. It must be stressed here, however, that the major aims of the economic reform movement were 1) to improve the existing system of planning and management and <u>not</u> to replace it and 2) to formulate regional development policies.

Yugoslavia with its multinational population, ever since the introduction of workers' self management and the reforms since the 1950s has moved toward a new planning system, with the reform of 1965 initiating an ultimate complete withdrawal of all centralized (federal) economic decision-making functions. Decision-making powers were shifted to individual enterprises and lower administrative units, but the Federal government retained some responsibility for the setting of national targets and important investment decisions. Since 1965 much effort has been devoted to determining whether these basic planning changes really had the desired results on the economy and the distribution of the standard of living of this multinational society. The great differences in the standard of living between the developed and underdeveloped republics, Slovenia, Croatia and Serbia proper vs. Bosnia and Herzegovina, Montenegro, Macedonia and the autonomous province of Kosovo, pose serious economic and political problems for the viability of the country. It has therefore been of top priority to Yugoslavia's decision-makers throughout the whole postwar period to eliminate these great regional disparities by a variety of regional development policies which are constantly adjusted to changing conditions (25). In spite of this emphasis, regional indicators such as the average national per capita income between 1971 and 1981 have not indicated the hoped-for reduction in the interregional economic inequalities. Various indices for Yugoslavia's regions still show a sizable gap in most economic and social indicators.

All Eastern European countries experimented with a variety of reforms in their planning apparatus. It became clear that the reform was not to overturn the political monopoly of the Party, the basic socialist system, the trend toward industrialization and the goal of <u>socialization of the countryside</u>. The various reforms did not affect the basic principles of central planning, which included a comprehensive national planning with central decision-making. With the exception of Hungary, the movement toward economic reform slowed down drastically after the mid-1970s. The slow-down of economic expansion, stagnation in industrial production and the desperate needs for an advanced technology together with a growing awareness of the oncoming serious energy situation and the political risks of economic liberalization, made all Eastern European countries extremely cautious in tampering with the existing planning apparatus in spite of many indications of their awareness of the outdated planning methods.

Western Europe - the European Community. The Treaty of Rome did not contain a special reference to a regional economic policy, but it did refer to the "unity of the member states' economies and ensure their harmonious development by reducing present differences between the various regions and by mitigating the backwardness of the less favored." Questions concerning a regional policy for the members of the European Economic Committee were raised and in 1965 the European Commission discussed broad policies for regional development (26). It took several years and the growth of structural problems within the individual regions of most countries of the enlarged European Community to focus on regional problems rather than on national plans which have a more limited policy objective. Final agreement was reached on an overall plan for a Community solution to regional problems and the plan was officially enacted on January 1, 1975. It deals with the degree and character of the principal regional disequilibria, the aims and instruments of the regional policies of member states, and the regional trends in the Community countries. The recognition that common policies in agriculture, freedom of movement for workers, technology, transportation, industry and energy, etc. greatly effect the inherent spatial and regional structure of the member countries, has been a decisive factor in the establishment of Community regional policies. Unfortunately, the funds available thus far are totally insufficient to make a long-term impact in view of the area involved (55 percent of the surface) and the size of the population (38 percent) that qualifies under the Community's rule for aid. The regional affairs directorate of the Community proposed at various times a reallocation of the quota section of the European Regional Development Fund by reducing the number of countries benefitting from the funds and thus increasing funds to the four so-called poor members - Italy, Ireland, Greece and Britain - but France and Belgium opposed such a reallocation.

In addition, the criteria for regional aid are very restrictive, 1) agriculture must predominate in the area eligible for assistance, 2) structural underdevelopment must exist, 3) industrial change is taking place, and 4) the Regional Fund can only be applied in those areas where "national rules for regional aid apply." While the size of the development areas has been criticized, it was agreed that the Community's contribution could only be made to larger projects of member states if those member states also made contributions, while smaller projects were financed exclusively by the individual member country. Perhaps the most important point made in setting up this Fund was that 1) aid given must lead to the creation of new employment or to guarantee existing employment, 2) contribute to the economic development of the region receiving aid, and 3) attention must be given to the environmental impact of the development project. A rather unique and important priority provides aid to investment projects established on the frontiers of two or more member states, thus developing "regions forming a natural economic connection."

It was clear as the Community regional policy evolved and emphasized new employment needs, environmental problems and aid to peripheral regions (aid to core regions was to be limited to 20 percent of total investment costs), that existing funds would be insufficient to support all the tasks required. A positive contribution by the Regional Development Fund of the European Community toward alleviating regional inequalities certainly would be a major step toward mitigating regional grievances (27).

One of the basic problems facing the Community at an early time was selecting indicators which would define "problem or priority regions" at the Community level rather than separately for each of the ten members. Several studies were completed during past years analyzing the situation of the regions of the Community beginning with the so-called Thomson Report of 1973 and the recently published report The Regions of Europe covering the period 1970 to 1977 with particular references to the years before and after 1974 (i.e. corresponding roughly to the period before and since the economic crisis of the mid-seventies). Based on the findings of this report the Commission is "preparing proposals as regards priorities and guidelines for a Community regional policy." With a possible expansion of a Community regional policy, studies have examined the level of the geographical unit best suited for analysis of regional problems and regional economic capacity. Regions which are chosen for special attention:

> should be sufficiently significant from the point of view of levels of population, to enable an assessment to be made of the over-all socioeconomic situation of the regions in question. With the aid of such an assessment the Commission would be in a better position to consider whether and where Community intervention would eventually be necessary (28).

With increased Community-wide action and perhaps an enlargement of Community regional responsibilities, Community regional policy could play an expanding role in the future development of its regions. This would include increased responsibilities for its newest member, Greece, and future members Spain and Portugal. Because of the great regional disparities within Greece, Portugal and Spain, regional problems will be accelerated in the Community of Ten or even Twelve. The restructuring of several industries

43

(such as steel, shipbuilding, textiles) will leave its impact on weaker regions and no one is as yet certain of the impacts on Community regions of the rapid advances in technologies, especially in the fields of micro- and bio-technologies in the years ahead. The main objective of the Regional Development Fund presumably is to narrow the gap in economic wealth and performance within the Community, but with the Fund totally inadequate when measured against the size of the problem, 7.6 percent of the total European Community budgetary commitments for 1982, an increase from 4.5 percent since 1978 - the impact of the Regional Development Fund is small indeed. Regions where GDP per head is below the Community average include most of Greece, Italy and the United Kingdom regions, Ireland, south and west France and the Massif Central, some regions of Belgium, the Netherlands and Germany as well as Greenland. But 95 percent of the available funds are allocated for priority areas as defined by national governments, the four least prosperous member states, Greece, Ireland, Italy and the United Kingdom receive 78 percent. Why West Germany and France receive 18.3 percent can only be explained by political exigencies. It also should be noted that within the Community member states, regional disparities of GDP per head were either reduced or remained about the same during the 1970s. But, the fact remains that a considerable number of regions in each member state have a GDP per head significantly below the respective national average (29).

Finally, it should be pointed out that one reason for the difficulty in solving the regional problem in the Community is the fact that the member states have different systems for regional aid which pre-date the introduction of a Community regional policy. These specific regional problem areas have for some time relied on domestic sources of finance. Projects for which Community regional aid is sought are forwarded to the Commission at Brussels by each national government which at the same time establishes its own priority region. The Regional Fund administrators determine the potential value of the project for the region involved - it complements national programs of regional aid - and whether the project diversifies the economic base of the region in question (30). Since 1978-80 the slightly increased Fund is distributed according to a revised criteria, though the Mezzogiorno, Ireland, Northern Ireland, the French Caribbean departments and the industrial agricultural areas in France, as well as in the United Kingdom continue as the major beneficiaries. A smaller amount (approximately 5 percent of the Fund) is now allocated to assist regions near national boundaries with the Member States "that have suffered because of progressive integration in the Community or have experienced particularly severe difficulties in response to the economic recession (31)."

With the further enlargement of the Community new regional problems will necessitate a basic rethinking of the regional development policies. Based on the experience in establishing the present regional policies, it is hoped that the member states will be able to meet the new challenges during the last part of this century. Many efforts are now under way after seven years of extremely modest achievements to put the Community's regional programs on a more effective track. For example, at present quota funds can be used only for physical investments, but in the future the strategy would be to fund small and medium-sized business development, sectoral or market studies, management improvements and the dissemination of information on modern techniques. Such an approach would certainly contribute to strengthening the regions' indigenous development potential according to the Commission "in other words to encourage growth activities that are already underway or can be launched locally (32)."

Another effort in regional development is the unique cooperation among 24 European transnational frontier regions which has been encouraged by the Conference on European Border Regions under the sponsorship by the Council of Europe. The main effort of this international cooperation is to overcome the problems created by national borders. The best known of these cooperative ventures is the trans-national frontier development of Regio Badiliensis of the Upper Rhine Region with northwestern Switzerland centered in Basle, the French province of Alsace and West Germany's southern region of Baden participating. As interest in this concept of regional cooperation has grown, it has emphasized numerous joint ventures and studies, such as future prospects for business in the region of 10 million people, environmental impact studies, transportation studies in view of the location along Europe's important North-South Axis and the road through the newly opened Gotthard Tunnel in the Swiss Alps and the bullet train development, searching for common working conditions for the more than 30,000 French and German workers who commute to jobs in Basel and for other transnational employees. Of great concern also are the 14 nuclear plants on stream or contempleted for this area, most of which will serve Paris and other distant regions, but leaving the area with serious environmental consequences. Other regional cooperation schemes are between Bavaria, the Austrian provinces of Varalberg and Tirol, Alto Adige (Italy) and Graudunden (eastern Switzerland) and the Austrian provinces of Carinthia and Styria, Yugoslavia's northern Republic of Slovenia and the Italian province of Udine with Trieste its most important center (33). Regional cooperation is increasingly recognized by Western European countries, the

45

European Community and slowly by Eastern European nations.

Increased attention has been given by the various governments of Europe to regional policies. Hopefully this will result in an improved distribution of spatial activities and to more attention being given to the grievances in areas where people often fell "they have been wronged." In Western Europe and to a lesser extent in Eastern Europe people have increasingly demanded from their governments an alteration in the spatial allocation of resources in favor of patterns more desirable than those that would result from market forces or from the priorities of national economic strategy in the prevailing institutional setting. Regional development policies in Western European countries generally focus on the development of a particular region or one or more specific problems. In Eastern Europe, development policies are part of all overall development plans with central authorities making the key decision. Yugoslavia, and to a lesser degree Hungary are the exception, but other countries have increasingly stressed the need for more decentralized decision-making. In both Eastern and Western Europe it is mainly the economic measures which serve as incentives to regional (national) development policies. Regional planning in the past in both subregions of Europe was growth-oriented, a development era which probably has come to an end. Therefore, future regional development policies will have to assist in adapting to new production methods demanding different approaches in planning and greater inter-European cooperation. In both subregions planning needs will have to address the modernization of obsolescent industry and the retooling of labor which is increasingly becoming involved in high technology activities.

Finally, it must be stressed that the serious economic slow down, with its associated social and political problems in both Western and Eastern Europe, demands new policy measures for existing regional inequalities. Neither of the subregions is homogeneous and existing regional problems demand different and innovative policies for individual countries. The emphasis on economic growth during the last decades must be supplemented by the introduction of advanced technology, greater specialization in production, and most of all, a retooling of its labor force to meet the demands of the latter part of the 20th century and the beginning of the 21st century and participate in the many innovations which will greatly influence every aspect of the social and economic life of its population.

NOTES
1. George W. Hoffman, "Regional Policies and Regional Consciousness in Europe's Multinational Societies," Geofor-

um, 8 (1977) pp. 121-129.

2. George W. Hoffman, "Variations in Center and Periphery Relations in Southeast Europe," in Centre and Periphery, Spatial Variation in Politics, ed. by J. Gottmann (Sage Publications, Beverly Hills, CA, 1980), pp. 111-133.

3. Gyorgy Enyedi, "Quality and Quantity of Regional Development Indicators in Eastern and Western Europe," in G. Demko (ed.) loc. cit., 1984.

4. I. S. Koropeckyj, "Equalization of Regional Development in Socialist Countries: An Empirical S t u d y ," Economic Development and Cultural Change, 21 (1972), pp. 68-85.

5. Roland J. Fuchs and George J. Demko, "Geographic Inequality under Socialism," Annals of the Association of American Geographers, 69 (1979), pp. 304-318; and George J. Demko and Roland J. Fuchs, "A Comparison of Regional Development Policy Instruments and Measures in Eastern and Western Europe," in G. Demko (ed.), loc. cit., 1984.

6. Bohdan Gruchman, "Key Features of Regional Development and Planning in Eastern Europe," in Regional Development and Planning: International Perspectives, A. R. Kuklinski (ed.), (Sijthoff, Laydan, 1975), p. 259.

7. Ibid, p. 260.

8. Kosta Mihailovic, Regional Development Experiences and Prospects in Eastern Europe (Mouton, The Hague, 1972).

9. George W. Hoffman, "Regional Development Policies," in A Geography of Europe: Problems and Prospects, 5th edition (John Wiley, New York, 1983), Chapter Four.

10. Gruchman, op. cit., p. 4.

11. Mihailovic, op. cit., p. 146.

12. Radio Free Europe Research, Decree on Developing Backward Regions (September 1982) pp. 1-5.

13. Laszlo Lacko, "Assessment of Regional Policies and Programs in Eastern Europe," in G. Demko (ed.) loc. cit. 1984.

14. William H. Berentsen, "Austrian Regional Development Policy. The Impact of Policy on the Achievement of Planning Goals," Economic Geography, 54 (1978), pp. 115-134.

15. J. Monod and P. Castlebajac, L'amenagement du Territoire (PUF, Paris, 1980); see also the discussions in Hoffman, op. cit., (1983) Chapter 6.

16. The European Community, p. 203.

17. Niles M. Hansen, "International Cooperation in the Field of Regional Policies," in Regional Development and Planning: International Perspectives, A. R. Kuklinski (ed.) op. cit., p. 425.

18. Koropeckyj, op. cit.

19. Frances L. Millard, "Problems of Applied Spatial Planning: A Note on the Polish Experience," Planning and Administration, 7 (1980), pp. 21-30.

20. Gruchman, op. cit., p. 261.

21. Ibid, pp. 264-265.

22. Mihailovic, op. cit., Chapter III.

23. George W. Hoffman, Regional Development Strategy in Southeast Europe. A Comparative Analysis of Albania, Bulgaria, Greece, Romania and Yugoslavia (Praeger, Special Studies in International Economics and Development, New York, 1972), Chapters 7 and 8.

24. Gruchman, op. cit.

25. Pepeonik, 1983; Dennison I. Rusinow, Unfinished Business: The Yugoslav National Question, 8 (DIR 2-81, American Universities Field Staff Report, No. 35, Europe, 1981); George Hoffman, "The Problem of the Underdeveloped Regions of Southeast Europe: A Comparative Analysis of Romania, Yugoslavia and Greece," Annals of the Association of American Geographers, 57 (1967), pp. 637-666); and George Hoffman and Ronald L. Hatchett, "The Impact of Regional Development Policy on Population Distribution in Yugoslavia and Bulgaria," in Population and Migration Trends in Eastern Europe, H. L. Kostankck (ed.), (Westview Press, Boulder, CO, 1977), pp. 112-116.

26. Norbert Vanhove and Leo H. Klaassen, Regional Policy - A European Approach (Montclair, Allanheld, Osmun, 1980).

27. Warren J. Nystrom and George W. Hoffman, The Common Market, Second Edition (New Searchlight Series, D. Van Nostrand/Wadsworth Publishing, New York, 1976).

28. Commission of the European Communities, The Regions of Europe, First Periodic Report on the Social and Economic Situation of the Regions of the Community (1980).

29. Ibid, p. 114.

30. A. J. Kerr, The Common Market and How it Works (Pergamon Press, Oxford, 1977).

31. Hugh D. Clout, Regional Development in Western Europe, Second Edition (John Wiley, Chichester, New York, 1981), Chapters 2 and 19.

32. John Wyles, "EEC's Spending Still Far Too Low," Financial Times 3 (April 27, 1982).

33. Niles M. Hansen, "International Cooperation in the Field of Regional Policies," in Regional Development and Planning: International Perspectives, A. R. Kuklinski (ed.), op. cit., pp. 423,431.

QUALITY AND QUANTITY OF REGIONAL DEVELOPMENT INDICATORS IN EASTERN AND WESTERN EUROPE

György Enyedi

Introduction

In this paper, the discussion will focus on the following issues: a) goal formulation in regional policy, b) implementation of regional policies, and c) the set of indicators established for regional policy purposes. It is assumed that the nature of regional development indicators depends on the goals and applications of regional policies. Presumably every country can establish a suitable set of criteria for their planning purposes; the differences come from the different goals and development techniques.

The Aims of Regional Policies

Generally speaking, the various development policies have a common goal: the leveling of regional disparities. The meaning of leveling and its importance in economic policy vary greatly not only between East and West, but within the capitalist and socialist part of Europe, depending upon the stage of development, spatial economic structure of the individual countries, etc.

Regional planning first started in the Soviet Union in the 1920s as a consequence of the nationalization of private enterprises and as a part of the comprehensive economic planning. Rapid industrialization has been the central aim of economic planning for a long time, based mostly on natural resource utilization. Most of these natural resources have been explored during the Soviet period. Development of mining industry, energy and other heavy industry in scarcely utilized and sparsely inhabited areas represented the main aim of regional planning in the 1920s and 1930s. Industrial location in a new urban frontier was the engine for regional development at that time. Regional policy has been essentially production-oriented.

Regional planning was introduced almost 10 years later in Western Europe under different circumstances. Planning (government intervention into the economy) was stimulated by the great economic crisis of 1929-32. Regional policies were formulated for relieving areas seriously hit by unemployment and industrial decline. Social goals such as reducing striking regional disparities in employment and income received most emphasis in the first western regional plans.

Growth of production is still an important goal in regional development of the East. In the socialist countries, regional planning embraces the whole national territory, and provides a framework for regional redistribution of development funds. In Western Europe, regional planning focuses on problem areas while there is very limited government intervention in regions where local communities and the private economic sector are strong enough to solve problems. This is a very simplified view and in reality - concerning the national policies and the opinion of regional economists or planning geographers - is much more complex.

Equalization is the subject of frequent debate. What type of regional disparities should be reduced? Economic level? Economic structure? Personal incomes? Social mobility? For what kind of regional units should leveling be planned? Is a total leveling possible and desirable? Is equalization a consequence of normal economic development or must it be forced by political necessity?

Egalitarianism is an important element in the ideology of Eastern Europe. Equalization among social classes, equal opportunity for culture and education, income leveling as well as the equalization between town and village have traditionally been cornerstones of Marxist societal policy. All these goals might be achieved by the continuous growth of production - since all the wealth is produced by labor - hence the original one-sidedness of production goals in socialist regional planning. Industrial expansion has been in the center of regional policy in less developed, Southeast European socialist countries where there still are large traditionally rural, peripheral areas. The more developed northern part of Socialist Europe pays more attention to social goals. In 1971, for example, Hungary officially formulated two basic aims of regional development: a) optimal utilization of local/natural and economic resources and b) regional convergence of living conditions of the population. The importance of the growth of production has been diminishing in socialist regional policies since the second half of the 1970s, with the general slowdown of the economy.

The economic philosophy of the Western market economies are based on differences rather than equalization - differences stimulate competition. Nevertheless, the social goal of regional development (more income and more employment) lead indirectly to a similar type of industrial decentralization (France being the closest case) to what is happening in Eastern Europe. Industrial decentralization was made possible by rapid economic expansion of the 1960s, and the new industrial locations were mostly attracted by the manpower resources of the backward areas. Local and regional authorities offered cheap infrastructure in industrial parks, tax reduction, etc. for the relocated industry in Western Europe as well as in Hungary and Yugoslavia. Central government agencies (ministries) directly ordered new industrial locations or relocations in target regions in most Eastern countries. This method was known in the important state industrial sector of Western Europe, too.

Another much discussed issue is the welfare character of regional development. There is a widespread opinion that a number of elements of regional equalization diminish economic efficiency (that is industrial location in backward areas, where the infrastructure is underdeveloped, and only low quality manpower is available). According to this opinion, regional policy expresses welfare aspects rather than economic reasons. In the long run, the social goals of regional development and efficiency of national economy are not contradictory although it is almost impossible to prove it quantitatively. The short run economic advantages of a concentrated industrial location might be overrun, in the long term, by the environmental, social and even economic disadvantages of urban-industrial overconcentration. In practice, the economic decisions - in enterprise as well as in government - are of short run character, especially under the pressure of the present economic difficulties. Consequently, government subsidies for regional development have been cut in many countries.

Paradoxically, the social elements of regional development get more political emphasis in critical economic periods. In Hungary, there is a growing concern for improving the basic elements of living conditions (health, housing, education) unless economic stagnation would render such concerns politicaly unsupportable. Presently, coordination of economic and social priorities are becoming more and more difficult.

The third debated question is whether regional policy aims at equalization among territories or among people? The answer is, evidently, that the intention is to diminish differences among the groups of people living in various regions. For this purpose, economic development of backward areas doesn't represent the only solution. Speeding up out-migration from backward areas may serve social equalization, despite the growing territorial differences.

The above mentioned problems are similar in East and West. There are two aspects, which are definitively different in the two blocs: a) the role of agriculture is more important in the East and b) because of full employ-

ment, there are no regional unemployment problems in the
East (except in Yugoslavia). But, general regional policy
formulation has to face similar types of problems everywhere
on the continent. The real differences between East and
West are found in policy implementation.

The Implementation of Regional Policies

Collective ownership and planned economy on one side,
private ownership and market economy on the other: these
are the basic elements which give rise to different ways of
policy implementation. The main differences are as follows.

In Eastern Europe, regional plans form an organic part
of a comprehensive national plan and its execution is
mandatory for different party and state organizations. In
most Eastern European countries all socioeconomic development is managed by central planning directives. The Central
Planning Office and the ministries locate new investments in
industry, agriculture and transport as well as in public
health and education. Consequently, the main path of
regional development is defined by the location decisions of
individual sectors and their coordination is difficult due
to the limited power of local (regional) authorities.

In Hungary and Yugoslavia the decision making is more
decentralized at enterprise or lower administrative units
and levels. Perhaps the Polish economic reform will
introduce similar forms. Government intervention means
primarily investment, subsidization and extension of credit
instead of planning directives.

In Western Europe government interventions are directed
mostly at the tertiary and not the production sector in
making the developing region attractive for private
investments in productive sectors. There is a large set of
economic stimuli (subsidies, favorable credits, tax exemptions, etc.) for regional development.

The role of local (regional, city or village) communities is much more important in the West than in the East.
It is a logical consequence of the planning methods and
organization. Historically, the role of local communities
was always more reduced in Eastern Europe. Government
subsidies usually have strict conditions and prescriptions
in Western Europe. Local communities have a mostly
executive and lobbying role in government subsidies and they
can decide how to use it; in most Eastern European countries
local resources are directed to the central budget and they
are redistributed among local communities by government
agencies. The decision-making role of local communities is
very limited and consequently they are not interested in
efforts to raise local funds.

Regional plans in Eastern Europe cover all aspects of
socioeconomic life, and the execution of the plan is
expected by different government sectors. The direct

government economic interventions in the West focus mostly on public services. The meaning of public services differs from country to country. In Eastern Europe, even the retail trade, at least in part, is included in public services. In the West, public services are characterized by a certain government involvement, but in most cases (defense and state security represent perhaps the only exceptions) there is also private participation (e.g. education, health services). Government involvement is stronger in public services, which forms a national network, while other public services (urban transport, garbage collection, etc.) are run by local communities.

Regional plans in Eastern Europe cover all the regions of the country, and provide a framework for regional distribution of planning targets and development funds. In the West - at least in most cases - regional planning is a tool for helping underdeveloped regions. The background of this difference has been discussed earlier.

Generally speaking, regional plans have no international character, despite the strengthening economic integration within the Common Market and the COMECON. The Common Market established a fund for subsidizing backward areas, but the planning remained within a national framework. In certain COMECON countries, there are common bilateral plans, mostly physical, for coordinated development of the border zones (e.g. between Czechoslovakia and Hungary), but the execution of plans is expected to be done separately, by each government. Neither West nor East is yet prepared to face the fact that economic integration will necessarily lead to regional integration and to the formation of multinational macro-regions within Europe.

Regional Development Indicators

Regional development indicators are similar in East and West, since they are designated for similar purposes. We can group the indicators into the following - population, production, consumption, economic indices (market, prices, investments), interregional connections and qualitative indicators. All indicators but the last have a quantitative character.

Population has traditionally been treated mostly from an economic point of view (labor supply, employment). Certain social aspects are now getting more emphasis. Migration has been frequently examined as a general indicator of the economic health of a given area and of interregional relations.

Living conditions are treated from various aspects: in a very detailed manner in the East including location of different services, infrastructure, institutions, retail trade and primarily income in the West.

Production functions are much more detailed as defined

by indicators in socialist countries. There are prescriptions for investments, cost-benefit analysis, expected output, labor productivity, etc. Production capacities are judged by the market potentials in the West but by investment and manpower potentials in the East. The market seems to be unlimited in centrally planned economies.

Although regional plans sometimes contain cost-benefit and other economic analyses, they are not very meaningful because of the artificial price system and other reasons. Finally, the indicators in kind (weight of products, number of newly employed workers, etc.) are the most important.

Consumption is viewed as a market potential in the West and as a satisfaction of the needs of population in the East. For the definition of these needs, there is a long set of norms, from the square meters of housing surface for one person to the number of hospital beds or the retail trade surface per 10,000 persons. Consumption is planned from two aspects: from the point of view of production of the consumer goods and the establishment and development of services. While consumption is carefully planned in the East, certain <u>economic indices</u> connected to the market are more carefully taken into consideration in the West.

Interregional connections are carefully analyzed everywhere in forms of flow of goods, migration and regional input-output analysis. They have perhaps more importance in socialist countries, where the whole national network of interregional connections is directly planned.

Qualitative indicators may have a double meaning. Quite frankly, we cannot handle such indicators as <u>quality of life</u>, <u>attractive</u> <u>environment</u>, etc. We can name <u>qualitative</u> indicators such indices (although they are quantified) which express new, qualitative changes and processes taking place in various regions (e.g. decisive structural changes, the propagation of innovations, etc.).

A set of recommended or generally applied set of indicators has been avoided here. Regional analyses are frequently overfed by data and many regional planners try to put as much information into a regional model as possible, which makes data gathering too long and the data processing too expensive. It should be added that environmental indicators are sometimes treated separately, but mostly they are associated with productive functions (as resources) or to living conditions.

Regional indicators are usually compared to the national average or to certain norms. In Eastern Europe, egalitarian aspects are continuously stressed (although they are not always achieved). There are spectacular results in economic levelling among regions in most of the countries. It should be noted that pre-war Eastern Europe had a predominantly agricultural economy with strong spatial disparities. At the same time, however, the urban/rural dichotomy is still a reality.

Equalization is usually measured by diminishing deviations from the national average which is a rigid interpretation of equalization. It would be more meaningful to compare regional development indicators of a given region to the needs of the local population. But how does one measure the exact social stratification of the local society and its level of need?

Conclusion

There are a number of similarities between regional planning indicators in Eastern Europe and in other developed countries. There are similar problems with a common spatial nature. The differences are important in the decision system of planning. Public ownership of the means of production is the basis for these differences.

What has been written in this paper is almost historical. Until now, regional planning was growth oriented. The era of rapid economic growth has ended and although the painful adaptation of a macro-economy to the new economic period is more or less successful, there is no such adaptation in regional policies. There are a few ideas regarding innovation-oriented regional policy which have remained rather theoretical. The implementation of a new type of regional policy will change the set of indicators, too. This may be one of the most urgent research tasks of regional economics in the 1980s.

REFERENCES

Burghardt, A. R. (ed.) (1975) Development Regions in the Soviet Union, Eastern Europe and Canada, Praeger, New York

Coates, B. E., R. T. Johnson and P. L. Knox (1977) Geography and Inequality, Oxford University Press, Oxford

Enyedi, Gyorgy (1979) Economic Policy and Regional Development in Hungary, 22, No. 1-2, Acta Oeconomica, pp. 113-126

Ewers, H. J. and R. W. Wettman (1980) Innovation Oriented Regional Policy, Regional Studies, No. 3, pp. 161-179

Faber, B. L. (ed.) (1976) The Social Structure of Eastern Europe, Praeger, New York

Fuchs, R. and G. Demko (1979) "Geographic Inequality under Socialism," Annals of the American Association of Geographers, 69, No. 2, pp. 304-318

Hägerstrand T. and A. Kuklinski (eds.) (1971) Information Systems for Regional Development, Lund Studies in Geography, Series B, Human Geography No. 37, Lund

Kornai, J. (1980) The Shortage, KJK, Budapest
Kuklinski, A. (ed.) (1975) Regional Development and Planning International Perspectives Sijthoff, Leyden
Kuklinski, A. (ed.) Regional Development Planning in the European Countries, PWN, Warszawa
Kuklinski, A. (ed.) (1977) Social Issues in Regional Policy and Regional Planning, Mouton, Paris - The Hague
Mihailovic, K. (1972) Regional Development: Experiences and Prospects in Eastern Europe, Mouton, Paris - The Hague
Nyekraszov, N. N. (1978) Regional Economics, Kossuth, Budapest
Obshaya metodika razrabotki generalnoi schemy razmeshcheniyz proizvoditelnych Syl SSSR na 1971-1980 gg. (1966) Ekonomika, Moscow
Pertsik, E. N. (1973) Raionnaya planirovka/geograficheskie aspekty, Misl, Moscow
Phlipponeau, M. (1981) Décentralisation et régionalisation, Calman-Levy, Paris
Romus, P. (1974) Economie régionale européenne, Presses University de Bruxelles, Brussels
Secomski, K. (1974) Spatial Planning and Policy: Theoretical Foundations, Polish Scientific Publishers, Warsaw

THE NEW REGIONALISM AND EUROPEAN ECONOMIC INTEGRATION

Niles Hansen

A Preliminary Overview

The postwar emergence of the Common Market, an inter-dependent world-wide economic system, modern transportation and communications facilities, and integrated global military alliances have served to diminish the importance of national boundaries and to weaken the traditional found-ations of the nation-state. A major counterpart to this evolution has been the remarkable growth of regional feeling and activism in Europe. Thus, Lasuen maintains that although the nation-state has been essential for the development of industrial society, it has been surpassed not only technically but also emotionally:

> It has little attraction for the younger generation, only a small percentage of whom - authoritarians of the right and left - are nationalists in the old sense. For the rest, the great majority, the territorial unit that evokes strong loyalties and establishes genuine emotional ties, producing the same kind of self-sacrifice that the nation-state inspired in the older generation, is the region, and to a much lesser extent (and only as an intellectual reference) the continental framework (1).

It is frequently argued, moreover, that Europe cannot become truly integrated without a strong regional renais-sance. Belgian law professor Francois Perrin states that:

> The base of Europe must be the region, where people feel that they can influence their destinies. The top is Europe. It is the nation-state in the middle that is bankrupt. The state is losing power to Europe on top and to the regions below. The old centralized state of

57

Napoleon is too distant from people (2).

Ardagh similarly points out that:

> In discussions about the future of the
> European Community it has often been argued
> that, as Europe moves haltingly towards some
> eventual integration, and as national
> sovereignties therefore dwindle, so not only
> will the regions assume more power and
> significance, but it will be essential for
> them to do so in order to provide smaller
> human-scale units that can balance the
> anonymity of the new larger one (3).

In reponse to the demands of people for greater
participation in and management of their own affairs, most
Western European governments have granted more decision-
making powers to regional authorities. Moreover, the new
regionalism is not an artificial growth but is, on the
contrary, typically rooted in cultural realities that
predate the nation-states of modern Europe. Consciousness
of ethnic distinctiveness can readily be found in, for
example, Great Britain (Wales and Scotland), Belgium
(Flanders and the Walloon region), France (Alsace, Flanders,
Brittany, Corsica, the Basque and Catalan areas, and
Occitania), Spain (Catalonia, the Basque provinces, and to a
lesser extent Andalusia and Galicia), Italy (Sicily,
Sardinia, the Aosta Valley, and Alto Adige), Germany
(Bavaria and other southern regions), and all the regions of
Yugoslavia. Even where the importance of ethnic factors is
not a major factor, local pride and traditions have con-
tributed to the development of regionalism.

Increasingly, too, emerging communities of mutual
interest transcend national boundaries. The Rhine-Rhone
axis, which many observers regard as the economic heartland
of the Common Market, provides two cases in point. One
involves Lyon and Grenoble, in the French Rhone-Alps region,
and Geneva and Lausanne in Switzerland - four cities brought
together by proximity, a common language, and common commercial interests. Another involves Alsace, Baden-Wurttemberg,
and Basel. Here the Regio Basiliensis, an organization
based in Basel, provides a mechanism for tri-national
cooperation and the common language is German, which is
understood by most Alsatians and, in its local form, used by
many of them on a daily basis.

The present paper critically evaluates the nature and
significance of the new regionalism from an economic perspective, taking into account the fact that non-economic
factors also provide major incentives for regionalism. In
some cases, issues involving language and culture represent

the principal justification for regional movements. But even so, regional demands are economically motivated to some degree; and national and international responses to these demands have economic consequences, both intended and unintended.

While this study is primarily concerned with Western Europe, attention is also given to the Soviet Union and the socialist countries of northeastern Europe. Regionalism in five Western European countries - France, Spain, Belgium, Great Britain, and Italy - and in the Soviet Union is discussed in some detail. Then a summary of regional development issues in Czechoslovakia, the German Democratic Republic, Poland and Hungary is presented. In the final section the more general national and international implications of European regionalism are considered.

Regional Economic Grievances

Regionalism usually arises from the existence of local grievances, which are translated into demands that may or may not be addressed adequately by regional policies. Although the redress of regional grievances is often presented as being consistent with economic efficiency from a national viewpoint, the more fundamental issue is likely to be equity. Some regions may feel that they are being expoited by having to subsidize less wealthy regions. (To avoid reification, "region" as used here should be regarded as a shorthand term for articulate regional interest groups. Similar liberties are taken throughout this paper). However, the more common source of friction between region and nation is rooted in the demands of regions with relatively low per capita income and/or high unemployment that something be done. Such regions tend to fall into one of two categories. The first involves rural areas characterized by relatively low-productivity agriculture, or by surplus labor that has been released from agriculture as a result of technological advance but is unable to find other local employment opportunities. The second involves older industrial regions with an overdependence on declining sectors. Finally, in many countries it has been argued that one or more large metropolitan areas are too big or too crowded in the sense that the social costs of growth outweigh the social benefits. The implication is that public policies should stem the growth of such areas and direct population and economic activity to other regions. Even though the rationale for decentralization policies implies national benefits, large cities have rarely promoted their own decline. Their de facto dominant position is probably reflected in the fact that they do not exhibit the kind of regionalism found in the provinces. In any case, the growth of large metropolitan areas has abated in recent years and significant decentralization of population and economic activity has taken place, though not necessarily to the benefit of the more peripheral regions.

Western European Case Studies

France. From the time of Hugues Capet (987-996), Paris has been the political, economic and cultural capital of France. Initially the monarchy encouraged the urban bourgeoisie in order to weaken the feudal authority of the barons, but to facilitate the collection and management of tax revenues it eventually destroyed the local powers it had initially promoted. A bureaucracy dependent directly on the king was used to govern the provinces throughout the Ancien Regime. The uniform rule of Paris was reinforced when Napoleon abolished the old provinces and created the departments, each (until recently) administered by a prefect appointed in the capital. Moreover, a bureaucracy totally centralized in Paris exercised more power than locally elected officials.

Unlike the situations in Germany, Italy, and most other European countries, the French state preceded and in fact made the nation. In the eleventh century France was roughly equivalent to the present-day Ile de France, but over the centuries new territories were conquered and annexed: Languedoc and parts of the center in the thirteenth; Aquitaine and Provence in the fifteenth; Brittany in the sixteenth; Franche-Comte, parts of Alsace and Flanders, and a number of regions in the Pyrenees in the seventeenth; Lorraine, Corsica, and the Comtat-Venaissin in the eighteenth; and Savoy and Nice in the nineteenth. Despite political centralization, the assimilation of these gradually added populations proceeded slowly. The modern view of a nation as a people voluntarily united and having common social and historical attributes was scarcely applicable to the France of 1870, "in which French was a foreign language for half of the citizens (4)."

Weber (5) has thoroughly documented the extent to which colonial references were applied to many parts of France in the last century. In the Alpine provinces and in much of the south and west the people generally knew themselves to be French subjects, but to many this status was no more than an abstraction. Brittany provides a particularly cogent example of the exploitation of colonial opportunities in the strict sense of settlers moving from one country to another. After its forced union with France, Brittany's towns were invaded by Frenchmen who dominated or replaced native merchants and imposed the French language and French customs on the people they employed or otherwise influenced. The term colony was frequently used to describe the royal ports of Brest and Lorient, garrison towns in a foreign territory. The rapid development of agriculture in Brittany in the nineteenth centry was also largely directed by external entrepreneurs, using cheap and abundant local labor. Helias' (6) vivid recollections of life in a Breton village prior to World War I clearly illustrate how the inexorable centralization of the Third Republic (especially the school system) worked to destroy provincial identity.

The internal colonialism theme has also been expounded by numerous contemporary advocates of regional autonomy (7). Lebesque (8) holds that Brittany is still an internal colony, while others (9) make the same case with respect to Occitania. Lafont (10), perhaps the most influential proponent of the view that the centralized capitalist state has impeded development in peripheral regions by a process of internal colonization, has argued on behalf of decentralization of political and economic power and regional self-management.

However, internal colonization does not really explain the economic dynamics of contemporary France. By the end of World War I regional differences had already been substantially reduced as a result of improved communications, mass education, and military service (11). Modernization has accelerated again since the 1960s. Towns that were quiet provincial backwaters are now energetic and receptive to change, mass consumption has replaced an artisanal economy, and the old-style peasant has virtually disappeared. Although colonialism typically implies underdevelopment with respect to the colony, what the autonomists actually are reacting to is modernization and the complex processes involved therein: regional specialization and exchange, uneven sectoral and spatial development, urbanization, increasing interdependence among both regions and nations, and the consolidation of firms into larger national and international corporations. Moreover, there is little connection between ethnic specificity in France and level of regional economic development. Some ethnically distinct regions are relatively poor but some - particularly Flanders and Alsace - are relatively developed; and there are both relatively poor and rich regions that are not ethnically distinct.

On balance, recent regional changes in France have tended to favor those regions where autonomist activity has been greatest. The Fifth Economic and Social Development Plan (1966-1970) included provisions for increasing economic activity and reducing population outmigration from the program regions of the West: Brittany, Lower Normandy, Pays de la Loire, Center, Poitou-Charentes, Limousin, Auvergne, Aquitaine, Midi-Pyrenees, and Languedoc. Between 1954 and 1962, all of these regions but one (Center, adjacent to the Paris region) had net outmigration. In contrast, between 1975 and 1980 all of the regions of the West except Lower Normandy, Poitou-Charentes and Auvergne experienced net in-migration (12). The evolution of regional economic

61

activity is reflected in change over time in the value of
the turnover of industrial and commercial enterprises. For
France as a whole, this value increased at an annual rate of
15.1 percent between 1966 and 1976. The corresponding
growth rate was higher in each of the regions of the West
except Languedoc (15.0 percent). Brittany recorded the
highest rate (18.7 percent) among all French regions; and
the six highest-ranking regions were all in the West (13).
Similarly, between 1963 and 1973 income per household grew
more rapidly than the national average in eight of the ten
Western regions (14).

In the light of such evidence, Beer is probably correct
in attributing regional-ethnic militancy in France to rising
expectations. In ethnic regions that are relatively
prosperous, insofar as there is any ethnic discontent the
discontented will vote for their representatives rather than
resort to violence. The relatively disadvantaged regions
are catching up rapidly, but with consequent disruption of
social structures. When previously disadvantaged groups
begin to experience improved conditions, their sense of
injustice will increase because they will expect more than
they had. "Internal colonial status is an explanation of
how ethnic regions were preserved in otherwise modernizing
states; it is the <u>end</u> of internal colonialism that explains
violent ethnic dissent today (15)."

Spain. In Spain, which is on the track toward
integration into the Common Market, the centralized
bureaucracy of Castile (Madrid) never succeeded in achieving
genuine national integration. Following the political
unification of Spain by the marriage of Ferdinand and
Isabella, the former kingdoms and provinces continued to
retain many of their own institutions and practices. The
Basques and Catalans in particular have long nurtured
separatist ambitions.

In the sixteenth century the Basques were granted a
degree of local autonomy in matters of trade, taxation, and
military service. These were incorporated in bodies of
traditional law known as the <u>fueros,</u> which determined the
rights of the popular assemblies and the rules of
inheritance. For generations the Basques showed their
strong attachment to this framework of their political and
social organization. In the nineteenth century they
resisted the attempts of the central government to encroach
on local privileges. In 1894 a Basque Nationalist Party was
founded to promote political independence. During the 1930s
most of the Basque population was loyal to the Republic, in
spite of its anti-Catholic policies, because the right-wing
forces were opposed to their relatively autonomous status.
Bilbao became the center of republican government and also
of Basque nationalism. Thanks to Picasso, the remembered
event of the Civil War is the bombing of Guernica, the

traditional assembly place of the province of Vizcaya and a symbol of Basque nationalism. Following their defeat, many Basques went into exile, and a Basque government-in-exile was created in Paris.

Catalonia has always played an important part in Spain's history, and since the seventeenth century – when Catalans placed themselves under the protection of the French king in opposition to <u>foreign</u> Castilian troops – it has been the center of a separatist movement often dominating Spanish affairs. In the eighteenth century Catalonia lost nearly all of its previous autonomy, but it gained economically by the encouragement that the Bourbons gave to industrial and commercial development. Catalan separatism re-emerged in the nineteenth century, largely through the impetus of a literary renaissance that began in the 1850s. Politically, Catalan nationalism again became a serious force after 1876, when it became a predominantly right-wing movement; but during the 1920s it shifted to a leftist orientation in reaction to repression on the part of the dictatorship of Primo de Rivera. Under the Republic Catalonia was granted a relatively high degree of autonomy, but repression of Catalonian nationalism returned with the triumph of General Franco.

Although regional economic grievances usually are associated with relative underdevelopment, in the case of Spain a major source of disagreement between region and nation has been the wealthier regions' resentment concerning their exploitation by the rest of the country, and by Castile in particular. In the nineteenth and twentieth centuries, mining, smelting, textile manufacturing and other industries developed around Bilbao and Barcelona. On the other hand,

> Castile offered little in the way of economic advantages, while it absorbed a great deal, or could be made to appear to do so. Taxes siphoned money into the center, and prevented these two peripheries from developing the commercial policies suited to their nascent industrial-ization. To various elements of the peripheral populations the advantages of membership in the whole appeared dubious, and the arguments of separatism quite plausible (16).

While Catalonia continues to be Spain's wealthiest and most highly industrialized region, the Basque region has, since 1975, been experiencing an economic crisis without precedent in modern times (17). Table 2.1 shows the per capita income rank in 1967 and in 1977 of each of the Catalan and Basque provinces in relation to Spain's 50 provinces. Between 1967 and 1977, Barcelona maintained its

Table 2.1: Per Capita Disposable Family Income Rank (1967 and 1977) and Population (1975) of Catalan and Basque Provinces

	Per Capita Income Rank		Population (thousands)
	1967	1977	
Catalonia			
Barcelona	4	4	4,387
Gerona	7	1	442
Lerida	19	12	349
Tarragona	12	7	485
Basque Region			
Alava	3	5	238
Guipuzcoa	1	6	683
Vizcaya	2	8	1,152

Sources: Columns 1 and 2, Banco Espanol de Credito (BANESTO) Renta Nacional de Espana (BANESTO, Madrid), p. 60; column 3, BANESTO, Anuario Banesto del Mercado Espanol 1981 (BANESTO, Madrid), Part Six.

ranking and each of the other Catalan provinces substantially improved its relative position. In contrast, the rankings of all of the Basque provinces declined during this period; Vizcaya, the most populous, fell from second to eighth, while Guipuzcoa, the next most populous, dropped from first to sixth. Vizcaya and Guipuzcoa also ranked first and second, respectively, in terms of net outmigration of population in the late 1970s (18).

Heavy industry in the Basque region has been protected and subsidized but not modernized. Lack of investment as well as high wages have led to a situation where the major steel, naval construction, and capital goods sectors are no longer competitive in international markets. The crisis also has spread to numerous smaller enterprises dependent on the large dominant firms. Moreover, conversion to more competitive activities is being severely hindered by the social unrest generated by Basque nationalism (19).

Modern Basque nationalism is a highly complex phenomenon (20). Vizcaya, and Bilbao in particular, industrialized rapidly between 1876 and 1900. The need for in-migrant labor was such that by 1900 about half of Bilbao's inhabitants were non-Basque, and many Basques felt themselves to be a social minority (though the Basque oligarchy never questioned Spain's unity). Thus, Basque nationalism initially was concerned with the problems of industrial Bilbao, and only later spread to other areas as they industrialized. From 1898 to 1936 - when a short-lived autonomous Basque government was formed - the Basque Nationalist Party was characterized by numerous tensions, separations, and reunifications between nationalist intransigents and moderate liberals willing to make economically advantageous compromises with Madrid. In reaction to Franco's attempts to suppress everything Basque, postwar nationalism took on the attributes of the revolutionary Third World model, the main elements being independence, armed struggle, and socialism. A second great wave of Basque industrialization occurred during the 1950-1965 period, and it too was accompanied by a large influx of Spanish workers who were viewed as economic and cultural competitors, particularly in recently-industrialized areas. Basque nationalism has increasingly created two antagonistic communities, cutting across class and rural-urban distinctions. Moreover, in the multi-ethnic climate of the region, who is or is not considered a Basque is determined not by descent but by whether or not a person adheres to the symbols of Basqueness. In the worsening regional crisis, it appears that more effort is being devoted to gaining differential access to the economic pie than to making it grow for the benefit of all concerned.

Belgium. As an independent nation, Belgium has been in existence for 150 years, and for most of this time regional disputes have strongly conditioned the country's social, political, and economic development. The northern provinces are populated by Dutch-speaking Flemings, whereas French-speaking Walloons inhabit the southern provinces. Brabant, where Brussels is located, is part Flemish and part Walloon. Brussels, as the seat of the constitutional monarchy and a symbol of national unity, is in principle neutral ground.

At the time of Belgium's formation, Wallonia was becoming one of the first areas of Europe to experience the Industrial Revolution, largely because of its rich iron and coal resources. But although emerging industrial enterprises were concentrated in Wallonia, Brussels - where large holding companies were based - became the center of actual economic decision-making. By 1850, Brussels accounted for 84 percent of the nation's banking assets. Moreover, capitalism in Belgium was long dominated by a French-speaking industrial bourgeoisie, which also controlled the political decisions of the highly centralized national government system. The industrialization of Flanders began in the late nineteenth centry and accelerated sharply in the 1920s. Despite the expansion of the port of Antwerp and the discovery of coal in Limburg, the rise of Flanders to a position of economic dominance has been primarily the result of a convergence of social factors: the emergence of a self-conscious Flemish industrial bourgeoisie; the creation of specifically Flemish financial institutions; and a Flemish populist ideology that has cut across social classes in its opposition to French-speaking domination and to militant socialism, which is largely associated with the old industrial areas of Wallonia. By the 1970s, the center of gravity of both political and economic power had clearly shifted in favor of Flanders, which also attracted most of the international investments flowing into Belgium (21).

In 1981-82, the Belgian economy was in a state of crisis. Belgium had Europe's highest levels of wages and unemployment insurance protection but many of its products were being priced out of world markets. The unemployment rate rose to 10 percent - the highest in Europe - and borrowing from abroad verged on being out of control. Corrective policies implied a cut in real incomes, which in turn further exacerbated Flemish-Walloon differences. The incidence of old and depressed industries is greatest in Wallonia and the Flemish chafe at having to subsidize their inefficiency. On the other hand, the President of the Walloon Socialist Party reflected the prevailing sentiment in his region by arguing that "the Belgian state has already proven its chronic incapacity to resolve the problems of our regions - all the more because one party tries to establish a hegemony profitable to Flanders alone (22)."

In recent European press commentaries it has been suggested that Belgium may be ungovernable and even that the nation may break up, though the precise form that the <u>new</u> political units would take is never specified. But similar speculation has occurred in the past and no doubt Belgium will continue to muddle through once again. Yet it is apparent why the notion of a Europe of the Regions is relatively attractive in the Belgian setting. It also should be pointed out that the Europeanism of the Belgians is in part a result of the fact that, despite internal conflicts, Belgium itself is a separatist region. If Belgium were a part of France - as might well have been the case - Brussels today would likely be a modest provincial city such as Bordeaux, rather than the headquarters city of NATO and the Common Market.

   <u>Great Britain</u>. Great Britain consists of four separate units: England, Scotland, Wales and Northern Ireland. Each has its own distinctive historical and cultural roots and the relationship of each to the government of Great Britain is somewhat different in each case. Wales has been under English control for 700 years and has been governed on the English model since the sixteenth century. In Wales there is a substantial Welsh-speaking minority with a cultural heritage more related to the other Celtic areas than to England. Scotland was an independent kingdom until 1707 when for economic reasons it gave up its statehood and joined the rest of Great Britain. The Celtic minority is too small to be of real political importance in Scotland, but there is nonetheless a strong feeling of separateness. In Northern Ireland the Protestant religion is the most important binding force that has made the majority of the population feel distinct from the Republic of Ireland.

   The overall economic decline of Great Britain has particularly affected its peripheral regions; and it has been a major factor in the rise of influential nationalist movements in Scotland and Wales. The case for an independent Wales is relatively weak because of its small size. Moreover, although it has a strong economic base along the southern coasts, it is closely associated with the industrial areas of England, especially with Severnside of which it forms a distinct part.

   Superficially, at least, Scotland appears to have the potential economic strength for an independent existence. Its area is larger than that of the Benelux countries; its population is larger than those of Ireland or Denmark; the Glasgow metropolitan area is larger than all but three of the capital cities in the Common Market; the Scottish economic core region - which stretches from the Clyde to the Forth - is geographically quite separate from England and carries out a high volume of international transactions; and Scotland is a major energy producer, having coal, hydro-electricity and North Sea oil (23). In this perspective, the British case could be regarded as a classic illustration of peripheral reaction to the dominance of a declining core area. Thus, Gourevitch has argued that:

> the economic weakness of the core region under-
> mined the whole. The core has not been able to
> solve the problems of the peripheries, which
> increasingly blame it for this failure. Scotland
> is the outstanding case of the contrast between
> the rising periphery and sinking core, and it is
> therefore not so surprising that nationalism is
> strongest there, even though Wales retains a much
> larger percentage of bilinguals (24).

But the situation is really a good deal more complex than this. For one thing, the rising periphery in fact has more than its share of depressed industries. The Scottish nationalists have tended to oversimplify the nature of regional economic problems; and they have played down the real achievements of British regional policies that have benefitted Scotland as well as other lagging regions (25). As Firn has pointed out, even though regional policies have not been based on a full understanding of the development processes in question, "it cannot be disputed that the depressed areas of the United Kingdom would have suffered even greater economic and social decline in the absence of regional policies (26)." In addition, nearly 60 percent of the ownership and control of manufacturing employment in Scotland lies in other regions of Great Britain or overseas; and the faster-growing sectors have the highest degree of external control. Owing to Scotland's high degree of integration with other economic systems, it would be very difficult for an independent Scottish government to run an independent economic policy (27). In this light it is not surprising that Scottish labor and business groups have not backed independence. Another difficulty is the fact that within Scotland there is a great deal of economic and social heterogeneity. A Scottish Assembly endowed with any real powers would have to address the issue of internal redis-tribution, and this could be contentious to the point of dissolving the alliance against English "depredations." Finally, the absence of an ethnic or cultural revival paralleling the autonomist movement deprives it of the popular fervor that would be needed to overcome the interests of rival groups (28). There is ample evidence from a variety of polls that the Scottish population for the most part does not comprehend the nature and effects of devolution, federation, and separation, nor even the existing administrative system (29). In brief, "a credible threat of separation remains the missing component in the political expression of Scottish nationality (30)."

In the larger context of the British devolution debate,

Buck and Atkins (31) suggest that a large proportion of regional resentments may be associated with class differences manifested in major differences in regional occupational structures. The results of a national study by Knox (32), in which 1,450 respondents were asked to indicate their priority ratings with respect to various "life domains," are instructive in this regard. The most striking finding was the consistency with which significant variation in attitudes occurred among regional subdivisions. Scots, for example, attached relatively high importance to neighborhood qualities, social status, and financial situation. The Welsh attached high importance to education and leisure opportunities but not to financial situation. In London, family life was less valued than elsewhere; and so on. On the other hand, no significant variations in attitudes were found across the social classes. This suggests that both decision-making and the evaluation of social well-being at the regional level should be undertaken in the light of community values; and that it seems appropriate to cater to regional differences by increasing local autonomy through at least some devolution of power.

  Italy. The problem of regional disparities is more acute in Italy than anywhere else in the European Community. Its principal manifestation is the economic dualism that has long persisted between the north and the south, or Mezzogiorno. The lack of economic integration of the Mezzogiorno with the rest of the country has been partly a result of natural conditions and the region's peripheral location. When Italy was unified in 1861, agriculture was the predominant activity throughout the country, but because of unfavorable climatic and agronomic conditions in the south productivity there was well below that in the north. That the inherent disadvantages of the southern regions were aggravated by their peripheral location became evident when, in the 1890s, the rapid industrialization of continental Europe began to spread to the neighboring Piedmont, Liguria, and Lombardy regions of Italy. Here, in the upper Po Valley, evolved the Milan-Turin-Genoa urban-industrial complex that has dominated Italian economic life throughout this century. It should also be pointed out that poverty conditions in the south were aggravated by protectionist trade policies that indirectly favored large-scale wheat production at the expense of specialized small farmers (33).

  Perhaps the best known regional development program in Europe is that of the Cassa per il Mezzogiorno, which was established by the Italian government in 1951. Detailed consideration of this effort - which has involved land reform, agricultural development, industrial subsidies, state enterprise investments, and tourism promotion - is beyond the scope of this paper. Evaluations of the results achieved vary greatly, though few would argue that the

69

Mezzogiorno has attained a self-sustaining take-off. More typically the Cassa has been criticized for putting too much effort into projects that have been of little real economic value and for lacking a regional strategy. There is even extensive evidence that much of the $3 billion the Cassa has spent in the past decade has found its way to criminal elements: "almost everyone agrees that the Italian government's costly program to revive the impoverished South has failed - everyone, that is, except the Mafia (34)." A rather more balanced appraisal would admit, however, that because of transfers from the north, per capita income in the Mezzogiorno has risen at a more rapid rate than in the central and northern regions since 1951 (35). In other words, the south is less poor today but more dependent on the north, so whether one says that southerners are on the whole better or worse off depends on how much weight one attaches to living standards on the one hand and autonomy on the other (36). The fact that there is no autonomy movement in the Mezzogiorno suggests the nature of public sentiment in this regard.

In addition to the dominant north-south issue, Rome has had to deal with five regions containing active ethnic or separatist groups. A degree of autonomy has been given to the "special statute" areas of Sicily, Sardinia, the French-speaking Aosta Valley, the German-speaking Alto-Adige (formerly the Austrian South Tyrol), and Friuli-Venezia-Giulia, with its Slovene speakers who have cultural links with Yugoslavia. In 1979, an autonomist united electoral front - made up of special statute-area groups opposed to the centralized state and national parties - narrowly missed electing a member to the European Parliament.

On closer examination there are still other regional differences in Italy. Bagnasco (37), for example, distinguishes between the large-scale modern capitalism that characterizes Piedmont, Lombardy, and Liguria and the rapidly growing, small business, light-industry economy that predominates in Tuscany, Marche, Emilia, and Venetia. There are even significant differences among the various sub-regions of the Mezzogiorno; the positive changes that have taken place have been concentrated in a relatively few areas, for the most part flatlands and coastal sites (38).

In 1972 a step toward greater federalism was taken by the establishment of regional entities with elected councils and powers over local matters. Nevertheless, the strength of the central government and its bureaucracy remains great, and Italy is still far from federalism as it is understood in West Germany or the United States. As Emiliana (39) has pointed out, "in spite of vast pressures from inside and outside the country, democracy in Italy has a solid base. What it needs is machinery more suited to the realities of a diverse nation of regions."

70

The Soviet Union. In spatial terms, planning in the Soviet Union, as in the Socialist countries of Eastern Europe, has among its objectives:

> the attainment of a high economic and social effect in the course of urbanization; the absence of antagonism of interests between town and countryside and between the towns themselves, and the successive planned union of town with country- side; (and) the socialist drawing together of nations and nationalities in the process of urbanization (40).

From the time that the Bolsheviks broke open Czarist Russia's "prison house of the nations," Soviet leaders have attempted to achieve the primacy of social solidarity over regional loyalties. Lenin relied on education to reach this goal. Stalin resorted to violence. When Khrushchev was ousted from power it was widely maintained in the Soviet Union that the federation had achieved its historic task, because almost two generations had known nothing but the Soviet system, its ideology and institutions. In place of dispersed and divided ethnic groups, the era of a Soviet people had dawned (41). And in 1972 President Brezhnev declared that "the problem of equalizing the levels of economic development of the national republics has been in the main solved (42)." In fact, however, marked regional economic disparities have persisted and over a hundred nations and peoples within the Soviet Union continue to maintain their languages, customs, religions and aspirations for some degree of autonomy (43).

About 60 percent of the Soviet population is Slavic; Great Russians, that is, the basic Russian stock, account for about half of the total. In principle the union republics have the constitutional right to secede if their grievances are not properly redressed, but this guarantee has been shown to be a fiction. To the ethnics of the Ukraine, the Baltic states, the Caucasus, and other regions, Great Russian dominance is the rule. In 1974, for example, fourteen Armenians were sentenced to long prison terms merely for suggesting a referendum on secession (44). More recently the Polish example has encouraged Baltic dissidents to protest food shortages and Soviet political repression (45). But Moscow still continues to purge poets, editors, and even party leaders in Tallinn, Riga, Tashkent or Kiev on charges of <u>bourgeois nationalism,</u> <u>feudal tendencies</u> and <u>chauvinism,</u> though no one ever purges Moscow of Great Russian chauvinism.

The existence of regional economic disparities is implicit in much of the Soviet literature on migration. Soboleva, for example, points out that

the problem of maintaining a stable labor force in
the less-developed regions of the country occupies
a particular place in the decision-making that is
focused on this problem. The stimulation of the
material welfare of the population of the
country's less-developed regions is principally
carried out by means of allocation of privileges,
of which there are two kinds (46).

Basically they involve a host of economic incentives as well
as release from certain obligations, including in some
instances military service. Soboleva (47) also remarks that
"this system of privileges aims to attract people to live
permanently in less-developed regions of the nation." But
Ball and Demko (48) show that while large numbers of persons
moved from European Russia to Central Asia and Kazakhstan
during the push to develop these areas in the 1960s, more
recent data indicate a reversal of this trend. A similar
phenomenon appears to have occurred in the massive movements
between the eastern regions and European Russia. In other
words, the evidence suggests that migrants from the European
areas are temporarily moving eastward and then returning to
their native areas.
     The future overall growth of the Soviet economy will be
conditioned by the fact that increases in the labor force
will come almost exclusively from peripheral Soviet
republics, particularly Kazakhstan and the republics of
Central Asia and of the Transcaucasus. The Russian,
Ukrainian and Baltic republics will experience a net decline
in labor force. Because the native populations in the
peripheral regions are reluctant to emigrate, Moscow may
have to incur large costs in making industry available in
these areas (49). Moreover, by the late 1980s almost 40
percent of the prime draft-age males will be non-European
(50). These processes may hasten the assimilation of ethnic
minorities; but it seems no less likely that they could lead
to insistence on a genuine federal system with greater
political and cultural autonomy for the regions.
     Eastern Europe. In comparison with the Soviet Union
(and even some western European nations), the socialist
countries of northeastern Europe are relatively homogeneous.
The most diverse country in this group is Czechoslovakia,
which is comprised of the Czech regions of Bohemia and
Moravia, and, in the east, Slovakia. Ethnic issues have
also been associated with shifts in political boundaries,
which have entailed population movements (e.g. when the
Soviet Union acquired Polish territory and when Poland
acquired German territory) and the division of ethnically
homogeneous peoples (e.g. significant Hungarian minorities
are found in Yugoslavia, Romania, and Czechoslovakia).

Nevertheless, substantial efforts have been made to reduce regional economic disparities.

In Czechoslovakia regional inequalities have been reduced by the priority given to the development of relatively lagging Slovakia. Among the northeastern European countries, regional inequalities are probably the least in the German Democratic Republic. Though a distinction can still be made between the more agrarian and less-developed north and the more industrial-urban south, regional planning in the GDR stresses the notion that egalitarian goals are not inconsistent with regional specialization and division of labor. With respect to the "basic principle" of an "even distribution of production over the whole country," Ludemann and Heinzmann remark that:

> the systematic development of industrial agglomerations and the utilization of their economic powers is part of this principle, just as the creation of predominantly agricultural production complexes in certain areas. The formation of a regionally differentiated but highly developed economic base in all parts of the country according to different historical, natural, and demographic conditions is a universal problem faced by most countries, though in varying degree according to specific conditions. Such a regionally differentiated structure of the economic base brings about regionally differing starting points and objectives for the dynamics of the human settlement systems (51).

In this context, the GDR has particularly stressed the articulation of functional economic areas and equality of opportunity in terms of education, culture, health, and recreational facilities.

In Poland the urban and western areas tend to rank high with respect to per capita income, whereas the rural and eastern areas tend to rank low. It is not clear whether these disparities are increasing or decreasing (52). In any case, despite a relatively well-developed urban network, there is a need to provide growth and service centers in the northeast and northwest, where such centers are few and the agricultural hinterlands are large and thinly populated (53). More generally, settlement system planning in Poland needs more specific policies concerning population, housing, and services; and "it should be stressed very strongly that such national policies should be regionally adjusted and diversified (54)."

Hungary's development has long been marked by the primacy of Budapest. More recently, however, significant shifts have been taking place in the geographic distribution of the industrially-employed population, which decreased by 120,000 in Budapest between 1965 and 1975. Meanwhile, it has been growing relatively rapidly in the economically-lagging regions of the Hungarian Plain and South Transdanubia; the increase in these areas was 16 percent between 1970 and 1975. In general, the economic base of Budapest and other larger urban centers has been shifting in favor of the tertiary sector, that is, these places have been entering the post-industrial phase of development. Medium-size towns have the highest growth rates, but the economic situation of many small towns has improved because of industrial decentralization and improved service functions. These changes have been brought about by two factors. First, industrial enterprises now make many independent decisions based on market considerations. Because of a lack of labor in Budapest, many factories have been set up where workers are available, chiefly in the Hungarian Plain. Second, a central fund for regional development has been established by the government to promote industrial decentralization; two-thirds of these outlays have gone to four regions of the Hungarian Plain. It is expected, however, that the rate of decentralization will slow down as the national settlement system becomes better articulated (55).

Implications of Regionalism

The regions of Europe have cultural roots that go back for centuries, yet until recently it was widely assumed that they had for all practical purposes been absorbed by the nation-states. Thus, it might seem ironic that regional issues should have gained prominance during a period when the regions were lowing their particular characteristics in the face of an increasingly integrated and homogeneous international economic system and the leveling effects of mass communications. In many respects, however, regionalism can be seen as a natural response to such phenomena.

Class and Region. Inevitably the Marxist view is that regionalism is a reaction to the breakdown of traditional social and economic elements to the benefit of monopoly capitalism (56). But regional movements cannot be comprehended in terms of the class distinctions that are fundamental to Marxism. For example, Flemish regionalism "reflects the populist character of Flemish society as well as the 'consensual nature' of class relationships (57)." The behavior of the Scottish National Party, and of Scottish politics in general, "is remote from the relatively simple equations between economics, class and political behavior (58)"; "political activity is now a matter of personal conviction and inclination, no longer of class and status and life-style (59)." In France, "ethnicity is a social category that cuts across class lines, and is capable of appealing to the interests of any or several of its constituent classes at the same time. That is why it is not correct to characterize ethnic activism as 'left' or 'right,' because it can be both (60)." The Spanish Basque "nationalists came to perceive themselves as a separate social groups regardless of their class and other differences (61)." Generally speaking, "Twentieth-century cross-class appeals on the basis of ethnic groups identity have repeatedly clashed with appeals to class solidarity, and the former have usually won (62)."

Diverse Regionalisms. Beer (63) argues convincingly that social strains resulting from rapid modernization and rising expectations that cannot be fulfilled immediately have given rise to regional activism in France's economically and ethnically marginal regions, e.g. Brittany, Corsica, and Occitania. While these arguments may have some relevance to other countries, they are inadequate as general explanations for European regional movements. For example, Spanish Catalonia and Belgian Flanders are relatively prosperous; here regional grievances are related to resentment at having to subsidize other regions. Scottish nationalism was given a boost by the potential prospect that oil wealth could be retained by an independent Scotland. The Italian case is complicated by the fact that the heavily-subsidized mainland Mezzogiorno has no regional movement, whereas Sicily and Sardinia have active autonomist parties. And the relatively rich but declining Spanish Basque region - where Basqueness is no longer necessarily an ethnic matter - is clearly a unique case.

Among the many complex factors associated with regionalism, perhaps the most pervasive is simply a democratic desire on the part of local populations to have more control over their own affairs - to be maitres chez nous, as they say in Quebec. Ardagh (64) recently examined life in provincial Europe as reflected in Stuttgart, Bologna, Newcastle-upon-Tyne, Toulouse, Ljubljana, and their respective regions. None of these places had any autonomist movement, yet each was characterized by a growth of regional feeling engendered by a wish for more local decision-making authority.

It may have been remarked that little has been said about West Germany in this paper. This has nothing to do with an absence of teutonic regionalism. Rather, it reflects the fact that the eleven Lander have a great deal of autonomy within a genuine federal system. Moreover, West Germany has a well-balanced urban system - a legacy from the various states that came together in the last century to form the German nation.

Switzerland provides an even more remarkable example of regional autonomy within the context of a nation-state - and this by no means represents a mere historical curiosity. In response to local demands, the French-speaking Bernese Jura recently achieved the status of a separate canton through democratic processes.

Within the past decade, Great Britain, Italy, Spain and, most recently, France have also taken steps to devolve more powers to regional bodies, but these still lack the powers of the states of the United States or the Lander of West Germany. In each case the centralized bureaucracy has been retained - and central organizations are reluctant to effect authentic decentralization. In particular, it is questionable whether devolution has provided the means for regions to guide their own economic development.

Economic Viability. Given the increasing economic integration within and among nations, a region must have sufficient size to be capable to some meaningful degree of control over its own economic destiny. The question of size is not simply one of population or area, but rather should be understood in functional terms, that is, in the light of such considerations as natural resource endowment, infrastructure facilities, quality of human resources and entrepreneurial talent, and the terms of trade for regional goods and services. Thus, many small European countries have per capita income levels that are among the highest in the world, whereas many of the world's largest countries are relatively poor.

Many of the administrative regions of France, Spain and Italy are too small to be competent economically and to form effective counterweights to central government power (65). In such cases it would appear desirable to consolidate existing units into larger regions, preferably structured around a metropolitan regional capital. As Jacobs (66) has remarked, it is possible for a culture to persist without its own metropolitan capital - but as a museum piece; to flourish culturally a region also needs an economically thriving metropolis. In the case of France, for example, Beaud (67) has proposed that the 22 program regions be regrouped into eight regions; each would have a major urban center and each would be relatively homogeneous internally. Unfortunately, there seems to be little movement in this direction in any of the countries where consolidation would strengthen regional independence. The central bureaucracies no doubt prefer the status quo because it permits them to follow a divide-and-conquer strategy in dealing with the regions.

Border Regions. One of the most important manifestations of the new European regionalism is transboundary cooperation. A good deal of spatial theory maintains that border regions are disadvantaged, but this conclusion is largely based on the assumption of hostility among nationstates; in fact border regions have been reaping considerable benefits from European economic integration (68). Some

76

fifteen regions are cooperating across the Rhine through such organizations as Euregio Nord, Ardennes-Eifel, Moyenne Alsace-Brisgau, and Regio Basiliensis. A Franco-Swiss commission has been established for the basin between the Alps and the Jura, and the Alpazur Region benefits from the support of elected officials in neighboring portions of France and Italy. The Triestine Region has the unique characteristic of uniting at the regional level the citizens of an Eastern country (Yugoslavia) and two Western ones (Italy and Austria). These and similar organizations are represented in the Association of European Border Regions, and a permanent border region organization is being created in Strasbourg in association with the European Parliament.

International Organizations, Nation-States and Regions. Among international agencies the Organization for Economic Cooperation and Development has been a leader in analyzing the economic and legal consequences of transborder environmental pollution in Western Europe (69). Recently it has been examining cooperative environmental protection measures in European border regions (70). The Council of Europe and the Commission of the European Communities have also stressed the importance of resolving such border region problems as labor market imperfections and international commuting; inadequate transportation facilities for trans-boundary traffic; international controls on environmental pollution; and the consequences of uneven inflation rates and of exchange rate fluctuations (71).

A European Regional Development Fund was established in 1975 by the Commission of the European Communities. Its purpose is to create or save jobs in economically lagging regions. Through 1978 it had granted 1.48 billion units of account to the nine members of the Common Market. The principal beneficiaries were Italy (35 percent), Great Britain (25 percent), and France (18 percent) (72). In fact the amount of assistance available from the Fund is very small in relation to the problems it is supposed to address. Some Community members regard it as only one among a number of financial instruments designed to offset what they consider to be the inadequate sums paid out by the Community's Agricultural Fund - which itself has averaged ten times the resources available from the Regional Fund. Credits from the Regional Fund have been thinly spread over many projects (some 5,000 between 1975 and June, 1978) without following any real regional policies. Moreover, because central governments alone can enter into dealings with the Community, little room is left for initiatives by regional or local bodies (73).

Transnational parties, transregional planning, and a multicameral European Parliament including a chamber of the regions represent possible vehicles for resolving complex triangular relations among the European Community, the member nations, and the regions. But at present a Europe of the Regions does not have an institutional basis; and regional autonomists have rarely attempted to spell out the details of how regional demands could be met within the context of a Western European federation. Would a directorate in Brussels be more responsive to the demands of, say, Brittany than a government based in Paris? In any case, the creation of new institutions at the Community level would still require the assent of the nation-states. Thus, in order to achieve their varied objectives, the proponents of regionalism will have to work through the respective nation-states for the foreseeable future.

Conclusion

It is perhaps ironic that the processes of modernization that have encouraged regional movements have also made it easier for the nation-states of Western Europe to respond positively to regionalism. France represents a case in point. As Burguiere (74) points out, "France, having passed through the mixer of modernization in the 1960s, is perhaps in the process of losing its cultural diversity. Having become more homogeneous it can, without risking its unit, let regional aspirations be expressed." Moreover, regionalism viewed in this light is likely to reach a more mature level of expression - that of the civic community rather than just the ethnic community.

In the east the situation is of another order. In the Soviet Union, regionalism among the nations originally colonized by the Czars has been a continuing problem. Efforts to achieve autonomy - which all of the union republics have in principle - have been countered from Moscow by persuasion, violent repression, and, in recent times, the leveling effects of the Russian language and Communist politics, society and economic. Nevertheless, assimilation is still a remote prospect. Rather, demographic disparities are likely to reinforce regional-ethnic dissidence. In Eastern Europe, suppressed but nonetheless active national feelings will, in the face of Soviet hegemony, continue to transcend subnational regional issues even though the latter do receive attention. In this perspective, the regions of Western Europe would seem to be fortunate despite their real and imagined grievances.

NOTES

1. Jose Ramon Lasuen, <u>La Espana Mediocratica</u> (Editorial Planeta, Barcelona, 1979).
2. Perrin, <u>Time</u> (March 18, 1974), p. 28.
3. John Ardagh, <u>A Tale of Five Cities: Life in Europe</u>

<u>Today</u> (Harper and Row, New York, 1979), p. 98.

4. Eugen Weber, <u>Peasants Into Frenchmen: The Moderni-</u>
<u>zation of Rural France, 1870-1914</u> (Stanford University
Press, Stanford, 1976), p. 70.

5. Ibid, pp. 485-496.

6. Pierre-Jakez Helias, <u>Le Cheval d'Orgueil</u> (Plon,
Paris, 1975).

7. Jean-Pierre Richardot, <u>La France en Miettes</u> (Pierre
Belfond, Paris, 1976).

8. Morvan Lebesque, <u>Comment Peut-On Etre Breton?</u>
(Seuil, Paris, 1970).

9. C. Marti, <u>Homme d'Oc</u> (Stock, Paris, 1975); and
Parti Nationaliste Occitan, <u>Occitanie Libre</u> (Edicions Occi-
tanas, Paris, 1973).

10. Robert Lafont, <u>Autonomie: De la Region a L'Auto-</u>
<u>gestion</u> (Gallimard, Paris, 1976).

11. Eugen Weber, op. cit., pp. 493-494.

12. Institut National de la Statistique et des Etudes
Economiques, <u>Statistiques et Indicateurs des Regions Franc-</u>
<u>aises</u> (Collections de l'INSEE, series R, No. 45-46, 1981),
p. 52.

13. Ibid, p. 426.

14. Ibid, p. 369.

15. Beer, op. cit., p. 86.

16. Peter Alexis Gourevitch, "The Reemergence of Peri-
pheral Nationalisms: Some Comparative Speculations on the
Spatial Distribution of Political Leadership and Economic
Growth," <u>Comparative Studies in Society and History</u>, 21, 3
(July 1979), p. 312.

17. Julio Alcaide, "Los Desequilibrios Regionales en
la Economia Espanola," <u>Revista de Estudios Regionales</u>, 4
(July-December), pp. 193-208.

18. A. Bagnasco, "Labour Market, Class Structure, and
Regional Formations in Italy," <u>International Journal of</u>
<u>Urban and Regional Research</u>, 5, 1 (March 1981), p. 308.

19. <u>Cambio</u> (March 9, 1980), pp. 33-34.

20. Marianne Heiberg, "External and Internal Nationalism: The Case of the Spanish Basques," in Raymond L. Hall
(ed.) <u>Ethnic Autonomy: Comparative Dynamics</u> (Pergamon, New
York, 1979), pp. 180-200.

21. Michel Quevit, "Economic Competition, Regional
Development and Redistribution of Power in the Belgian Poli-
tical System," in Antoni Kuklinski (ed.) <u>Polarized Develop-</u>
<u>ment and Regional Policies</u> (Mouton, Paris, 1981), pp. 357-
377; and Aristide R. Zolberg, "Splitting the Difference:
Federalization without Federalism in Belgium," in Milton
Esman (ed.) <u>Ethnic Conflict in the Western World</u> (Cornell
University Press, Ithaca, New York, 1977), pp. 103-142.

22. Barry Newman, "Economy Overshadows Belgium Vote,"
<u>Wall Street Journal</u> (November 5, 1981), p. 27.

23. Donald Mackay, <u>Scotland 1980: The Economics of</u>

Self Government (Q Press, Edinburgh, 1977); and Geoffrey Parker, The Countries of Community Europe (St. Martin's Press, New York, 1979).

24. P. A. Gourevitch, op. cit., p. 310.

25. Gordon Cameron, "Regional Economic Policy in the United Kingdom," in Niles Hansen (ed.) Public Policy and Regional Economic Development (Ballinger, Cambridge, MA, 1974), pp. 65-102.

26. J. R. Firn, "External Control and Regional Development: The Case of Scotland," Environment and Planning A, 7 (1975), pp. 393.

27. Ibid.

28. Norman Furniss, "The Political Component of Scottish Nationality," in Raymond L. Hall (ed.) Ethnic Autonomy: Comparative Dynamics (Pergamon, New York, 1979), pp. 152-179.

29. John Mercer, Scotland: The Devolution of Power (John Calder, London, 1978), p. 230.

30. N. Furniss, op. cit., p. 174.

31. Atkins, op.

32. P. L. Knox, "Regional and Local Variations in Priority Preferences," Urban Studies, 14, 1 (February 1977), pp. 103-107.

33. Vera Cao-Pinna, "Regional Policy in Italy," in Niles Hansen (ed.) op. cit., pp. 137-179.

34. Jonathan Spivak, "Crime in Calabria," Wall Street Journal (December 29, 1980), pp. 1, 11.

35. Commission of the European Communities, Regional Development Programme Mezzogiorno 1977-1980 (CEC, Brussels, 1979), p. 16.

36. Robert Wade, "Fast Growth and Slow Development in Southern Italy," in Dudley Seers (ed.) Underdeveloped Europe: Studies in Core-Periphery Relations (Humanities Press, Atlantic Highlands, N.J., 1979), pp. 197-224.

37. A. Bagnasco, op. cit.

38. Commission of the European Communities, op. cit., p. 18.

39. Vittorio Emiliani, "The Stirrings of Political Reform," Europe, 228 (November-December 1981), pp. 2-4.

40. G. Lappo, "Geographical Aspects of Urbanization Studies," Soviet Geographical Studies (USSR Academy of Sciences, National Committee of Soviet Geographers, Moscow, 1976), p. 197.

41. Helene Carrer d'Encausse, Decline of an Empire (Newsweek Books, New York, 1979), pp. 45-46.

42. R. Fuchs and G. Demko, "Geographic Inequality under Socialism," Annals of the Association of American Geographers, 69, 2 (June 1979), p. 314.

43. H. Carrer d'Encausse, op. cit.; R. Fuchs and G. Demko, op. cit.

44. David T. Lindgren, "Racial and Ethnic Conflict in

Soviet Central Asia," in Raymond L. Hall (ed.) op. cit., pp. 245.

45. "Estonians to Strike Against Soviets," <u>Daily Texan</u> (November 23, 1981), p. 3.

46. Svetlana Soboleva, <u>Migration and Settlement: Soviet Union</u> (International Institute for Applied Systems Analysis, Research Report No. RR-80-36, Laxenburg, Austria, 1980), p. 64.

47. Ibid, p. 69.

48. Blaine Ball and G. Demko, "Internal Migration in the Soviet Union," <u>Economic Geography</u>, 54, 2 (April 1978), pp. 95-114.

49. Abram Bergson, "Can the Soviet Slowdown Be Reversed?", <u>Challenge</u>, 24, 5 (November-December 1981), pp. 33-42.

50. David T. Lindgren, op. cit., p. 245.

51. Heinz Ludemann and Joachim Heinzmann, "On the Settlement System of the German Democratic Republic: Development Trends and Strategies," in Niles Hansen (ed.) <u>Human Settlement Systems</u> (Ballinger, Cambridge, MA, 1978), pp. 122.

52. R. Fuchs and G. Demko, op. cit., p. 307.

53. G. Demko and R. Fuchs, "Demography and Urban and Regional Planning in Northeastern Europe," in Huey Louis Kostanick (ed.) <u>Population and Migration Trends in Eastern Europe</u> (Westview Press, Boulder, CO, 1977), p. 65.

54. Kazimierz Dziewonski, "The Structure of Population and the Future Settlement System of Poland," in Niles Hansen (ed.) <u>Human Settlement Systems</u>, op. cit., p. 154.

55. Laszlo Lacko, Gyorgy Enyedi and Gyorgi Koszegfalvi, <u>Functional Urban Regions in Hungary</u> (International Institute for Applied Systems Analysis, CP-78-4, Laxenburg, Austria, 1978).

56. Renaud Dulong, <u>Les Regions, L'Etat et la Societe Locale</u> (Presses Universitaires de France, Paris, 1978).

57. M. Quevit, op. cit., p. 374.

58. Christopher Harvie, <u>Scotland and Nationalism</u> (George Allen and Unwin, London, 1977), p. 165.

59. Ibid, p. 271.

60. Beer, op. cit., p. 39.

61. M. Heiberg, op. cit., p. 190.

62. P. A. Gourevitch, op. cit., p. 322.

63. Beer, op. cit.

64. J. Ardagh, op. cit.

65. Niles Hansen, <u>French Regional Planning</u> (Indiana University Press, Bloomington, 1968), pp. 1420150; J. Alcaide, op. cit.; G. Parker, op. cit., p. 115.

66. Jane Jacobs, <u>The Question of Separatism</u> (Random House, New York, 1980), p. 16.

67. Michel Beaud, "Une Analyse des Disparites Regionales de Croissance," <u>Revue Economique</u>, 27, 1 (January 1966),

pp. 55-91.

68. Niles Hansen, "The Economic Development of Border Regions," Growth and Change, 8, 4 (October 1977), pp. 2-8.

69. Organization for Economic Cooperation and Development (OECD), Problems in Transfrontier Pollution (OECD, Paris, 1974); OECD, Economics of Transfrontier Pollution (OECD, Paris, 1976); OECD, Legal Aspects of Transfrontier Pollution (OECD, Paris, 1977).

70. OECD, Environmental Protection in Frontier Regions (OECD, Paris, 1979).

71. K. T. Sherrill, "Economic Growth in West German Border Regions," unpublished Ph.D. Dissertation, Department of Economics, University of Texas at Austin (December 1979).

72. Commission of the European Communities, European Regional Development Fund Fourth Annual Report 1978 (CEC, Brussels, 1979), p. 83.

73. Jean Mayer, "The Regionalization of Employment Policies in Western Europe," International Labour Review, 118, 4 (July-August 1979), pp. 415-426.

74. Andre Burguiere, "Qui Avait Ligote la France?", Le Nouvel Observateur (July 18, 1981), pp. 28-29.

PART III: REGIONAL DEVELOPMENT INSTRUMENTS AND THEIR
EFFECTIVENESS

A COMPARISON OF REGIONAL DEVELOPMENT POLICY INSTRUMENTS AND
MEASURES IN EASTERN AND WESTERN EUROPE

George J. Demko and Roland J. Fuchs

Introduction

Any perusal of the regional development literature
readily yields information on a bewildering array of
restraints and incentives utilized by governments in
attempts to solve or ameliorate regional problems. Although
there have been attempts to catalogue such measures and
compare them for some groups of nations such as the European
Economic Community (1) and the Organization for Economic
Cooperation and Development (2), there are few other such
efforts for other nations and regional groups. For example,
little or no work has been done explicitly on this issue for
the socialist nations of Europe (3) and clearly no
comparison of Eastern and Western Europe has been completed
(4).

At the international scale, it is also noteworthy that
few if any comprehensive attempts have been made to identify
and compare regional policy measures and instruments. There
have been cross-national studies and comparisons of
particular policy interventions such as growth center
policies or new city programs. Less spectacular, less
costly and more practical measures, however, have not been
fully identified, evaluated and compared.   Such an effort
may be very revealing and useful. For example, it may be
more effective to utilize regional social security payment
concessions than to fund a growth center policy in a lagging
region.   However, policy makers must first be aware of such
options and their associated costs where they have been
applied. The main goal of this paper then is to identify
and compare the regional development policy measures which
are utilized in both Europes. Such an analysis should
presumably yield insights into the policy emphases, the
differences and the trends in regional policies across
Europe.

The Classification of Policy Instruments

In Europe in general, all regional measures may be
classified into one of five general types. The first of

these, infrastructure investments, may be oriented to rural or urban regions which are intended to act as facilitating or enhancing measures to attract industry or stimulate agricultural progress.   Secondly,   and   perhaps   most widespread and numerous, are monetary incentive measures ranging from capital grants to removal-cost assistance and through the entire range of fiscal and financial aids.   The third group include the location of state-owned or controlled firms and services for target areas.   The fourth type is the control or disincentive type, legal or financial, which attempt to divert activity from pressurized or congested areas to targeted regions of underdevelopment. The fifth general type of measure, in contrast to the types above, are manpower/migration policies aimed at people – attempts to influence them to move to jobs or to stay and acquire skills for jobs.

The classification of policy instruments and measures employed in this paper distinguishes primarily between those characterized as positive or <u>incentives</u> which encourage growth in a specific locale and those which are negative or <u>disincentives</u> to increased agglomeration or growth.   A secondary distinction may also be made between those measures which are directed to individuals or families and those which are targeted at employing institutions.   Such a typology is, of course, arbitrary and many other systems may be used in organizing the policy measures.   In addition to simplicity, however, the system used here has merit in that it focuses on the objectives of the policy instruments, which, despite the vast differences in national goals, perceptions of regional problems, planning systems and political ideologies, can be ultimately reduced to attempts to either encourage or limit growth in specific regions or urban places.

Policy Instruments in Eastern Europe (5)

A summary of the major policy instruments employed in the socialist countries of Eastern Europe is shown in Table 3.1.   It should be noted that this list contains only the documented and discrete measures.   Since the economies of most of the European socialist nations are centrally planned, regional concerns may be addressed in very direct ways through the sectoral planning which predominates in these systems.   There is a large body of literature on the issue of economic efficiency versus regional equity in socialist countries which will not be addressed here (6).

Considering first the incentive measures, those designed to stimulate economic activity and employment in problem regions, the majority are economic in character and directed toward employing organizations: direct investment in job-creating enterprises, both industrial and non-indus-trial, and the indirect measure of investment in various

Table 3.1: Regional Development Policy Instruments of the Socialist Countries of Eastern Europe

Directed Toward	Policy Emphasis	
	Incentives	Disincentives
Employing organizations	-State investments in new industrial and non-industrial enterprises. -Investment in expansion of existing state enterprises. -Investments in public and industrial infrastructure. -Investment in rural and agricultural infrastructure. -Favorable transportation rate adjustments.	-Bans on new industrial investments in designated cities and areas. -Restrictions on industrial expansion in designated cities. -Removal of existing enterprises. -Investments in labor-saving equipment. -Differentiated urban "rents" discriminating against large cities.
Individuals and Families	-Work assignments for higher education and technical institute graduates. -Job transfers.	

Table 3.1 (cont'd)

Directed Toward	Policy Emphasis	
	Incentives	Disincentives
Individuals and Families (cont'd)	-Increased housing investments, provisions, and assignments in particular regions. -Increased investments in services and social overhead capital for particular regions or cities. -Increased provisions of educational opportunities in specific regions and cities. -Regional wage differentials and bonuses. -Regional differences in retirement ages and benefits. -Relocation allowances. -Creation of national and regional organized labor recruitment system. -Mass exhortation and persuasions campaigns.	-Residence registration and related administrative controls. -Administrative and legal controls on in-migration to designated cities. -Penal and other corrective removals and transfers. -"Underurbanization" and commuting.

forms of infrastructure. Such investments may occur in
lagging regions, inexisting centers or in "new towns (7)."
        Secondarily, but growing in importance, are a range of
incentive measures directed toward individuals. These
include investments in various types of social overhead
capital projects, especially housing. Investment in housing
as a labor inducement has increased in recent years as the
significance of housing availability in migration decision-
making has become more widely recognized (8).   Regional
differentials in wage and pension benefits are employed
overtly in the USSR. In the other socialist nations,
however,   since   sharp   wage   differentials   exist   by
occupations, and since many occupation groups are regionally
concentrated, unintended regional wage differences exist.
        The last two incentive measures identified are
information and propaganda measures designed to influence
labor migration. Organized labor recruitment is found in
all socialist countries under study, although an organized
national labor recruitment system has developed surprisingly
late in the USSR. Mass exhortation and persuasion campaigns
are characteristic only of the Soviet Union particularly
among certain groups such as the Young Communist League
(Komsomol).
        With   regard   to   the   disincentives,   they   may   be
characterized as utilizing the knout rather than the sweet.
Some caution, however, should be exercised in such an
interpretation because difficulties have already been
experienced in enforcing some of these measures (9).
Spatially selective bans on new or expanding industrial
growth are growing in importance in these countries and are
employed most frequently in the USSR, Hungary, and, to a
lesser degree, Poland. An even stronger control measure is
the actual removal of existing enterprises such as occurred
in Budapest where, between 1958 and 1970, industrial plants
employing 20,000 workers were removed and relocated
elsewhere in Hungary (10). An emphasis on "rationalization
of industry in larger cities, eg. on capital investments
stressing labor-saving equipment, is now widely employed in
the socialist countries as a means of limiting growth in the
labor force requirements of large metropolises (11)." The
USSR is apparently experimenting with urban "rents" - e.g.
charges   to   industrial   enterprises   for   infrastructure
services - differentiated by size of city in order to reduce
the appeal of large cities (12).
        With respect to individually directed disincentives,
residence registration, and related administrative measures
such as work documents, these measures are widely employed
in most of the socialist countries. Restrictions on
in-migration   to   designated   cities   usually   involve   a
selective process with special exemptions for certain skill
categories and other reasons. Such restrictions have been

utilized primarily in the USSR, Poland and Hungary.

A comprehensive but rarely identified measure employed in some socialist countries to limit growth in larger cities is that of "underurbanization" combined with commuting. Investments in housing and social infrastructure have been deliberately limited in selected large cities, permitting diversion of capital to more "productive" sectors of the economy (13). The limitations in housing and services, combined with administrative and legal measures restricting residence, have served to limit growth of resident populations, while the industrial and productive capacity of the cities has continued to grow at a rapid rate. The labor needs of the centers have been met by utilizing the surplus labor concentrated in surrounding villages, small towns and satelite cities through the mechanism of commutation (14).

The practice of assigning graduates of universities and technical institutes to their initial post for several years permits planners to direct specialists to localities requiring personnel with special skills and away from centers considered to have adequate numbers of such personnel or under growth controls. Work assignments, and the related measure of job transfers, can therefore be employed to encourage growth or control growth as required in specific locales.

In addition to the individual measures and instruments identified in the table there do exist special programs which utilize combinations of measures. The most often cited of these is the growth center program designed to identify latent or incipient urban centers in undeveloped or lagging regions (15). Such package programs include a number of the measures cited and primarily the infra-structure investment and housing instruments as well as direct capital investment for state industries.

In some of the socialist nations and particularly in the USSR, new towns or new cities have been planned and built in remote areas based on a resource. In the USSR the most recent example of such a city is Ust-Ilimsk on the Angara River in Eastern Siberia. In this case the city is essentially run by the pulp and paper combine around which the city is organized.

Policy Instruments in Western Europe

Major policy instruments that have been employed in the nations of Western Europe are summarized in Table 3.2 (16). The dominant emphasis in Western Europe are the numerous incentives that have been directed toward employing organ-izations. Commonly, special promotional or coordinating agencies have been established for areas targeted for growth and development, e.g. the Mezzogiorno development package in Italy. Clearly the primary mechanisms relied upon in Western Europe are the various economic measures designed to

Table 3.2: Regional Development Policy Instruments in Western Europe

Directed Toward	Policy Emphasis	
	Incentives	Disincentives
Employing Organizations	-Special promotional and co-ordinating agencies. -Public infrastructure development for industry, including new towns and industrial parks. -Agricultural infrastructure programs. -Grants and loans for industrial development, including capital investment subsidies. -Tax incentives, including special depreciation allowances for industrial development. -Tax rebates and concessions for industrial relocation. -Tax and manpower subsidies for relocation of tertiary sector. -Rent subsidies. -Land expropriation and reclamation.	-Permits and licenses or other controls on new industrial plant construction. -Permits and licenses for office building construction. -Tax or other financial penalties for investments in congested areas. -Rationing of building materials. -Dispersal and relocation of government, industries, offices, agencies. -Disclosure of major new industrial investment or expansion plans for approval. -Compulsory government supply contracts to companies and industries in lagging regions.

Table 3.2 (cont'd)

Directed Towards	Policy Emphasis	
	Incentives	Disincentives
Employing Organizations (cont'd)	-Technical assistance. -Employment or labor-cost subsidies to industries. -Transport adjustments and subsidies. -Preferential government procurement policies. -Social security payment concessions. -Municipal and community loans for buildings, sites, etc. -Export profit tax relief.	
Individuals and Families	-Job training and human resource programs. -Relocation and settling-in grants. -Social infrastructure investments (hospitals, universities, cultural services). -Housing (public and loans for private). -Physical planning and environmental amenity improvement programs.	-Imposition on metropolitan residents of full costs of water and sewage utilities, and other services. -Zoning practices. -Discriminatory treatment of non-residents, e.g. local government employment, education, etc.

90

entice employing organizations to invest (and thereby create
jobs) in desired areas. These measures include an array of
grants, loans, tax rebates, incentives, and subsidies
intended to overcome the perceived disadvantages of problem
areas targeted for economic growth or stabilization.   In
addition to such economic incentives made directly to the
employing organization, there are also employed other
measures intended to increase the attractiveness of specific
regions.   Included are such measures as land development
projects, public investment in industrial infrastructure
(often in the form of industrial estates and new towns),
transport facilities and subsidies, technical assistance
programs, and government procurement programs providing
preferential treatment for designated areas. Moral suasion
directed toward organizational decision-makers may be
attempted on a sporadic or even permanent basis.

Incentives immediately directed toward individuals and
families are far fewer in number and have been less
emphasized than measures directed toward organizations.
With the exception of often quite limited relocation grants
and housing loans, relatively few financial incentives are
extended directly to individuals (17).   The individual-
directed incentives instead tend to be indirect and include
measures such as job training and other human resource
development programs, public investment in social and
cultural forms of infrastructure, and physical planning and
environmental amenity improvements.

Disincentives, designed to limit further congestion and
growth in a specific locale, in general are less common, and
often less well enforced, than incentives.   Those directed
to employing organizations are not generally outright legal
bans on development in spec-ified cities or regions,
although this may occur.   Such constraints tend rather to
involve permits, licenses or similar controls limiting the
extent of expansion or new investment, and taxes or other
financial penalties are levied to discourage such
development in areas perceived as pressured or congested. A
potentially strong disincentive, more often proclaimed than
implemented, is the relocation and dispersal of government
offices and agencies to regional centers outside the core
area of the major metropolis.

The disincentives directed toward individuals are fewer
and milder; even when promulgated they may prove legally or
administratively unenforceable.   Included in such
individual-directed disincentives are special utility or tax
surcharges for residence in congested areas, zoning
practices designed to limit population growth, and
discriminatory treatment of non-residents (or more properly
new residents), intended to discourage in-migration.   The
restriction of in-migrants to designated locations is
simultaneously a measure designed to control growth of

certain centers and to stimulate growth in target locations.

In general, in Western Europe the fiscal and financial incentives to organizations have been over-whelmingly more important than disincentives and aid to individuals. The main financial incentives have been, in order of importance, capital grants, interest subsidies or discounts, tax concessions and depreciation allowances. A relatively new trend appears to be the use of such incentives by service (tertiary) industries in addition to secondary type activities.

In addition, the measures used are decidedly oriented to taking jobs to workers, although as Yuill, et. al. state, "it must be recorded that the movement of labor has in fact probably done more to balance regional demand and supply than has movement of jobs (18)."

Western European nations also have experimented with packages of instruments including growth center programs, and the development package for the Italian south embodied in the Mezzogiorno Laws, to name a few.

Comparison of Western and Eastern European Policy Instruments

There exists some overlap of policy measures in Eastern and Western Europe when the two are compared. In both areas there is a decided emphasis on economic measures as the principal policy instruments. Both groups basically rely on job-creating capital investments or stimuli to capital investment as the major means of fueling economic growth in desired areas. Economic incentives under this category, directed at the employing organizations, dominate the list of measures employed in both the West and East, and take precedence over social, administrative, and legal measures, as well as other economic measures, including incentives aimed at individuals and disincentives, whether aimed at organizations or individuals.

It should be noted, however, that while there is a general similarity in approach, there are also very significant differences in detail which stem from the substantial differences in the economic and political systems involved. The socialist states, with direct control over the greater part of their economies, are able to intervene much more directly in the spatial economic processes than are the Western nations, characterized by market economies in which the publicly-owned sector is relatively small. Also the socialist nations generally appear less sensitive to the ethical-political problems posed by restrictions on movement and residence taken in the public interest at the expense of individual choice.

With regard to incentives directed at employing organizations, both West and East share certain approaches, including public infrastructure investments and transport rate adjustments. The major distinction is between the socialist states' emphasis on job creation through direct investments in state-owned industries and enterprises, and the reliance in the Western nations on a vast array of incentive measure such as grants, allowances, concessions, loans, tax benefits, and other advantages designed to induce private organizations to invest, expand or stay in designated problem regions.

In the case of incentives directed to individuals and families, both groups employ investment in social infrastructure to attract migrants and retain labor. Similarly, both groups of nations use state employment and recruitment agencies to provide information on employment opportunities to potential migrants. In the socialist countries, however, with a much greater proportion of housing in the public sector, intervention is more massive and made more direct through housing construction, assignments, and provision while the Western nations must generally depend on more limited public housing programs supplemented by indirect incentives such as housing loans or subsidies.

In the category of incentives directed toward individuals, the socialist countries utilize many more than their Western counterparts. Given again the more centralized and collectivized societies of the East, measures such as exhortation and, in the case of the USSR, regional wage differentials (neither of which have precise equivalents in Western policies (19)) are common.

Regarding disincentives directed toward organizations, it may be noted again that the socialist countries intervene directly through outright bans on new construction or expansion, and even the shutting down or removal of employing enterprises. This contrasts with the preference in Western nations of relying upon less direct disincentives such as permits, licenses, and tax penalties.

Perhaps the greatest contrast exists in the case of disincentives aimed at individuals. In the Western nations these are rarely invoked, fairly mild, indirect measures such as tax penalties, land-use zoning, and discriminatory hiring practices. The socialist states, however, may employ administrative and legal controls, such as residence permits, bans on in-migration, and student-graduate assignments - measures which in the West would generally be considered ethically or politically intolerable. Also the socialist nations, unlike the market economies, may employ comprehensive policies fostering underurbanization, with commuting substituting for migration.

Finally, it may be noted that there appear to be few fiscal incentives to enterprises in the Eastern European nations. It is difficult to determine whether this is a function of the centrally-planned economic systems. It may be that there exist tax, price, and wage relationships between the central governments and the ministries, Kombinats, firms and other economic institutions in these systems. We know, for example, that many industrial ministries in the centrally-planned economies have and use their own funds to provide housing for their workers and to erect social infrastructure. We do not know, however, if and on what basis they may build-in regional biases or whether such ministries or trusts are allocated special funds for problem areas. Clearly there is much more to be learned about the Eastern European regional development measures and the intricate relationships among the Government Planning agencies, regional governments, industrial ministries and plants and city authorities.

Conclusion

The identification and comparison of regional development policy instruments and measures clearly leads to a number of generalizations. There is a very heavy dominance of <u>economic measures</u> especially aimed at organizations and institutions. There is a qualitative difference between Eastern and Western Europe in that the former is characterized by measures aimed at State-enterprises whereas the latter group is characterized by a large number of indirect incentives targeted at private enterprises. In both areas, incentives are more important than disincentives.

In general, in the East there is a relatively greater emphasis on moving people to jobs than in the West although both areas utilize predominantly "jobs to people" measures.

Overall there is clearly a bias in that regional development problems are perceived in nearly pure economic terms. This emphasis is noteworthy, for many of the regional problems in both areas have ethnic and/or linguistic overtones. Examples are the Central Asian region in the USSR, the Walloon and Flemish areas of Belgium, Czech and Slovak republics of the CSSR and Brittany in France.

There is an emerging body of development work which indicates that the economic emphasis may cause as many problems as it resolves. Legasto, for example argues that "real societal development can be achieved only through 'enrichment strategies' . . . which rather than displace existing social benefits with material benefits . . . enrich the social with the material (20)."

Appell uses education as an example of an often misunderstood regional policy:

The act of education assumes that the teacher has knowledge or skills to impart to pupils who do not have, at least within the educational environment, anything equivalent to offer in exchange. However,

the knowledge and skills imparted by the teacher are
derived from the more sophisticated centers of the
country and have little or no relevance to the local
ecosystem in which the education act occurs; except
in that they may encourage the pupils to accept an
exploitive view of the natural world . . . As local
knowledge is not included in the educational process
its relative status is implicitly devalued, if not
explicitly, in certain cases (21).

The argument focuses on the fact that regional
development problems are more than spatial economic
inequalities. Indeed, the cultural, linguistic or social
separation of a region and its people from the rest of the
nation may require more than economic palliatives.
Educational, social and related cultural measures may indeed
reduce regional tensions and even facilitate economic
equity.

Finally, the incredible array of measures employed in
both Eastern and Western Europe by their very number and
continual change testify to the fact that we know precious
little of their efficacy. Indeed, it is almost conventional
wisdom that such measures cannot work in isolation but
rather that combinations provide reinforcing impacts.
Until, however, we have a much better idea of the costs and
benefits of regional measures and packages we shall continue
to grope uneasily on our path of regional aid. Obviously
there is a pressing need to set about assessing and
comparing effectiveness of regional instruments in a
rigorous and comprehensive manner. Such a plan must be
placed high on the research priority list as well as the
need to compare and cooperate in such work across national
and ideological boundaries. It would seem that the problems
and measures found in Eastern and Western Europe are similar
enough and important enough to provide an invaluable
laboratory for such a cooperative experiment!

NOTES

1. D. Yuill, K. Allen and C. Hull, <u>Regional Policy in
the European Community</u> (St. Martin's Press, New York 1980).
2. Organization for Economic Cooperation and
Development, <u>Re-Appraisal of Regional Policy in OECD
Countries</u> (OECD, Paris, 1974).
3. For a related effort focused on population policies
see R. Fuchs and G. Demko, "Spatial Population Policies in
the Socialist Countries of Eastern Europe," <u>Social Science
Quarterly</u>, 58, 1 (June 1977), pp. 60-73.
4. Again, for a related analysis of population
redistribution policies see G. Demko and R. Fuchs,
"Population Distribution Policies in Developed Socialist and

Comparison of Policy Instruments

Western Nations," Population and Development Review, 5, 3 (September 1979), pp. 439-470.

5.   This section is based in part on R. Fuchs and G. Demko, "Population Redistribution Policies in Developed Western and Socialist Countries: A Classification and Comparison of Policy Instruments," Symposium on Population Redistribution Policies (Oulu, Finland, 1978); and Demko and Fuchs, "Spatial Population Policies in the Socialist Countries of Eastern Europe," Social Science Quarterly, 58, 1 (June 1977), pp. 60-73.

6.   For a brief overview of the efficiency/equity issue see G. Demko and R. Fuchs, "Geographic Inequality Under Socialism," Annals of the Association of American Geographers, 69, 2 (June 1979), pp. 304-318.

7.   New towns in the Soviet Union are discussed in J. A. Underhill, Soviet New Towns: Housing and National Urban Growth Policy (U. S. Department of Housing and Urban Development, Washington, D.C., 1976); and O. A. Konstantinov, "Role of New Towns in the Development of Settlement Systems in the USSR," Geographia Polonica, 37 (1977), pp. 115-120.

8.   The role of housing in labor migration is discussed in G. Bendemann, "Graphische Fortschreibung der Bevolkerungsbewegung und des Wohnungbestandes als Hilfmittel zur moglichst realen Einschatzing der zu erwartenden Bevolkerungsentwicklung," Petermanns Geographische Mitteilungen, 113, 3 (1969), pp. 194-200; G. Bose, "Entwicklungstendzen der bennenwanderung in der DDR im zeitraum 1953 bis 1970," Geographische Berichte, 64/65, 3/4 (1972), pp. 187-204; R. Ivanova, "Concerning the Development of the Eastern Regions and Their Manpower Supply," Problems of Economics, 16 (June 1973), p. 5; and V. A. Protsenko, "Problemy upravleniya migratsiey naseleniya Evropeyskogo Severa," Sotsial'nye Problemy Migratsiya (Institute of Sociological Investigations, Soviet Sociological Association, Academy of Sciences, Moscow, USSR, 1976), pp. 115-125.

9.   See R. J. Osborn, Soviet Social Policies: Welfare, Equality, and Community (Dorsey, Homewook, Illinois, 1970).

10.   Cited by G. Enyedy, "Development Regions on the Great Hungarian Plain," Development Regions in the Soviet Union, Eastern and Europe and Canada, A. F. Burghardt, ed. (Praeger, New York, 1975), p. 67; and A. Tatai, "The Selective Industrialization and the Removal of Factories to the Country from Budapest as an Economic Policy Influencing the Growth of Agglomeration," Hungarian-U.S. Seminar on Geographical Characteristics of Urban Development (Budapest, 1975), mimeo, p. 36.   The removal and relocation of factories may also occur as a response to areal patterns of labor availability as in the case of the relocation of 340 factories in Czechoslovakia from Bohemia to Slovakia. F. E.

I. Hamilton, "Changes in the Geography of East Europe Since 1940," Tijdschrift voor economische en sociale geografie, 61, 5 (September/October 1970), p. 304.

11.   O. A. Kibalchich and V. Y. Lyubovniy, "Regulating the Development of Big Urban Agglomerations in the Soviet Union: Experience and Problems," Geographia Polinica, 37 (1977), pp. 169-196.

12.   Ibid., p. 195. A Polish author, however, suggests that the socialist countries have yet to develop an adequate economic mechanism to replace land rent in market economies. R. Karlowica, "Mechanism for Controlling the Development of Urban Agglomerations," Geographia Polonica, 37 (1977), p. 173.

13.   Gur Ofer, "Economizing on Urbanization in Socialist Countries," International Migration: A Comparative Perspective, Alan A. Brown and Egon Neuberger, eds. (Academic Press, New York, 1979), pp. 277-303.

14.   Roland J. Fuchs and George J. Demko, "Commuting and Urbanization in Socialist Countries of Europe," Bulletin, Association for Comparative Economic Studies, 19, 1 (1977), pp. 21-38.

15.   See A. Kuklinski (ed.) Growth Poles and Growth Centers in Regional Planning (Mouton, Paris, 1972) for a discussion of such programs in the USSR and Poland, and K. Mihailovic, Regional Development Experiences and Prospects in Eastern Europe (Mouton, The Hague, 1972).

16.   Particularly useful sources in identifying instruments in the nations of Western Europe include Organization for Economic Cooperation and Development, Regional Problems and Policies in OECD Countries (OECD, Paris, 1976); L. S. Bourne, Urban Systems: Strategies for Regulation (A Comparison of Policies in Britain, Sweden, Australia, and Canada) (Clarendon, Oxford, 1975); Robin J. Pryor, op. cit., 1976; and Terence Bendixson, ed., The Management of Urban Growth (OECD, Paris, 1977); D. Yuill, K. Allen and C. Hull, op. cit., 1980; OECD, Restrictive Regional Policy Measures (OECD, Paris, 1977); OECD, Re-Appraisal of Regional Policies in OECD Countries op. cit.

17.   Employment or labor-cost subsidies, a form of wage subsidy, are paid to the employing organization to stimulate job creation and hiring. N. M. Hansen, ed., "Preliminary Overview,"   Public   Policy   and   Regional   Development (Ballinger, Cambridge, MA, 1974), pp. 25-26; also see D. Yuill, K. Allen and C. Hull, op. cit., pp. 200-240.

18.   D. Yuill, et al, op. cit., p. 216.

19.   It may be, however, that regionally based cost-of-living allowances or nationally or regionally uniform union wage scales or minimum wage standards may have indirect, if unintended, effects on population distribution in market economies.

20.   A. Legasto, Jr., "Towards a Calculus of Development

Analysis," <u>Technological Forecasting and Social Change,</u> 14
(1979), p. 1.
    21. G. Appell, "The Pernicious Effects of Development,"
<u>Fields with Fields,</u> 14 (1975), p. 35.

AN ASSESSMENT OF REGIONAL POLICIES AND PROGRAMS IN WESTERN EUROPE

Brian Ashcroft

Introduction

From the late 1950s through the 1960s and early 1970s many governments in Western Europe sought to expand the size and range of their regional policy programs. In Britain, for example, total government spending in real terms (1975/76 prices) rose from £34 million in financial year 1960/61, through £75 million in 1964/65, to £612 million in 1969/70. The persistence of regional disparities in key economic indicators, particularly unemployment, had led governments to seek a more active role in influencing the spatial distribution of economic activity. These developments revived a debate among many regional analysts as to the economic consequences of such policies and, in particular, whether there was an economic case for regional policy.

The debate was conducted between the proponents of the resurgent policies, who advocated a <u>work to the workers</u> strategy and those in favor of a <u>workers to the work</u> strategy. The advocates of the newly expanding policy regime justified their views in terms of national economic efficiency arguments, as well as the more usual appeals to interregional equity and the preservation of regional cultural identities. There was evidence that labor markets in the core regions were experiencing the inflationary pressures associated with excess labor demand. Moreover, it was believed that increasing concentration had led to diminishing returns, rising private costs and the creation of the harmful externalities associated with congestion. The peripheral regions of Western European countries were in contrast suffering from an excess supply of factors of production, leading to unemployment and the underutilization of resources. Spatially unbalanced growth, often considered necessary to maximize national economic development, had gone too far.

It followed that an interregional policy which sought

to compensate for imperfect market adjustment, both within and between spatially separated factor markets, would reduce regional imbalances, raise national employment and so increase the productive potential of the economy as a whole. The shadow price of resource use, particularly labor, in the assisted areas could therefore be considered to be below the market price and so some subsidization of investment and employment was held to be justified.

For the advocates of the workers to the work strategy, a regional policy diversion of labor demand, if it could be justified at all, was purely a 'second-best' strategy. If labor could not be induced to migrate from depressed to prosperous areas, then a policy of firm relocation would only be justified if the net present value (NPV) of output lost through unemployment in depressed areas was greater than the NPV of the output gained by firms choosing to remain in their original more productive locations. Differential regional unemployment and hence the regional problem itself, was a necessary but not a sufficient condition for the regional economic policies that were adopted in many Western European countries in the 1960s.

The debate was conducted largely on the basis of a priori judgements concerning the effects and efficiency of regional policy. Little was known about how regional policies would actually work in practice. Many questions were begged which at that time had little prospect of a satisfactory answer. Would regional policies providing a mixture of carrot and stick, inducements and controls, influence the location and investment decisions of private firms in favor of the assisted areas? Would regional policies work where the non-assisted areas were experiencing unemployment? If regional policies did work in these conditions, would they harm the non-assisted areas, lowering national production and output, while exacerbating incipient spatial problems in areas such as the inner cities? Would efficient assisted firms beat the cost of regional policy by being "forced" to make sub-optimal location decisions? Would regional incentives act as welfare payments to "featherbed" ailing firms and so retard resource reallocation in the economy? Would the expanded regional policies, by making large claims on the public finances, divert resources from more highly valued uses in both the public and private sectors?

We now have much experience with and some knowledge of, the operation of these regional policies. The last decade has seen a rapid growth in the number of regional policy evaluation studies in Western Europe. These studies, which are frequently imperfect and often suffer from serious methodological deficiencies, do, nevertheless, provide an opportunity to reopen the debate about the economic case for regional policies in mixed market economies. Some judgements can also be made about the composition of the regional policy package.

This paper surveys critically the evidence on the effects and efficiency of policy obtained largely, but not wholly, through the construction of empirical models and the application of quantitative techniques. We begin by examining the effects of regional policy on the assisted areas. This is followed by a consideration of regional policy and the assisted firms. In Part III the effects of regional policy on non-assisted areas are examined. Part four discusses the opportunity costs of regional policy. The paper concludes by highlighting some of the implications of the assessment for the formulation and operation of regional policy.

Regional Policy and the Assisted Areas

<u>Estimates of the Effects of Policy</u>. If the evidence is to be believed, regional policy has been successful in creating jobs and stimulating investment in assisted areas. Table 3.3 presents some of the key estimates available for nine EEC countries. The estimates have been standardized compared with their original sources to facilitate cross-country comparisons. The estimated effects do appear to be remarkably similar. However, we must be extremely cautious before drawing conclusions from these estimates about the absolute and relative effectiveness of regional policy in the different countries.

First, the scale and intensity of policy has varied between the countries. Table 3.4 summarizes the major instruments in use in 1979, their method of application, their effective values and coverage. These instruments account for over ninety percent of the expenditure on regional incentives. The information on instruments largely for the single year 1979 is not of course directly comparable to the extended study periods of the policy evaluation studies. These studies have of necessity had to estimate the effects of past policies primarily in the 1960s and early 1970s. The use of a single year in Table 3.4 simplifies comparison and is indirectly relevant because the broad nature of the instruments used and the intensity and scale of policy have not changed dramatically. Moreover, what is perhaps more important here, the relative position of each country both in terms of the scale and intensity of policy, appears hardly to have changed at all.

Ranking the six countries for which we have both job creation estimates and per capita expenditures, we find Italy ranked first on per capita expenditures and maximum effective subsidy but ranked sixth in effects; the Republic of Ireland is ranked second and fourth; Great Britain is ranked third and second; the Federal Republic of Germany is ranked fourth and third; the Netherlands ranked fifth and

Table 3.3: Estimates of the Direct Effects of Regional
Policy on Manufacturing Employment and Investment in the
Assisted Areas of EEC Countries

Country	Employment[1] (Jobs p.a. per 10^3 pop.)	Investment[2]
Belgium	n.e.[3]	n.e.
Denmark	0.79[4]	n.e.
Federal Republic of Germany	1.27[5]	6 to 15[6]
France	n.e.	n.e.
Great Britain	1.30[7]	16 to 25[8]
Italy	0.36[9]	n.e.
Luxembourg	n.e.	n.e.
Netherlands	1.50[10]	17[11]
Republic of Ireland	1.24[12]	n.e.

Notes to Table 3.3
(1) Estimated manufacturing jobs created per annum per thou-
     sand of the population, at mid-1977, in main assisted
     areas.
(2) Percentage of manufacturing investment per annum created
     by regional policy, in main assisted areas.
(3) n.e. = no estimate
(4) Source: IVTB Erhvervsudvikling i Nordjylland, 1974.
(5) Source: E. Recker, Erfolgskontrolle regionaler
     Aktionsprogramme durch Indikatoren (Bonn, Forschungen
     zur Raumentwicklung Bd. 6) 1977.
(6) Source: E. Recker, op cit; Thoss et al (1975); Bolting
     (1976).
(7) Source: Moore and Rhodes (1973,1974,1975,1976a,1977)
     and Moore, Rhodes and Tyler (1977).
(8) Source: Moore and Rhodes (1973); Begg, Lythe and
     Macdonald (1976); Ashcroft (1979); Rees and Mall (1979).
(9) Source: Del Monte (1977).
(10) Source: Netherlands Economic Institute (1975).
(11) Source: Van Delff, Van Hamel and Hetson (1977).
(12) Source: Moore, Rhodes and Tarling (1977).

Table 3.4: Regional Policy in Nine EEC Countries: Major Instrument Type, Intensity and Scale of Policy (1979)

Country	Major Instruments			
	Capital Investment Subsidies (1)	Labor Subsidies (2)	Output Subsidies and Profits Tax Concessions (3)	Disincentives (4)
Belgium	Capital Grant (1966) (D) Interest Subsidy (1959) (D)	Labor Grant (1975) (minor) (A)		
Denmark	Company Soft Loan (1972) (D) Investment Grant (1969) (D) Municipality Loan (1962) (D)			
Federal Republic of Germany	Investment Grant (1969) (D) ERP Regional Loan (1969) (A) Special Depreciation Allowance (1953) (A)	Investment Allowance (1969) (A)		
France	Regional Development Grant (1972) (A) (PDR) (A/D)	Service Location Grant (PLAT) (1967) (A/D)	Local Business Tax Concession (1976) (A)	Agrement (1955) (D) Redevance (1960) (D)
Great Britain	Regional Development Grant (1972) (A) Selective Financial Assistance (1972)(D)	Regional Employment Premium (1967 to 1977) (A) Office and Service Industries Scheme (1973) (D)		Industrial Development Certificate (1947)(D) Office Development Permit (1965) (D)

Table 3.4 (cont'd)

Major Instruments (cont'd)

Country	Capital Investment Subsidies (1)	Labor Subsidies (2)	Output Subsidies and Profits Tax Concessions (3)	Disincentives (4)
Italy	Cassa Grant (1976) (A) 'National Fund' Soft Loan (1976) (A)	Social Security Concession (1976) (A)	Tax Concessions (1947)(1957) (1965) (A)	Authorisation (D) (1971)
Luxembourg	Capital Grant (1973) (D) Interest Subsidy (1973) (D)		Tax Concession (1962)(1967) (1973)(D)	
Netherlands	Investment Premium (1967) (A/D) WIR Regional Allowance (1978) (A)	Lelystad Premium (minor)(1968)(A)		Selective Investment Regulation (1975) (D)
Republic of Ireland	IDA Capital Grants (1969) (D)		Export Sales Relief (1956) (A)	

Table 3.4 (cont'd)

Intensity and Scale of Policy

Country	Maximum Effective Subsidy (%) (5)	Spatial Coverage(6)	% Population	% Area	Expenditure (7) (English pounds per capita in AAs)
Belgium	11.2	Development Zones	39.5	33	19.6
Denmark	14.2	Special Development Regions	17	33	10.0
		General Development Regions Total	31	52	
Federal Republic of Germany	18.6	Zonal Border Area	13	?	20.0
		GA Areas Total	36	60	
France	12.0	PDR Award Zones	32	47	6.3
Great Britain	20.9	Special Development Areas	12.4)	60	20.7
		Development Areas	10.1)		
		Intermediate Areas	18.3)		
		Assisted Areas	40.8	60+	
Italy	47.3	Mezzogiorno	34.2	41	39.5
Luxembourg	8.3		100	100	7.6
Netherlands	16.0	Northern Development Area/South Limburg, which includes WIR			12.9
		Regional Allowance Areas	17	26	

Table 3.4 (cont'd)

Assessment in Western Europe

Intensity and Scale of Policy (cont'd)

Country	Maximum Effective Subsidy (%) (5)	Spatial Coverage (6) % Population	% Area	Expenditure (7) (English pounds per capita in AAs)
Netherlands (cont'd)		IPR Areas Total 28	31	
Republic of Ireland	34.5	Designated Areas 27	50	32.0

Notes to Table 3.4

(1) Major Instruments

The date in brackets indicates when the instrument was introduced. The letters in brackets denote the degree of administrative discretion: (D) = (for incentives) administrative discretion in award rates up to a maximum; (for disincentives) discretion to refuse a permit; (A) = little or no administrative discretion in award, rates fixed; (A/D) = automatic but with an element of discretion for large projects and/or cases of special regional importance.

(2) Maximum Effective Subsidy

These calculations refer to the effective values as a percentage of initial capital costs using maximum incentive combinations in maximum rate zones. In Ireland it assumes that the Export Sales Relief is awarded, but it does not include the value of the relief. In the United Kingdom the estimate excludes the higher value of the package available in Northern Ireland. The SFA grant is included rather than the SFA laon, which is an alternative. The loan has a smaller effective value than the grant.

The effective values are the nominal values of the Capital/Investment subsidies adjusted for tax, delays in payment, and eligible items of expenditure.

106

Notes to Table 3.4 (cont'd)

(3) Spatial Coverage

In Ireland incentives are available nationally but rates are differentiated in favor of the Designated Areas. In the United Kingdom the population average is in terms of the working population. The figures are for January 1979. In July 1979 it was announced that the Assisted Areas are to be reduced by August 1982 to 25 percent of the British working population.

(4) Expenditure

Average annual expenditure in pounds sterling, at 21 November 1980 exchange rates, per head of recipient region population during 1975 to 1979 in current prices.

(5) Sources

Much of the information in Table 3.4 has been obtained from Allen and Yuill (1980, 1981).

first and Denmark ranked sixth and fifth. For the three countries where there is evidence of the impact of policy on investment, we find, taking midpoints from the range of estimates, that Great Britain is ranked first on per capita expenditures and maximum effective subsidy and ranked first in terms of estimated effects; the Federal Republic is ranked second and third and the Netherlands third and second. Can we conclude that the regional policies operated in the Netherlands, Great Britain, the Federal Republic of Germany and Denmark have been superior in creating jobs to the policies in the Republic of Ireland and Italy? Further, has regional policy in Germany, while creating jobs, failed to secure an increase in assisted area investment comparable to Great Britain and the Netherlands? Alternatively, could we conclude that the higher policy expenditures and rate differentials in favor of the depressed regions of Ireland and Italy have not been sufficient to offset the relative unattractiveness of those regions to economic development? It is perhaps tempting to draw some of these conclusions. Unfortunately, it would be dangerous to make these inferences.

Regional policy often amounts to more than financial subsidies: controls and public infrastructure expenditures can play an important role. Differences in the composition of the policy package might in part account for the differences in the rankings between intensity and scale of policy and estimated policy effect. Moreover, since the estimates of policy impact were obtained over somewhat different time periods and refer to different countries, we cannot be sure that other non-policy conditions were similar. This is important because many non-policy conditions interact with the policy instruments to increase or decrease their effect. The most obvious example is the strength of the national pressure of demand. The volume of mobile jobs and investment available to be influenced by a given policy stance will in any one period be greater the higher the pressure of demand. This effect, coupled with changes in the absolute intensity of policy or the policy stance, accounts at least in part for some of the variations in the estimated effects within one country. Countries experiencing a higher than average demand pressure are likely to show greater than average estimated effects and, where automatic instruments are employed, higher than average policy expenditures for a given policy stance. Indeed, the estimated policy effects are likely to increase in greater proportion than the policy expenditures because of the influence of the non-financial components (controls) in the policy package.

How reliable are the results obtained from the policy evaluation studies? Several authors have surveyed the methods employed and the results obtained by these studies

for Britain in particular and Western Europe as a whole (1).
Methodological problems inherent in many of these studies
have been discussed elsewhere and the topic is the subject
of another paper in this volume. It is sufficient to note
the conclusion of a recent survey, that the:

> comparative studies . . . do suggest that a
> reasonable consensus can be formed in an number of
> countries in terms of whether policy has had a
> major or minor effect and, despite the many
> reservations which can be made with respect to
> individual studies, it would be unwarranted to
> conclude that they have all 'got it wrong' (2).

<u>Unanswered Questions</u>. There are significant areas
where the light has still to shine, before we can have a
full appreciation of the effects of regional policy on
assisted areas. First, we know little of the success
achieved in realizing the ultimate objectives of regional
policy. This is in part due to the objectives being vague
and unclearly specified (3). However, it is surprising that
there is a dearth of evidence concerning the effects of
policy on unemployment. Many researchers have avoided
examining the implications for unempoyment because of the
necessary costs involved in the estimation and construction
of a multiequation evaluation model. Regional policy in
creating jobs affects migration and activity rates as well
as unemployment. The impact on all sources of labor supply
should therefore be examined.
    The limited evidence available suggests that when jobs
are created by regional policy in assisted areas, the main
effect is on net-outward migration, rather than activity
rates or the registered unemployed (4).   This is an
important conclusion which requires further investigation.
It is important because it raises the question whether labor
migration in the long-run serves to maintain a pattern of
equilibrium unemployment rates at different levels in
depressed and prosperous areas. In these circumstances,
following the creation of a job by regional policy,
outmigration will be reduced until the initial unemployment
rate in the assisted areas is restored. The shadow wage
will in equilibrium be equal to the market wage and <u>ceteris</u>
<u>paribus</u>, national employment and output will be unchanged.
If migration is equilibriating, the net national employment
effect of regional policy would be positive only during the
period of adjustment to equilibrium (5). And, if other
things are not equal, so that, for example at the given
production technique labor productivity is lower in the
assisted areas, then regional policy could reduce the
equilibrium levels of national employment and output.
    A second area where we have limited knowledge, concerns

the composition of the estimated regional policy effects. The studies are largely concerned with the aggregate net effects of policy on, for example, manufacturing employment and investment in the assisted areas. Little research has been undertaken to disaggregate the effects of policy either by type of unit affected or by type of change. If consistent, differential and systematic relationships can be identified between policy and particular types of assisted area employment and employment change then, by targetting policy towards the most responsive components, government might increase the cost-effectiveness of regional policy and raise the speed of adjustment to economic change in the assisted areas. One problem is that it is often not clear which criteria to use to decompose the data. For example, employment can be disaggregated by type of unit into a large number of different categories: area, industry, occupation, plant ownership, plant size, age of plant and so on. And for each category chosen there remains the question of the appropriate level of disaggregation within each category. Similarly, employment change can be decomposed in many different ways, given the chosen type of unit and level of disaggregation, for example, jobs created and jobs lost, or jobs created in expansions, openings, inward movement and jobs lost in contractions closures and outward movement.

Some research has been undertaken to identify the impact of policy on particular components of employment change. The measurement of the impact of policy on mobile employment has been a popular choice.

In the United Kingdom, it appears that inward foreign investment has been more responsive to regional policy incentives than inward domestic investment (6). Incoming foreign firms are less subject to the inertia which ties domestic forms to non-assisted area locations and they are more likely to adopt expensive and sophisticated site search procedures to identify suitable locations offering minimum operating costs (7). The studies also suggest that approximately 50 per cent of incoming employment was induced by regional policy (8). Questionnaire surveys of the influence of regional policy on firms' location decisions are much less clear cut. A recent survey of this work concludes that "with the major exception of the U.K., regional policy . . . hardly ever receives a ranking above 4 and often much lower, although there are occasional exceptions (9)."

There is, however, no direct evidence of the impact of policy on the other components of net employment change. We can obtain indirect estimates of the contribution of net indigenous employment by subtracting induced mobile employment from the estimated net policy effect. In Britain, estimates range from 20 to 60 per cent of the net effect (10). But what has not been identified is the policy-induced interaction between each component of employment change as well as the direct effect of policy on each component. For example, in addition to our lack of knowledge of the direct effects of policy on the components of indigenous change, we do not know whether induced mobile firms have favorable or unfavorable effects on local economies. We do not know if these firms generate indigenous expansions and births via multiplier and linkage effects, or whether the effect of increased competition in local product and factor markets leads to indigenous contractions and closures. Many studies simply apply income and employment multipliers to the estimate of the direct policy effect without questioning the assumption of positive indirect effects.

If regional policies can be said to have had positive effects on employment and investment in the assisted areas of Western Europe, the evidence on the longer-run effects of these policies is much less conclusive. In theory the existence of regional incentives making production relatively more attractive in assisted areas, should increase <u>ceteris paribus</u> the proportion of national output produced in those areas. The evidence does suggest that the distribution of economic activity has moved in favor of assisted areas. This is particularly the case in Britain (11). However, it is not clear whether continuing aid would be required to maintain this higher proportion. Some insight into this question can be gained by considering the effects of regional policy on the assisted firms.

Regional Policy and the Assisted Firms

We have noted the evidence that regional policies have attracted firms to assisted areas who would otherwise have expanded in and/or maintained their production in non-assisted areas. If the regional policy stimulus to investment and employment is to be self-sustaining, then the prospects for future development will depend on the suitability of the assisted areas for the operations of assisted firms and the characteristics of the assisted firms themselves.

Locational Disadvantages of Assisted Areas for Assisted Firms. An important question raised in the debates concerning the economic case for regional policy related to the prospects for viable production in certain economic activities in assisted areas. It is important to ascertain whether regional policy is necessary to overcome real as opposed to perceived locational disadvantages to production in assisted areas. Many people believe that areas have to be assisted by regional policy because of the extra real cost incurred by firms in locating and producing there. If this is in fact the case, then it would be necessary for regional policy to provide a continuing subvention to maintain the policy created jobs in those areas.

It is virtually impossible to generalize for the assisted areas of Western Europe as a whole. Some areas such as the Mezzogiorno suffer more severe locational problems than others. The nature and extent of the regional problem must obviously determine the degree of locational disadvantage experienced by incoming and new indigenous firms. Nevertheless, from the limited evidence available it is not certain that regional policy has in general 'forced' firms to choose unacceptable and inefficient locations. Indeed the wide spatial coverage of the assisted areas in Western Europe may, as we note below, have allowed assisted investments to follow national locational trends, such as the recent evidence concerning the urban-rural shift in Britain in particular and in other Western European economies (12).

The available evidence does suggest that firms induced to locate in assisted areas often experience higher operating costs. However, it is not clear whether these extra costs are temporary, transitional costs or whether they are likely to be permanent. In Denmark, Kolind and Matthiesen's survey (13) found that for locations in provincial areas, costs could vary from +3.5 percent to -3.5 percent of total costs and +6 percent to -5 percent of value added. For firms in receipt of regional incentives costs would be reduced by on average approximately 2 percent of value added. In general, it was found that costs did not vary by much between locations, provided that the firm did not depend on a specific local raw material or a local market. In some cases the value of the incentives was not sufficient to produce a net decrease of costs following re-location. The incentives have, nevertheless, been found to make a significant contribution in offsetting higher operating costs where these have occurred following an assisted area location (14). No evidence is available concerning the question whether apparently higher operating costs in a Danish assisted area location are simply temporary dislocation costs or whether they are permanent.

In the United Kingdom, the only other country for which there is much detailed information, there is evidence that some firms who relocated to assisted areas experienced higher operating costs (15). Opinions varied amongst the firms in this survey as to whether the cost penalty was temporary or permanent. Indeed, it is often not clear whether the performance comparisons are in fact reliable. Some of the evidence on higher operating costs have been found to result from a comparison of a new plant in an assisted area with an established plant in a non-assisted area (16). Survey research undertaken by academics has found that higher operating costs are often a temporary phenomenon (17). Where ostensible regional differences in efficiency have been subjected to rigorous analysis, as in the study by O'Donnell and Seales (18) of the mechanical engineering industry in the U.K., the differences have been found to be attributable to non-regional specific factors. In sum, as a recent study of the effects and costs of U.K. regional incentives points out,

> we cannot conclude that there is any evidence that diversion of activity through regional incentives leads to any long-term reduction in the efficiency with which resources are used, not that creation of additional activity in the assisted areas is in any way a less efficient use of resources than its location elsewhere (19).

  <u>Characteristics of Assisted Firms.</u> The characteristics of the assisted firms induced to locate and expand in assisted areas are likely to be crucial to the prospects for future development. Unfortunately, economic theory does not provide us with a clear idea of the characteristics that are likely to be important. Many researchers have identified certain attributes of firms, and the environment in which they are located, which are considered beneficial or harmful to regional economic development. Emphasis is sometimes placed on the interactions between firms and the limiting and the liberating effects of a region's spatial structure (20). The sectoral structure of firms has been emphasized. For example, whether the firms influenced by policy are concentrated in the modern growth sectors of the economy or in the less dynamic sectors. Alternatively, stress is sometimes placed on the organizational and ownership characteristics of the firms. A high proportion of externally-owned branch plants is frequently considered to be prejudicial to regional development in the long-run (21). Finally, the operating characteristics of firms are often considered to be important. For example, the factor intensity of the techniques used, the size of the establishment and the employment and wage structure.
  The characteristics of the firms influenced by regional policy in each country can be considered under four headings: their spatial and locational characteristics; their sectoral composition and performance;   their organizational and ownership patterns and their operating characteristics. It should be noted that the limited information available largely concerns the characteristics of firms investing in the assisted areas.   If the characteristics of those firms induced by policy to invest in the assisted areas differ from those firms investing in the assisted areas for non-policy reasons, any conclusions drawn here are likely to be inaccurate.
  <u>Spatial and Locational Characteristics.</u> It is to be

expected that firms investing in the assisted areas would not be spread evenly throughout space. In Ireland, O'Farrell (22) found that the probability of an area obtaining an establishment per head of the population declined as town size increased. He found that 50 percent of all projects went to towns with less than 5,000 population. The possibility of a location in a town with less than 5,000 people was estimated to be 0.6 compared with 0.2 for a town of 25,000 to 150,000 people.

For Great Britain, Keeble (23) and Fothergill and Gudgin (24) appear to draw similar conclusions. These studies refer to the periods 1971-1976 and 1959-1971, respectively. Both studies found, having standardized for spatial differences in industrial structure, that the more rural or the less urbanized the sub-regions the greater the proportionate increase in employment. Regional assistance did not appear to alter the dominating effects of relative and absolute growth in non-urbanized sub-regions containing major free standing cities and relative and absolute decline in conurbations. However, Moore, Rhodes and Tyler (25), note that the effect of regional policy in the British assisted areas is likely to have retarded the urban-rural shift in those areas even if the dominating effect of the shift was not removed. Their view is based on the evidence for Britain provided by industrial movement data which suggests that regional policy attracted a significant amount of manufacturing employment to conurbations in the assisted areas. Although it is the periphery of the conurbations rather than their centers which appears to have provided the most suitable locations (26).

In Denmark, the evidence suggests that policy-assisted investments were not located in the large towns in the assisted areas but in the middle-sized towns (27). The centers of major cities also appear to have been avoided by those firms in the Federal Republic of Germany in receipt of regional assistance. The evidence suggests that firms located in the periphery of cities when land was the main constraint on expansion, and in urban areas and in rural areas when labor shortages occurred in the cities. Nevertheless, in the Federal Republic urban areas and regions have perhaps retained their attractiveness to assisted investments to a greater degree than elsewhere. Between 1955 to 1967, admittedly somewhat earlier than the results from the other studies, 20 percent of assisted areas locations and 33 percent of jobs, were concentrated in four congested areas, 11 urban sub-regions and the Zonenrand-gebiet of Hamburg. The underdeveloped rural areas of the GA areas appeared to be less attractive to mobile employment (28).

In general, however, it does appear that assisted investments have followed national locational trends by seeking to avoid the centers of major conurbations. Medium-sized towns in non-urban areas and the periphery of larger cities, are the locations that best satisfy the current locational preferences of modern industrial firms. Regional policy, in the form of financial incentives, does not seem to have altered these basic locational preferences. The wide spatial coverage of many Western European assisted areas appears to have allowed assisted firms to follow national locational trends.

Sectoral Composition and Performance of Assisted Firms. Another important characteristic which has possible implications for the future performance of the assisted investments, and the assisted areas as a whole, is the sector in which in the investments occur. The evidence is again rather limited. In Table 3.5 some industrial sectors in Belgium are ranked by their propensity to invest in the depressed regions, their growth performance and stability. In Table 3.6 certain industrial sectors in Great Britain have been ranked by their estimated investment shift to the three main Development Areas and their growth performance and stability. The tables are not strictly comparable. The sectors are defined differently. The growth and stability rankings are derived from different measures. In Great Britain the rankings of industry investment are based on an estimate of the policy induced shift to the DAs, while in Belgium the rankings of industry investment simply reflect the proportion of industry investment in the DAs. Nevertheless, perhaps we can say that in Belgium the main industries (the first three) investing a greater proportion in the DAs had a tendency to be relatively growth orientated and cyclically unstable (excluding metallic products). In Great Britain, the policy induced shift of investment was greater in those industries with relatively low average annual growth and low cyclical stability. However, it would be unwise to make too much of this comparison.

In both Belgium and Great Britain metal manufacturing appears to have been important for investment in the assisted areas. It should be emphasized, however, that in Belgium the basic metal industry dominated industry in Wallonia before the regional development program. Nevertheless some 70 percent of the employment provided by new foreign firms entering Belgium and the assisted areas was concentrated in the metal and chemical industries (29). Also in both Denmark and Ireland metal manufacture was a major recipient of regional/industrial assistance. In Denmark, metals, engineering, food and drink received more than 50 percent of the regional assistance. In Ireland, metals and engineering constituted one-third of the total employment provided with assistance from IDA grants. Food, clothing and footwear constituted another third. In Germany, metals ranked fourth of those sectors whose

Table 3.5: Sectoral Characteristics of Investments in the
Assisted Areas in Belgium

Industry	Rank[I] PIDR	Rank[II] Growth	Rank[III] Stability
Basic Metals	1	1	8
Chemicals	2	1	7
Metallic Products	3	3	2
Construction Materials	4	5	4
Textiles, Clothing	5	7	5
Food, Beverages	6	6	1
Other Industries	7	2	6
Wood, Paper	8	5	3

(I) Source: Deblaere (1979), period 1967-1977. PIDR is the
proportion of industry investment in the DAs.

(II) (III) Source: National Accounts 1968-1975. Instability
has been measured by the change in the rate of growth of
output from 1974-1976.

Table 3.6: Sectoral Characteristics of the Policy-Induced
Shift of Investment to the Three DA Regions of Great Britain

Industry	Rank[I] Policy Shift	Rank[II] Growth	Rank[III] Stability
Paper, Printing	1	3	4
Metals	2	6	6
Textiles	3	8	8
Vehicles	4	2	1
Chemicals	5	1	2
Bricks	6	5	7
Food	7	7	5
Engineering	8	4	3

(I) Source: Rees and Miall (1979), period 1966 to 1976.

(II) Source: <u>Index of Industrial Production</u>, period 1948 to
1972 annual average growth rates.

(III) Source: Thirlwall (1966). Instability measured in
terms of the regression of the first differences in
percentage <u>unemployment</u> in the industry on the first
differences in the U.K., period 1949 to 1964.

investments received respectively more regional assistance. There is evidence also in Germany that expanding sectors were less likely to be assisted. For example, from 1969 to 1973 only 28.6 percent of the total assisted investments were undertaken in expanding sectors (30). Once again we should not set too much store by these comparisons because they are not made on exactly the same basis. Perhaps the least contentious conclusion that we can draw from these sectoral comparisons is that there does appear to be evidence, in at least three countries: Belgium, Germany and the United Kingdom, that the main sectors influenced or aided by regional policy were relatively more cyclically unstable than other sectors.

Organization and Ownership of Assisted Firms. Many of the establishments induced to locate in assisted areas have been branch plants. In Great Britain approximately 80 percent are likely to have been branch plants (31). For the Federal Republic of Germany, there is some, albeit very much weaker, evidence that branch plants have contributed in a major way to the policy effect (32). Incoming foreign firms have also played an important role. In Ireland, at least 45 percent of the policy effect in the Designated Areas appears to have been provided by firms moving from abroad (33). In the United Kingdom DAs 19 percent of all mobile jobs, that is jobs created as a result of both policy and non-policy influences, were provided by new firms from abroad. A higher percentage figure was recorded for Scotland. Foreign firms also appear to have been a major source of employment and to have been more responsive to the incentives available in Belgium's assisted areas. Conversely, foreign firms do not appear to have contributed in any significant way to job creation in Denmark's assisted areas (34). Furthermore, in Denmark some 80 percent of assisted investments were extensions to factories already located in the assisted areas (35). This does appear to be in sharp contrast to the other countries considered here.

The importance of branch plants and foreign subsidiaries to the regional policy effect is considered by some to be a factor that is likely to inhibit future regional development (36). This view is based on the evidence that branch plants and the subsidiaries of foreign firms are likely to be solely production units with decisions concerning purchasing, marketing and research and development being made outside the region (37). In Ireland, for example, McAleese (38) found that 60 percent of the foreign firms in his sample left research and development to the parent firm. Branch plants and particularly foreign owned establishments are thought to be more likely than the parent plant to suffer closure or contraction during a recession. This, coupled with the evidence that regional policy seems to have attracted firms in more cyclically unstable sectors, might suggest that regional policy has contributed to an increase in the cyclical sensitivity of assisted areas. However, the very limited evidence available suggests that branch establishments are no more likely to close or contract in a cyclical downturn than either their parent plants or indigenously owned plants (39).

Operating Characteristics of Assisted Firms. The main information on the operating characteristics of the plants influenced or assisted by regional policy, concerns the factor intensity of the techniques used, the relative size of the establishments and their employment and wage structure.

In Belgium and Germany, it appears that assisted investments were generally more labor intensive than non-assisted projects (40). In contrast, in Denmark, it appears that firms receiving regional incentives employed more capital intensive techniques (41). Similarly, in the United Kingdom industries employing higher capital intensive techniques were found to be more likely to invest in the assisted areas (42). A partial explanation for these differences between countries is that where discretionary policies are in operation they are more likely to operate in favor of those firms that will provide the most jobs in the assisted areas. This explanation cannot, however, be applied to Denmark, given the absence of automatic policies there. Nevertheless, in Ireland, Ruane (43) found, using econometric methods, that the grant package negotiated by the IDA was higher for labor intensive firms. Ruane attempted to identify whether the IDA varied the grant offered according to firms' capital-labor ratios and whether firms responded to the variability of the grant by altering the capital intensity of their production technique. Her estimates suggested that the IDA did influence and was influenced by, the capital intensity of the applicant firms.

In the absence of work comparable to Ruanes' in other countries, there is no satisfactory evidence to support the traditional view of neoclassical production theory, that regional factor subsidies have induced firms to change their production technique. We must rely for the most part on less direct evidence. So, in Denmark there is evidence that assisted investments were more capital intensive than the technique currently employed by the firm making the investment. However, this effect might simply by explained by the investment enabling a more capital-intensive new technology to be introduced, rather than substitution towards a more capital intensive technique within an existing technology.

There is also some evidence that policy has been more effective in influencing larger firms rather than the small firm (44). Also in Denmark, firms applying for incentives were on average some 33 to 66 percent larger than those not applying (45). One possible explanation for this phenomenon, is that the larger firm is more likely to use investment appraisal techniques and to incorporate regional assistance within the appraisal (46). Another reason is that for many firms a location in the assisted areas requires a long-distance move. The smaller firm is more likely to be tied to the local economy of which it is part and so be unable to move the required distance (47). In these circumstances, it is the larger firm with the ability to locate a branch plant in the assisted areas, that is more likely to profit by the assistance (48).

One other feature of interest where there is some information concerns the employment and wage structure of the firms influenced/assisted by policy. In Denmark, Thorvildsen (49) found that the projects aided were more likely to employ the higher educated, higher salaried, office employees. In addition, relatively fewer female workers were employed by the supported firms. Whether this reflects a specific bias in the operation of discretionary policy in Denmark in an attempt to diversify the local labor market, or whether it indicates that firms employing more skilled workers are more likely to be investing and therefore eligible for assistance, is not clear. The evidence from the Federal Republic of Germany contrasts with Denmark, because assisted firms were found to be more likely to employ unskilled female workers receiving relatively low wages. Klein (50) found that, on average, assisted firms employed 17.4 percent skilled workers compared with a national average of 29.6 percent. In the United Kingdom the employment structure of the firms attracted to the assisted areas has probably been more similar to the German structure than that of Denmark. In Cameron and Reid's survey (51) of 79 firms that moved into the assisted areas between 1958 and 1963, the main locational influence was the available supply of unskilled but trainable labor. The availability of trained labor ranked only eighth out of seventeen identified locational factors.

In sum, the limited evidence on regional policy in Western Europe and the firms influenced and/or assisted by policy suggests rather tentatively the following conclusions. First, we cannot conclude that firms have been forced or induced to choose unacceptable and inefficient locations. Second, there is no evidence that regional policies have largely supported ailing firms that would have closed in the absence of policy. From the evidence concerning the structural and operating characteristics of assisted firms it appears that the typical firm or plant aided by policy is relatively larger, more cyclically unstable, using a production technique with a different factor intensity and requiring a different level of skills from its workforce, than the national average plant or firm. We must be wary of generalizations from such sparse information. However, one cannot conclude from this evidence that assisted firms are necessarily marginal offering little prospect of a favorable impact on the future economic performance of assisted areas. Indeed, many of the firms attracted to assisted areas have often been expanding firms (52). Many of these firms became mobile because of supply constraints on expansion in the non-assisted areas (53). The existence of the regional financial incentives has served to induce many of these firms to satisfy their growing demands for land, premises and labor by locating in the assisted areas. One implication is that policy has denied to the non-assisted areas many firms who might have expanded or relocated there. This raises the question whether regional policies have actually harmed the economic performance of the non-assisted areas and the nation as a whole - an issue to which we now turn.

Regional Policy and the Non-Assisted Areas

A popular and perhaps reasonable misconception concerning the effects of regional policy, is that since the policy seeks ostensibly to influence the spatial distribution of production then any benefit to the assisted area must necessarily be at the expense of the non-assisted areas. While this might be the case in particular circumstances, there is much theoretical argument and some limited empirical evidence to suggest that this zero-sum relationship is by no means inevitable.

First, the evidence suggests that regional policy incentives have largely induced the diversion of additions to capacity, net new investment, from the non-assisted areas, rather than the transfer of existing capacity and replacement investment. Of course, this can still be interpreted as a loss to the non-assisted areas if the standard of comparison is what otherwise would have happened to capacity rather than the given levels of capacity in the non-assisted areas.

Secondly, there is the evidence that regional policy incentives have attracted foreign investment. For Belgium, Ireland and Great Britain regional incentives appear to have attracted some foreign firms both to the assisted areas and to the country itself (54). However, from the available evidence, this does not appear to be the case for Italy, where the incentives were found to play a role in steering foreign investments to the Mezzogiorno only after they had decided to locate in Italy (55). Where incentives do attract foreign firms to the country as well as to the assisted areas, then jobs will not be displaced in the non-assisted areas compared with what otherwise would have occurred. This assumes that there would be no financial

121

crowding-out effects of domestic jobs through incoming
foreign firms financing their investment in the domestic
capital market.

Thirdly, regional incentives have induced local
assisted area firms to expand. We noted above that in Great
Britain estimates range from 20 to 60 percent of the policy
effect. However, some local expansion might be the result
of linkages to incoming firms plus the effects of the income
multiplier. This indirect job creation will have as its
counterpart indirect job losses in the non-assisted areas.
The remaining indigenous job creation need not be at the
expense of the non-assisted areas.

The final point of relevance here concerns the
theoretical proposition that a spatial redistribution of a
national aggregate demand might in certain circumstances
raise the effective productive potential of the economy. A
Keynesian interpretation of this proposition would suggest
that moving employment from a region with a relatively tight
labor market to a region with relatively high unemployment,
might lower the rate of national inflation (56). If
Government demand management is constrained by a target
inflation rate then a policy which reduces spatial imbalance
in the supply and demand for labor might relax the
constraint, allowing the Government to raise national
employment and output. A quasi-monetarist interpretation
would suggest that a regional policy reduction in the
spatial imbalance in the supply and demand for labor might
lower the 'natural' rate of unemployment removing or
reducing the constraint on private market adjustments to a
higher level of national employment and output.

In reality the outcome is uncertain because it depends
on the satisfaction of the necessary assumptions. Nevertheless, there are some suggestions that a regional policy
diversion of labor demand will in practice raise the level
of national employment and output.

In Great Britain, Ashcroft and Swales (57), developed
a large empirical model to allow for several simultaneous
effects of a spatial diversion of demand on the national
rate of inflation. The operation of the regional labor
market was specified in some detail. The model was solved
using parameter estimates in the equations which were
obtained from previous empirical work on the U.K. economy.
The model, which was applied to identify the effect of the
dispersal of Civil Service posts to the DAs, predicted a net
national employment effect: for every 100 posts dispersed
29 full-time male equivalent jobs were expected to be
created in the economy as a whole. Simulations made with
the REGINA model of the French economy suggest that a
regional policy seeking to decentralize industries from the
Parisian region to the Province regions has a favorable
effect on national economic efficiency as well as

interregional equity (58).   Both models suggest that the
national effects depend on the national and regional
economic situation but contrary to popular belief, positive
national effects can be produced even when there is some
unemployment in the non-assisted areas.

Some support for these predictions is provided by Tyler
(59) who found, from econometric estimates of the effects of
past British regional policies, that these policies had
produced no harmful effects on employment in the West
Midlands: a major origin region for jobs diverted by
regional policy to the DAs. Further research is of course
still necessary in this area so that we can be clear about
the full range of regional and national economic circumstances that will enable a successful regional policy
diversion of labor demand to have favorable national
effects.

It should be noted that, if regional policy does raise
national employment and output, then the unfavorable impact
on non-assisted areas will be somewhat lower than the
measured policy effect in the assisted areas.   In certain
circumstances, there could be a favorable net effect on
employment in non-assisted areas.   However, this would not
preclude the possibility of unfavorable effects on
particular locations within the non-assisted areas. We have
very little evidence concerning the detailed spatial
incidence of the effects of policy.   One study in Great
Britain did find that only 9 percent of the decline in
employment in the inner-areas of London had been transferred
to the assisted areas (60). This might indicate that even
if regional policy was responsible for the whole of the
diversion, the policy itself has not contributed markedly to
inner-city decline in non-assisted areas.

The Opportunity Costs of Regional Policy

Can it be said that Western European regional policies
have been worthwhile?   In theory, many economists would
argue that all public projects and policies should be
accepted if they succeed in raising the net present value of
national consumption. This test would be subject to present
and future costs and benefits being identified and valued
correctly, including the use of the appropriate distributional weights and a suitable discount rate. If regional
policy has led to additional jobs and output in the nation
and if the policy resulted in no major long-term relocation
costs then, other valuation problems aside, this might be
taken as affirmative support for the policies.   However,
even if we could be certain about the effects of past
policies which, of course, is not yet, if at all, possible,
we cannot conclude either that existing regional policy
expenditures and programs should be expanded until the net
present value of the return from the last dollar spent is

zero, or that they should be maintained. If there are some policies that are mutually exclusive, or alternatively the public sector is subject to a form of capital rationing, which in effect could be public expenditure restrictions, then the alternative uses of public sector resources should be considered.

For regional policy, the mutually exclusive policies are all the different regional policies that might have been used. Here, other things remaining equal, the opportunity costs of regional policy turns on the question whether the regional policy objectives could be achieved more efficiently by different regional policy packages. And, if so, which package would be likely to generate the highest net present value. Unfortunately, researchers in Western Europe have not devoted much attention to the evaluation of alternative policy packages ex ante. We can, however, gain a limited insight into this question by examining the evidence concerning the relative impact of different instruments in policy packages adopted previously and the effects when these policy packages have changed in composition.

It should be remembered that there is no widely accepted theory concerning the choice of instruments and the composition of the policy package. The area is surrounded by controversy. There is controversy concerning the type of instrument that should be used. Are capital subsidies to be preferred to labor subsidies? Should whole-factor or marginal subsidies be employed? Are cash grants preferable to tax allowances? Are disincentives necessary to obtain a sizable policy effect? Does infrastructure play a permissive or propulsive role in advancing regional development? Questions also arise concerning the methods used to implement policy: the extent of the spatial and industrial coverage, the scale of assistance, whether policy should be automatic or discretionary and whether quasi-autonomous Government agencies are necessary to achieve the desired effects.

In general terms, Table 3.4 suggests that the main policy instruments adopted in Western Europe show a substantial bias in favor of capital and investment subsidies, compared with other possible incentives such as output and labor subsidies. Grants appear to have been more important that tax concessions. Disincentives are not generally used; and few countries operate completely discretionary policies.

The evidence suggests the following, if tentative, conclusions. Grants appear to be more effective than tax concessions, largely because the latter tend to be underestimated, or because only a limited number of firms are able to take advantage of them. An automatic policy tends to produce a greater effect than a discretionary policy

(61).   The increased certainty of an automatic policy is favored by many firms and so produces greater effect. Controls, such as the British Industrial Development Certificate, are important, perhaps crucially so, in inducing firms to leave a non-assisted area location, while financial incentives appear necessary to influence the choice of location.   Firms can more effectively be pushed then pulled, rather than pulled directly into an assisted area location.   Finally, infrastructure appears in previously developed regions to play a permissive rather than a propulsive role in advancing regional development (62).

It is clear that we cannot use the slight evidence available to suggest that policymakers have seriously got it wrong. It is also clear that the evidence does not allow us to draw conclusions about the relative efficiency of each policy instrument and method of application.   Policymakers must still, and probably always will, have to rely on their own judgement as to the content and composition, in given circumstances, of the optimal policy package.

During periods of low growth and national recession, some Governments often appear to pursue the regional equity objective with less enthusiasm than at times of national prosperity.   Questions about the division of the national cake are held to be less important than the issue of its size.   In these circumstances, regional policy can probably only be justified on economic grounds by its effect in raising national employment and output.   In the absence of different weights on the spatial distribution of new employment and output, one new job created by regional policy is valued equally with a new job resulting from other job creation policies.   Moreover, if Governments wish to curtail public expenditures to satisfy policy objectives other than job creation, then regional policy should be evaluated against the alternative policies.   In these circumstances it is not sufficient that the net present value of job creation is positive for any job creation policy to be undertaken. Rather, the Government must choose those policies that promise a greater return per unit of public expenditure, or alternatively provide a given return at minimum cost to the public finances.

There appears to have been little research in Western Europe to evaluate regional policy against alternative policies or even against alternative job creation policies. The only research known to this author which seeks to compare the public finance cost of regional policy with other job creation policies is by Judith Marquand at the British Department of Industry (63).   In this research, regional policy is assumed to create national jobs in the range of one-quarter to one-half of the jobs diverted to the assisted areas.   This assumption broadly corresponds with specific estimates of the national job creation effects of regional policies (64). Marquand further assumes a job life of 10 to 20 years and then using a suitable discount rate estimates the net public finance cost per job created to range from £9000 to £700 at 1978/9 prices. From the Treasury macro-economic forecasting model, most of the fiscal policies that could be used to create employment lie, in terms of cost per job, in the middle of this range. Other policies, such as increased public procurement, or decreases in direct taxation, lie above this range. Marquand therefore concludes that given the assumed national effects of regional policy ". . . the benefits to the national economy from regional incentives . . . would appear to be of the same order of magnitude as the benefits of other fiscal measures (65)."

Implications for Regional Policy

At the beginning of this paper we argued that the growth in regional policy evaluation studies in Western Europe provided an opportunity to reopen the debate concerning the economic case for regional policy in mixed market economies. It must be stressed that the evaluation studies do not allow firm conclusions to be drawn either for or against the regional policies and programs adopted in Western Europe. The evidence on the effects and efficiency of past policy programs is often tentative and occasionally dubious. Yet, these policies do appear to have resulted in more jobs in the assisted areas than would have been the case if policy had been absent. Evidence on the longer-run effects of regional policies on assisted areas is much less conclusive. It is not clear whether continuing aid is necessary to maintain policy created jobs in assisted areas or whether short-term job creation gains will be at the expense of self-sustaining indigenous assisted-area development.

The firms assisted by regional policies do not appear to be marginal firms offering little prospect of a favorable impact on the future performance of assisted areas. Many of the assisted firms have been expanding firms, although there are indications that this is the product of a greater cyclical sensitivity rather than superior growth perfor-mance. The policies also need not have worked at the inevitable expense of the non-assisted areas: some net new jobs appear to be created in the assisted areas and some jobs replaced in the non-assisted areas due to regional policy induced indigenous expensions, the attraction of mobile foreign firms and improvements in the working of the interregional labor market. Where jobs have been lost in non-assisted areas, perhaps as a consequence of regional policy, the loss does not appear to have been dispropor-tionately concentrated in particular regions or subregions such as the inner-areas of central cities.

The net national job creating effects of regional policy is a controversial subject and no hard conclusions can be drawn at this stage. Further research is necessary in this area. However, present research does suggest that positive national effects can be produced, contrary to popular belief, even when there is unemployment in the non-assisted areas. The creation of national jobs by regional policy suggests that the cost to the public finances is no greater and sometimes less than other job creation policies. If this conclusion is correct, there would appear to be no reason why regional policy expenditures should be viewed by Governments as a welfare handout which can be sacrificed to other economic policy expenditures during times of national financial stringency. Indeed since regional policy is essentially a structural policy it might be considered by some to be a more appropriate means of raising employment and output than traditional Keynesian policies which do so by stimulating aggregate demand.

The policy mix adopted by Western European Governments, favoring investment subsidies to labor subsidies, grants to allowances, incentives to disincentives and automatic to discretionary application, can be criticized on a priori grounds. The evidence on effects does not however enable one to conclude in favor of a particular policy mix. Nevertheless, it is evident that a given policy package produces a greater effect during a period of expansion in national aggregate demand. The evidence does not suggest that regional incentives pull firms into depressed area locations. Rather firms that are expanding are found to run up against supply constraints and the existence of financial incentives can serve to attract already mobile firms. Given this industrial movement and location process, the existence of controls can increase the number of mobile firms when the national economy is expanding and so reinforce the influence of the financial incentives. Since many moves to and expansions in assisted areas are often undertaken in relative haste, one can see the value of a policy consisting of automatic cash grants for certain activities rather than a discretionary policy of tax allowances. The simplicity and clarity of the former is likely to lead to an increased take-up rate which may or not offset the known disadvantages of such policies.

What are the implications for future regional policies in Western Europe? In recent years the general trend in Western Europe has been one of widening spatial, project and activity coverage, a relaxation of size conditions and an increase in the maximum award values of the financial incentives. The United Kingdom provides an exception to this trend. Largely as a result of the measures taken in

July 1979, the scale of regional policy in Britain has been
reduced, if not the intensity. Some commentators see these
changes as bringing the U.K. back into line with the rest of
Western Europe (66). However, the position is more
complicated than this.

The recent and continuing recession in Western Europe
has induced some Governments such as the British to seek
public expenditure restrictions, other Governments seem
likely to follow. Moreover, the regional problem in some
Western European countries appears to be changing. The
recession has narrowed percentage unemployment differentials
between depressed and prosperous areas, but all areas are
suffering from high absolute levels of unemployment. The
availability of foreign mobile investment has declined and
there are less mobile manufacturing jobs available for both
cyclical and secular reasons. In addition there is evidence
of structural changes favoring the less urban and more rural
areas at the expense of the conurbations and the inner-
cities. The effect of these changes is to produce areas of
severely localized depression in both the present assisted
and non-assisted areas and a perceived erosion of much of
the traditional rationale for regional policy.

The likely policy response is a reduction in the scale
of central regional policy expenditures, an increase in
urban policy and local initiatives, a reduced concentration
on the provision of incentives to manufacturing industry and
greater selectivity generally. Competitive bidding in terms
of rates of award between areas and countries for a much
lower level of mobile investment is likely to increase. If
this prognosis is correct then some of the conclusions of
the policy evaluation studies should be heeded.

A movement towards increased spatial selectivity can be
justified if, as in Britain, an increasing number of areas
have become eligible for assistance. However, if assistance
is targeted to very small areas this development might
seriously reduce the beneficial effects of regional policy.
The previous use of broadly-banded areas appears to have
created employment while allowing firms to follow national
locational trends. These broad assisted areas are less
likely to cut across functional economic regions. If
sub-functional areas are chosen for policy assistance then
there is a geater probability that say, the unemployment
rates in those areas do not reflect a lack of job
opportunities peculiar to the areas. In addition,
functional economic areas with low average unemployment
rates would be more likely to contain assisted areas than
functional areas with high average unemployment rates if the
adjustment processes in the former areas had produced a
wider dispersion around the mean rate than in the latter
areas. Moreover, it is less likely that policy will
actually be able to remove the problems in the smaller

128

areas. Offsetting adjustments between the area in question
and the other areas to which it is linked functionally are
liable to frustrate the aim of policy.

The British Government in reducing regional policy
expenditures and increasing spatial selectivity wishes both
to save expenditure and to treat different parts of the
country more consistently and fairly given the effect of the
national recession in raising unemployment rates in all
areas and the secular changes in the spatial structure of
production.   Other Western European Governments may
subsequently take this route. If so, these actual and
likely changes do not appear to take sufficient account of
the admittedly limited evidence that the effects of a
national recessions, producing unemployment in all areas, do
not necessarily remove the traditional economic rationale
for regional policy.   However, the evidence does suggest
that a national recession makes regional policy more
difficult to implement. Given the evidence that financial
incentives do not stimulate mobile manufacturing investment
directly, that a high level of aggregate demand accompanied
by controls possibly constitutes the necessary conditions
for a successful policy, then in periods of national
recession Governments should perhaps consider encouraging
the dispersal of some of the stock of existing private
sector fims in both manufacturing and service sectors. This
could be achieved by targetting financial assistance to ease
the transactions costs which are a major impediment to the
transfer of economic activity (67).   More direct intervention might be required, eg. Government office dispersal
policies and public procurement. Finally, if Governments
wish to maintain regional policy at a reduced level of
expenditures by increased selectivity it is perhaps better
on balance to be more selective, not as between small areas,
but between categories of project aided.

NOTES

1.   Brian Ashcroft, The Evaluation of Regional Policy
in Europe (C.S.P.P. No 68, University of Strathclyde, 1980);
J. A. Schofield, "Macro-evaluations of the Impact of British
Regional Policy: A Review of Recent Research," in Urban
Studies, 16 (1979), pp. 251-271; J. Marquand, "Measuring the
Effects and Costs of Regional Incentives," Government
Economic Service Workshop Paper No. 32 (Department of
Industry, 1980); W. Nicol, An Appreciation of Regional
Policy Evaluation Studies (International Institute of
Management, Berline, 1980); B. Ashcroft, An Evaluation of
Regional Policy in Europe op. cit.; C. P. A. Bartels, W. R.
Nicol and J. J. Van Duign, "Estimating the Impact of

Regional Policy: A Review of Applied Research Methods," <u>Regional Science and Urban Economics</u>, 12, 1 (1982), pp. 3-42.

2.   C. Bartels, W. Nicol and J. Van Duign, op. cit., p. 36.

3.   B. Ashcroft, <u>An Evaluation of Regional Policy in Europe</u>, op. cit.

4.   B. C. Moore and J. Rhodes, "The Effects of Regional Policy in the United Kingdom," in Sant MEC (ed.) <u>Regional Policy and Planning for Europe</u> (Saxon House, 1974); B. C. Moore, J. Rhodes and R. Tarling, "Industrial Policy and Economic Development: The Experience of Northern Ireland and the Republic of Ireland," <u>Cambridge Journal of Economics</u>, 2 (1978), pp. 99-114.

5.   B. Ashcroft and J. K. Swales, "Estimating the effects of Government Office Dispersal," <u>Regional Science and Urban Economics</u>, 12, 1 (1982), pp. 81-98.

6.   B. Ashcroft and K. P. D. Ingham, "The Comparative Impact of U.K. Regional Policy on Foreign and Indigenous Firm Movement," <u>Applied Economics</u>, 14, 1 (1982), pp. 81-100.

7.   D. Forsyth, <u>U.S. Investment in Scotland</u> (Praeger, New York, 1972).

8.   B. Ashcroft and J. Taylor, "The Movement of Manufacturing Industry and the Effect of Regional Policy," <u>Oxford Economic Papers</u>,29 (1977), pp. 84-101; B. Ashcroft and J. Taylor, "The Effect of Regional Policy on the Movement of Industry in Great Britain," in Maclennan and Parr (eds.) <u>Regional Policy Past Experience and New Directions</u> (Martin Robertson, London, 1979) Chapter 2.

9.   W. Nocol, op. cit.

10.   B. Ashcroft, "The Measurement of the Impact of Regional Policies in Europe: A Survey and Critique," <u>Regional Studies</u>, 16, 4 (1982).

11.   J. Marquand, op. cit.

12.   D. E. Keeble, "Manufacturing Dispersion and Government Policy in a Declining Industrial System: The United Kingdom Case," <u>Environment and Planning, A</u> (1980); S. Fothergill and G. Gudgin, "Regional Employment Change: A Sub-Regional Explanation," <u>Progress in Planning</u>, 12, 3 (Pergamon Press, New York, 1979); S. Fothergill and G. Gudgin, <u>Unequal Growth, Urban and Regional Employment Change in Britain</u> (Heinemann, London, 1982).

13.   L. Kolind and P. H. Mathiesen (1978), op. cit.

14.   Frederiksson and Lindmark (1975), op. cit.

15.   House of Commons Expenditure Committee, <u>Regional Development Incentives</u> (Trade and Industry Sub-committee Report, H.M.S.O., 1973).

16.   B. C. Moore and J. Rhodes, "Evaluating the Economic Effects of Regional Policy," in <u>Methods of Measuring the Effects of Regional Policies</u> (OECD, Paris, 1977).

17.   W. F. Luttrel, <u>Factory Location and Industrial</u>
<u>Movement</u>, 1 (NIESR, 1962); P. M. Townroe, "Settling-in Costs
in Mobile Plants," <u>Urban Studies</u>, 13 (1976).
18.   A. T. O'Donnel and J. K. Swales (1978), op. cit.
19.   J. Marquand, op. cit., p. 84.
20.   J. B. Parr, "Spatial Structure as a Factor in
Economic Adjustment and Regional Policy," in Maclennan and
Parr (eds) (1979), op. cit.
21.   Firn, "External Control and Regional Policy," in
G. Brown (ed.) <u>The Red Paper on Scotland</u> (1975), pp.
153-169.
22.   P. N. O'Farrell, <u>Regional Industrial Development</u>
<u>Trends in Ireland, 1960-1973</u> (IDA, Dublin, 1975).
23.   D. E. Keeble (1980), op. cit.
24.   S. Fothergill and G. Gudgin (1979), op. cit.
25.   B. C. Moore, J. Rhodes and P. Tyler, "Urban-rural
Shift and the Evaluation of Regional Policy," <u>Regional</u>
<u>Science and Urban Economics</u>, 12, 1 (1982), pp. 139-158.
26.   D. Maclennan, "Tolerable Survival in the City:
The Realities for Urban Policy," in M. Gaskin (ed.) <u>The</u>
<u>Political Economy of Tolerable Survival</u> (Croom Helm, London,
1981), pp. 165-189; Firn, "Economic Policies for the
Conurbations," in G. Cameron (ed.) <u>The Future of the British</u>
<u>Conurbations</u> (Longman, 1980) Chapter 12.
27.   IVTB, <u>Erhvervsudvikling i Nordjylland</u> (DTH, IVTD,
1974).
28.   <u>Der Bundesminster fur Arbeit und Sozialordnung</u>,
1973, 1974, 1975, 1977.
29.   De Sloovere and Van den Bulcke (1972), op. cit.
30.   E. Recker, <u>Erfolgskontrolle Regionaler Aktion-</u>
<u>sprogramme Durch Indikatoren</u> (Forschungen zur Raumentwick-
lung Bd. 6, Bonn, 1977).
31.   R. S. Howard, <u>The Movement of Manufacturing</u>
<u>Industry in the U.K.</u> (Board of Trade, H.M.S.O.,1968).
32.   D. Furst, K. Zimmerman and K. H. Hansmerey,
<u>Strandarfwahl Industrieller Unternehmen</u> (Schriftenreche der
Gesellschaft fur regionale Struktwentwicklung, Bonn, Bd. 1,
1973); F. Wolf, <u>Effizienz und Erfolgskontrolle der region-</u>
<u>alen Wirtschaftsforderung</u> (hrsg von der Hessichen Landevent-
wicklungsund Treuhandgesellschaft, Wiesbaden, 1974).
33.   B. C. Moore, J. Rhodes and R. Tarling, "Industrial and Regional Policy and the Republic of Ireland"
(mimeo).
34.   G. Deblaere, "De betekenis van de economische
expansiewetten voor de ontwiddleingsgebieden," <u>ECO -</u>
<u>Brabant</u>, 21 (1979), pp. 3-17.
35.   I.V.T.B. (1974), op. cit.
36.   N. S. Segal, "The Limits and Means of 'Self-
Reliant' Regional Economic Growth," in Maclennan and Parr
(eds.) <u>Regional Policy: Past Experience and New Directions</u>
(Martin Robertson, 1979).

131

37. N. Hood and S. Young, "U.S. Investment in Scotland: Aspects of the Branch Factory Syndrome," Scottish Journal of Political Economy, 23 (1976).

38. D. McAleese, A Profile of Grant Aided Industry in Ireland (Publication Series Paper 5, The Industrial Development Authority, Dublin, Ireland, 1977).

39. D. H. N. Atkins, "Employment Change in Branch and Parent Manufacturing Plants in the UK: 1966-1971," Trade and Industry (August, 1973), pp. 437-439.

40. G. R. Thomson, Foreign Investment and Regional Development. The Theory and Practice of Investment Incentives with a Case Study of Belgium (Praeger, New York, 1973).

41. I.V.T.B. (1974), op. cit.

42. R. H. Gleed and P. J. Lund, "The Development Area Share of Manufacturing Industry Investment 1966-1969," Regional Studies, 13 (1979), pp. 61-72.

43. F. Ruane, Trade, Fiscal Policy and Industrialization in the Small Open Economy: The Irish Experience (Oxford University, 1976).

44. U. Freund and G. Zabel, "Zur Effizienz der regionalpolitischen Industrieforderung in der Bundesrepublik Deutschland," in Raumordnung und Raumforschung, 36 Jahrgang (1978).

45. I.V.T.B. (1974), op. cit.

46. G. Walker, Regional Incentives and the Investment Decision of the Firm (Centre for the Study of Public Policy, University of Strathclyde, Discussion Paper, 1979).

47. D. E. Keeble, "Employment Mobility in Britain," in M. Chisholm and G. Manners (eds.) Spatial Policy Problems of the British Economy (Cambridge University Press,1971).

48. W. Luttrel (1962), op. cit.

49. M. Thorvildsen, Malkonflikter: Regional Politikken (Bilag i tel Nord, REFO, 1976).

50. H. J. Klein, Moglickkeiten und Grenzen einer operationalen Erfolgskon bei der Investitionsforderun von gewerblicke Produktionsbetrieven im Rahmen der regionalen Wirtschaftspolitik (Dissertation, Darmstadt, 1972).

51. G. C. Cameron and G. L. Reid, Scottish Economic Planning and the Attraction of Industry (Occasional Paper No. 6, Glasgow, 1966).

52. B. Ashcroft (1980), op. cit.; W. Nicol (1980), op. cit.

53. It should, however, be noted that this does not necessarily mean that these firms are the most dynamic firms. Tables 3.5 and 3.6 suggest that firms producing cyclically unstable products have tended to be attracted to assisted areas. Firms subject to a greater variability of demand are probably more likely to be subject to pressures to move than firms experiencing a higher but more steady growth rate. In the absence of rational expectations, the

former group appear more likely to move in haste without exploring other non-locational adjustments to a supply constraint.

54. G. Thomson (1973), op. cit.; B. Moore, J. Rhodes and P. Tyler (1977), op. cit.; B. Ashcroft and K. Ingham (1982), op. cit.

55. W. Nicol (1980), op. cit.

56. The national inflation rate must be more responsive to the reduction of one job in non-assisted areas than to the creation of one job in assisted areas. In addition, labour force migration should not be so responsive as to maintain a particular spatial pattern of differential unemployment rates. Also Government should not be constrained by objectives other than the rate of inflation or the difficulties of "fine-tuning."

57. B. Ashcroft and J. Swales (1982), op. cit.

58. R. Courbis, "Measuring Effects of French Regional Policy by Means of a Regional National Model," *Regional Science and Urban Economics*, 12, 1 (1982), pp. 59-80.

59. P. Tyler, "The Impact of Regional Policy on a Prosperous Region: The Experience of the West Midlands," *Oxford Economic Papers*, 32 (1980), pp. 151-162.

60. P. A. Stone, "Changing Metropolitan Structure," in Maclennan and Parr (eds.) (1979), op. cit.

61. This appears to be the case notwithstanding the slight evidence that a discretionary policy allows the Government to raise the number of jobs created by inducing firms to alter the capital-intensity of their proposed technique (Ruane, 1976). The probability of firms applying for the available assistance appears to be greater under an automatic policy. This conclusion can be drawn from the relatively low number of applications for Selective Financial Assistance in Great Britain from firms which were eligible to be considered.

62. B. Ashcroft, "The Evaluation of Regional Economic Policy: The Case of the United Kingdom," in K. Allen (ed.) *Balanced National Growth* (Lexington, 1979), Chapter 7; B. Ashcroft (1980), op. cit.; W. Nicol (1980), op. cit.

63. J. Marquand (1980), op. cit.

64. B. Ashcroft and J. Swales (1982), op, cit.

65. J. Marquand (1980), op, cit., p. 107.

66. K. Allen and D. Yuill (eds.) *European Regional Incentive Survey: 1979* (C.S.P.P., Glasgow, 1980).

67. B. Ashcroft and K. Ingham (1982), op. cit.

AN ASSESSMENT OF REGIONAL POLICIES AND PROGRAMS IN EASTERN EUROPE

Laszlo Lackó

Introduction

Regional policies may be evaluated and compared in at least two different ways at the international level: with regard to the achievement of formulated goals or compared to each other. Thus, it is possible to draw conclusions regarding their success, performance, etc. However, such evaluations are of little use in terms of future application. I should like to elaborate on this from two perspectives. One, experiences with regional policies can be roughly useful to a limited extent in international comparisons (e.g. policy objectives, conditions existing in a successful or unsuccessful period, the circumstances of goal realization, etc.). Both basic and applied science may draw much and often from comparisons in an indirect manner. Second, with regard to regional development and urbanization, the possibilities of international comparison are perhaps more difficult than in other subjects (e.g. technological development). The results of regional development policy are often determined only indirectly. They are not independent of other processes, are composed of several related elements, have long delays in relation to initial decisions, and the problems of measurement are very great. It is worth mentioning, moreover, that in the international technical literature the methods of evaluation allow only a five to six year time horizon.

Those concerned with regional issues assert that regional development depends on many things: the conditions of general socioeconomic development, on the given development level, on the specific regional structure, etc. On the other hand, they are also convinced that regional development plays also a strong active role in influencing general development.

Taking all this into consideration, this paper presents an assessment of regional development in selected East European countries - the GDR, Poland, Czechoslovakia,

Hungary, Yugoslavia and Rumania - covering a few general features in the form of a review by country in a traditional manner.

The first section outlines a few general features of regional development, the main similarities and a few characteristic differences in regional development levels of the countries included in the study. The second part contains a review of the results of regional policies by country.

A Few Comprehensive Issues of Regional Policies

A certain level of regional thinking had already evolved in Eastern-Central Europe prior to World War II. This was the result of activity associated with protection of the political frontiers, with the establishment of the state administration. The consideration of regional issues was required as a solution to certain issues of development and planning, primarily in connection with the development of large infrastructure networks (e.g. development of railway systems and river regulation systems) and for political reasons. In addition, the eradication of internal regional inequalities was motivated frequently by ethnic points of view. Between the two world wars, more complex studies, and monographs, occasionally stimulating ideas about social motivation were published which touched upon the different levels and aspects of regionality. However, the formulation of regional policy and the introduction of regional planning took place only after World War II.

The histories of each of the socialist countries, their modes establishing socialist social orders, the divisions of state administration and their other geographical conditions are significantly different and, accordingly, the system of objectives and means of their regional development policies are also varied. A common feature, however, is that they take into account the socioeconomic requirements of their regional differences, trying to influence them purposefully and systematically.

In these countries, regional policy forms an integral part of general economic policy and, in the different phases of economic development, regional policy is also modified in accordance with the given development phase.

It is well-known that regarding the historical path of the socialist countries following World War II, a number of development phases can be distinguished in broad outline:
1) a reconstruction period, including the post-war years;
2) a phase of extensive development, which can be characterized by an initially rapid and later decelerating rate of growth, lasting until the late 1960s and early 1970s; 3) a change-over to a phase of intensive development, which is characterized by a moderate growth rate since the mid-1970s in most socialist countries.

There are some objectives, guidelines and processes in regional development policies of the socialist countries which characterize almost the entire period, since they are essentially stable elements of the regional structure, economy and society. At the same time, there are short-term processes which accommodate particular development phases of the economy.

In the socialist countries, regional development policy generally has two objectives: it must serve the <u>efficient</u> <u>development</u> of the overall economy <u>and</u> the level of living conditions of the population living in the different areas. The main task of regional policy is to arrive at an appropriate compromise between these two different objectives.

Leveling has never appeared in political practice in the socialist countries as an absolute objective, and actual decisions have been generally aimed at solving problems involved at a given development stage. A dominant motive was the solution of the fundamental problems of employment, the raising of income or living standards, and the reduction of the differences in living levels among the individual regions, settlement types and/or nationalities of the country. At different levels of economic development, the regional problems - as tasks to be solved - have presented themselves with different emphases.

In the following section we shall briefly review what common features were and are in the nearly forty years of development in the socialist countries and what characteristics have asserted themselved in the different development phases.

Significant regional disproportions were characteristic of all socialist countries when power was initially established. A common and fundamental reason for this was that the socialist countries of Eastern-Central Europe inherited considerable internal regional development differences from the capitalist period. The difficulties were even more aggravated by the disproportions following the political adjustments of frontiers after World War I and World War II and by the losses and damages caused by the world wars and, for some, civil wars. Even in the GDR and Czechoslovakia with the most balanced regional situation today, the developed and backward regions are sharply demarcated. In the socialist countries of Southern Europe (Yugoslavia, Rumania, Bulgaria, Albania) only a few major towns and minor industrial zones have arisen out of the underdeveloped agricultural environment. Thus, the effort aimed at leveling regional differences in economic development has become a central issue of regional policies in the socialist countries; that is, the development of the economically backward, or formerly underdeveloped areas.

The reconstruction necessitated by the war did not

provide possibilities for improving regional structures. What is more, the attempt to start production as soon as possible preserved for the most part the old regional structure. The economic development during the past nearly four decades at an unprecedented rate resulted in significant changes in the regional economic structure as well. Development levels of the regions converged in almost all of the countries. Although this did not change the fundamental scheme of the inherited disproportions, the disproportions were reduced. The development of the most backward regions were generally raised to a higher level by the outstandingly rapid development of some minor regions and towns. This phenomenon reflects the common regional development principle - based for the most part on industrialization - that is, concentrated decentralization.

At the time of the extensive phase, only industry was regarded as a means suitable for regional development and regional leveling. Later, at the time of the change-over to the intensive period, leveling of profitability, the increasing wage levels in agriculture also contributed to regional leveling to a considerable extent. The improved regional proportions of infrastructural supply, recreation and foreign tourism, and, in recent years, intellectual life, also played a role in the leveling efforts. However, the principal factor in the regional leveling has been industry until recently, and in the less developed countries, industry will remain the main factor into the next decade.

It can be shown on the basis of analyses that the economically more developed four countries of the European socialist countries, the GDR, Czechoslovakia, Poland and Hungary, have undergone a significant regional leveling. The only European socialist country where there has not been substantial leveling since World War II is Yugoslavia.

In the group of the more developed countries there has been a tendency in recent years for the rate of leveling to be inversely proportional to economic development. At the same time, this also means that where leveling is highest, change is smallest, and vice versa. This exemplifies the general relationship - verifiable by comprehensive international comparative analyses - by which at higher levels of economic-social development the rate of change of regional economic-social proportion slows down and the regional structure becomes stable.

It is a characteristic feature of the regional policy in the socialist countries based on the development of the productive sectors that regional development depends to a great extent on the entire investment and sectoral development policy of the given country. It exerted a preserving effect on regional structure in the period of extensive development in that the requirement of ensuring maximum economic growth necessitated the intensive concentration of activities in areas and on growth poles, having favorable endowments and traditions. Generally, this was tantamount to the further development of the relatively developed industrial regions and an increase in their importance. The objectives of leveling were fundamentally formulated in terms of living conditions and thus meant another separate element of regional development. In the present phase of economic development, when the reduction of the growth rate can be observed, a similar regional effect is to be expected. Giving prominence to reconstruction also favored the developed regions.

It should be also mentioned that the productive and non-productive investments are for the most part realized through sectoral decisions which do not always take into consideration the interests of complex regional development. This has led to certain contradictions such that, in most socialist countries, agricultural accumulation provided the basis for the industrialization of the backward regions. That is, the basic economic sector of the backward regions got into a critical position because of the development of industry.

In addition, a characteristic feature of the change of the regional economic structure of the European socialist countries is the shifting of the regional center of gravity of the economies to the east. This fortunately coincided with the more intensive development of the most backward regions.

In addition to the systematic decentralization of the industrial productive forces, the socialist reorganization of agriculture resulted in increased profitability of agriculture released manpower. This created one of the most essential conditions for industrialization and played an important role in the reduction of regional disproportions in the majority of the countries.

Development over the past 37 years was accompanied in all countries by extremely intensive regional movement, and migration of the population (although at a greatly reduced rate in the more developed countries in recent years) which was directed mainly from villages into towns and from the underdeveloped, mostly agricultural regions into the industrial regions. Despite this, regional leveling resulted, not from the change of the regional location of population, but from the shift in proportions of the means of production and in the regional distribution of the value produced. This is associated not only with the fact that under the circumstances of a planned economy the investments can be relatively rapidly mobilized, but also with the fact that - especially in the socialist countries of South-West Europe - there are sharp regional differences in the growth of population - natural increase. While in most developed urban zones the birth rate has significantly decreased, in the underdeveloped regions it stabilized at a level corresponding to the formerly high birth rates. Thus, in the developed regions the scissors between the birth and death rates has closed and in many places, population growth is ensured only by in-migration while in the underdeveloped regions the high natural increase in some places increases the population to an extent exceeding by far the national average, despite migration losses. Because of this sharp demographic contrast in Yugoslavia there is no essential progress in terms of the liquidation of the regional disproportions. The regional distribution of population was most stable in the GDR, which is associated with the extremely low population increase (or decrease).

Urbanization policy of the socialist countries occupies a peculiar position in their regional policy. Efforts aimed at more proportionate and more rational regional location of the productive forces created favorable possibilities for the elimination of disproportions and deficiencies in the settlement system. In the period of reconstruction the urbanization levels of these countries varied greatly. Occasionally they pursued different settlement policies, varying periodically as well.

It is evident that the most important effect of socialist economic development on the settlement network was that the role of urban centers strengthened, the proportion of the urban population increased and the urban network became more proportionate regionally. The principal means of urban development was socialist industrialization. It was industrial development which stimulated the fundamental infrastructural development and the extension of services, while in the regions not affected by industrial development, the development of urban centers was slow.

Socialist towns - established primarily in the early 1950s - formed a peculiar chapter in the framework of the urban development efforts of the socialist countries. The rapid process of urbanization is reflected by the growth in the proportion of the urban population: presently in most of the countries it already exceeds 50 percent. The assessment of this, however, is made difficult by the fact that in the individual countries different criteria are used to define cities. In the East-Central European socialist countries, the rate of urbanization has generally fallen behind economic development, but it has been for the most part rapid compared to the development of the absorbtive capacity of the cities. Therefore, nowadays the main point of the management of the urbanization processes is transferred to improving the degree of infrastructure of urban centers. The six countries inherited a very varied rural settlement network. During the past decades village (rural) policy and the development of villages changed most frequently and often in opposite directions. The rural transformation after the liberation was determined by two factors - partly by the relative decrease of significance of agriculture and partly by the purposeful, systematic efforts to liquidate the differences between village and town.

In several countries, the concepts concerning urban and rural development are independent of each other, or even if there is a uniform concept for the development of the two categories, in practical application it rarely goes beyond the level of towns.

In socialist countries the planned economy provides the framework for the realization of the objectives of economic policy. In all European socialist countries, regional planning is an integral part of the national economic plan covering the entire socioeconomic life of the country.

In these countries - besides the several similarities - there were and still are significant differences even today. Perhaps from the viewpoint of regional policy, the most fundamental difference is in the general degree of development and infrastructural supply (thus for example between the northern and southern regions of the GDR and Yugoslavia). Significant differences can be shown between the economic development practices (e.g. how long they considered industry to be of exclusive importance), or their management concept. The differences are considerable also concerning the forms in which the regional differences within the countries fundamentally manifest themselves: in some cases, these are of regional character (e.g. in the GDR, Czechoslovakia, Yugoslavia), elsewhere they are associated with the traditional disproportions of the settlement system (Hungary). The characteristics of the regional distribution of natural resources, the natural endowments, the lack or abundance of a peculiar type of resource, etc. are also different bases or limits of regional development.

Review of Countries

Czechoslovakia. In Czechoslovakia, the sharpest dividing line in respect to economic development runs between the two large parts of the country: Bohemia and Slovakia. This is a historic heritage.

Czechoslovakia is a young state which came into being in 1918 as one of the successor states of the Austro-Hungarian Monarchy. Until then, her eastern and western parts belonged to the territory of the Monarchy under Hungarian and Austrian supremacy, respectively. Their historic development took place separately, and the economic relations between them were weak. Steps were taken in the period between the two world wars to unify the two large regions from the point of view of development by means of the development of the industry of Slovakia with the establishment of industrial centers.

Following the German occupation and the collapse of the fascist Slovak puppet state, Czechoslovakia was reborn largely within her pre-war frontiers; a significant change was the annexation of the Sub-Carpathian territories by the Soviet Union.

The population exchanges following World War II had a significant regional effect: Czechoslovakia became a country having two nationalities because the Czechs and Slovaks make up 94 percent of the total population. This also contributed to the fact that regional development — primarily the development of Slovakia - was given a great political emphasis.

The development of Slovakia is favorably influenced by her advatageous economic geographical situation, primarily by her nearness to the Soviet Union. Also as a consequence of the central situation of Czechoslovakia, socialist economic integration (through the Council of Mutual Economic Assistance) may play an extremely important role in regional development.

Of course, there are differences of development within the two large parts of the country, too. In Czechoslovakia, there are considerable differences at the level of the units of regional administration not only between the western and eastern parts of the country, but between her northern and southern parts as well. There is still a very close connection between the degree of development and the location of industrial employment. Accordingly, the most developed zones are the Northwest industrial zone of the central Czech region, from the Plzen agglomeration through Prague to the central reach of the Elba and the Moravian industrial region. In addition to the zones listed, other parts of the country are characterized by isolated development poles.

Regarding economic regions, the Czech part of the country is more homogenous because it is at a higher level of development. The rate of development of the Slovak regions is much higher. From this point of view, the Pozsony and Eastern Slovak regions are outstanding. Given the different growth rates, a significant leveling can be shown between economic regions as well.

The differentiation in demographic conditions has played an important role even in recent years in the trend of regional development differences. The natural increase of the Slovak regions is considerably higher than that of the Bohemian Republic (Eastern Slovakia is three times higher than the national average). On the other hand, in the Bohemian Basin, the population is virtually decreasing. Thus, Slovakia has ample manpower sources, and because even the rapid industrialization has been unable to absorb this, it also ensures a manpower supply for the more developed

Table 3.7: Population and Income Shares of Slovakia, 1929, 1950, 1970 and 1975

Year	Percentage Share of Slovakia of			Produced national income per capita in Slovakia as a % of Bohemia
	Population	Urban Population	National Income	
1929	23.8	15.2	15.0	56.8
1950	27.9	15.9	15.8	60.4
1970	31.6	23.5	26.7	78.8
1975	32.0	25.2	28.0	82.7

Czech regions.

In Czechoslovakia, Bohemia and Moravia also belong to the old urbanization zone. The urban development of Slovakia is somewhat different, though there are many towns of medieval origin there too. A dense network of small and medium-sized towns is characteristic.

Metropolitan concentration is not intensive and it is gaining strength only slowly. The problems of single-pole development concentrated on a single large city are not significant in Czechoslovakia, although purposeful efforts are made to restrict the growth of Prague to prevent overdevelopment.

Besides the small towns, Czechoslovakia is characterized by small, dwarf villages. The two settlement categories are only slightly different in function because their infrastructural supply has already made possible the location of certain kinds of industry there. The current objective of settlement policy is to bring about strong development poles suiting the conditions of the country best.

In its entirety, Czechoslovak regional development - because of its great political significance - was generally in the foreground of economic development. In addition to backward Eastern Slovakia, a certain degree of backwardness can be observed in Southern Bohemia and in some sections of Northern Bohemia which is characterized by out-of-date industrial structures. Undoubtedly, the regional structure of the economy of the country is much more balanced than that of the other socialist countries. Thus regional differences are no longer regarded as an outstanding problem of the Czechoslovak economy. The elimination of the existing east-west differences for their own sake is no longer an absolute objective at the present development level and under present economic conditions.

Yugoslavia. In the case of Yugoslavia, the historical background lends special significance to regional problems. The Yugoslav state came into being from parts of the former Austro-Hungarian Monarchy (within this, a part had been an hereditary province of the Habsburgs), and the Islamic Ottoman Empire. At the time of its formation the republics and provinces which were organized into the new state were at very different degrees of development and had different resource endowments. The six republics and two autonomous provinces differ from one another in ethnic, religious, linguistic, cultural and historical aspects.

After World War II, common economic development and regional equity came immediately into prominence. The high degree of disparity between northern areas (Slovenia, Croatia, Serbia, Voivodship) and southern areas (Bosnia and Herzegovina, Macedonia, Montenegro, Koszovo) were increased further by the fact that the country was liberated primarily by the less developed regions. A policy of leveling was stimulated also by the view that in the long run, there was a positive effect on the developed regions as well. Generally, any economic policy can be realized more easily in the homogenous, uniform economy than in a heterogeneous one. The support of the less developed regions became an element of national unity, solidarity and a part of the constitution.

Political decentralization, the independence of the federal republics and automonous republics were asserted in the field of regional development policy, planning, management and financing alike. At the level of the federal government, there has been one main regional development objective for 30-35 years - the reduction of the differences in regional development levels by supporting economic development in the republics of Bosnia and Herzegovina, Montenegro, Macedonia and in the Koscovo province of Serbia. In addition, special support is given in the backward regions for investment if conditions for development are at least as favorable there as elsewhere. During the last decade, the central support of development was primarily the exploration and exploitation of natural resources.

Regional development concepts also at a national scale, but not yet fully part of the federal program are: 1) development of two axes, the Sava Valley and the Morava-Vardas region (they join the Danube waterway system at their crossing at Belgrade); and 2) building a connection to the export-ports of the Adriatic Seacoast and to industrial centers; the Belgrad-Bar railway line was constructed in connection with this by 1978.

Despite efforts made at the federal level, the efficiency of the new investments is more favorable in the northern and particularly in the northwestern parts of the country than elsewhere because of the better utilization of the resources and infrastructure.

In spite of the efforts outlined, it has not been possible to reduce the differences in the development levels of the most developed northern federal republics and the southern backward regions. The variation in per capita national income has even increased, even though 76 percent of the coal fields, 96 percent of the iron ore reserves, 86 percent of the non-ferous metal resources are to be found in the less developed regions. The trend of GNP by region is illustrated in Table 3.8.

The variation of the value of GNP by region per capita unequivocally proves that the differences between the developed and less developed regions grow, which is aggravated by the higher population increase of the more backward regions. This occurs parallel with rapid national development and thus it follows not from the stagnation of the backward regions, but from the regional differences in

Table 3.8:   Regional Variations in GNP Per Capita, Yugoslavia,
1947, 1960, 1970 and 1978

Regions	GNP Per Capita (Yugoslavia = 100%)			
	1947	1960	1970	1980
Less Developed Regions	77.2	66.3	63.1	59.5
Posnia-Herzegovina	85.6	76.0	67.6	64.9
Koszovo	50.4	37.4	34.1	29.1
Macedonia	70.6	63.9	70.0	69.0
Montenegro	93.0	64.5	77.2	71.0
Developed Regions	109.9	116.5	119.6	123.5
Croatia	104.3	119.2	123.6	126.2
Serbia	100.3	96.5	96.5	98.3
Slovenia	163.3	180.4	193.7	203.6
Voivodship	99.8	107.9	107.4	110.4
Yugoslavia	100.0	100.0	100.0	100.0

rates of development.

In Yugoslavia, it is possible to conclude that in regional development policy - taking into consideration the economic-social organization of the country - it is necessary to shift to a greater intensification of interregional relations. Thus, the regrouping of resources would not only result in a more rapid development of the less developed regions, but it would also have positive repercussions on the more developed regions.

The centralized planning system based on economic plans was in force only until 1951 in Yugoslavia. Since then and in conjunction with more independent enterprises, self-government and self-financing of settlements (administrative units) has also taken place. The national medium-range plans of the national economy containing the comprehensive development objectives and the incentive-regulatory elements have been concerned with the issues of settlement development only since the 1976-1980 plan period.

There is no officially approved national settlement network development concept in Yugoslavia, but national settlement development guidelines have been in force since the mid-1970s. A settlement network development concept was elaborated by the republics and autonomous provinces in the early 1970s. The objectives are different, depending on the character and the development level of the given region: 1) in Croatia, the main objective is the development of a few large centers, primarily Zagreb; 2) in Serbia, the development of the centers outside of Belgrade is paramount; 3) in Bosnia and Herzegovina, the goal is the development of Sarajevo and four towns of medium size; and 4) the settlement network development of Macedonia, Montenegro and Koscovo is planned to be less concentrated.

The characteristics of the national settlement network development policy were summarized for the first time in the framework of the work entitled "The Long-Range Development Concept of Yugoslavia to 1985." This is not an official document, but professional material based on scientific research activities which influenced the sectoral policies affecting settlement development. The regional and settlement development plans will be elaborated at national, republic and local levels up to 1984.

Poland. The urbanization process started in Poland in the 19th century under the influence of the industrial revolution. At the end of the 18th century the country was divided among the three surrounding empires. One of the consequences of this, among others, was that the country had no capital city but rather regional centers - Warsaw, Wroclaw, Poznan and Gdansk.

Following World War I, the independent Polish state made enormous efforts to integrate the different regions which had developed separately for more than 120 years.

146

Integration meant the establishment of the network of roads became a primary requirement. Construction and extension of the railway network started, followed by the modernization of public roads.

In the field of settlement development - in the spirit of intervention by the state - some organized actions were initiated. Thus, the port of Gdynia was built, which was the largest city of the Baltic seacoast when World War I broke out.

The government also endeavored to regulate living conditions developing in the towns. Efforts were made to overcome the housing shortage and economic speculation partly through the stimulation of housing construction and partly by the legal protection of tenants.

Prior to World War II, Poland was an agrarian country. Between 1960 and 1975, the rural population was around 15-16 million compared with an urban population which had almost tripled between 1945-1980. The latter increased from 7.6 million to 21.5 million. One of the most important tasks of settlement policy in this period was the chanelling of large-scale migration and the establishment of new places of work.

During the entire period following liberation, the general principles of planning aimed at providing jobs, dwellings, recreation, and better living conditions corresponding to an urban milieu for all social groups.

Of course, the concrete objectives of regional policy have changed in the course of time. In the reconstruction period between 1945-1950, promoting a better economic life and the provision of the elementary conditions of life were the main objectives in all regions. In the 1950s, industrialization, primarily heavy industry, was given priority and all other aspects including infrastructure projects were concentrated around industrial centers. Regional development was a function of industrialization. This manifested itself mainly in the construction of the new industrial centers (Nowa Huta, etc.).

In the 1960s, industry still continued to enjoy priority, although not to the same great extent as in the previous years. Laws providing for settlement development, regional planning and the preservation of the natural environment were adopted in this decade. Settlement network development plans of the country and the individual regions were elaborated in the 1960s. The aim was the elaboration of an adequate plan of regional development, consistent with cost minimization as an important limiting condition. Since the second half of the 1960s, the Government has tried to restrict a huge increase in urban population. The national settlement network development plan proposed the establishment of a hierarchical urban system. Excessive development of the most important metropolitan regions was slowed down

147

by administrative means: employment and in-migration were restricted. Attempts were made to transfer some plants to smaller towns. The most important concept of the plan was the development of the network of towns of medium size. According to the notion, these towns would be the industrial and social centers of the given regions (microregions) in a district with approximately 30 km radius. This concept was based on the following preliminary assumptions: 1) the further growth of large cities would cause serious difficulties, especially in infrastructure costs; 2) only towns having especially favorable development potential were selected to be regional centers; thus, the cost of the development of the new industrial capacity was kept at a relatively low level; and 3) there was permanent manpower shortage in large cities, while some rural regions had manpower redundancy. If the industrial capacity shifts nearer rural regions, the more rational use of manpower would be realized.

Since 1970, a new urbanization policy has been worked out by the Government. The essence of this is that regional development was linked with the new strategy of socioeconomic development. The main objective of regional development policy in that period was the leveling of regional differences and the development of the backward regions. This was to be achieved primarily by the reduction of the differences in the living standard.

However, it was not possible to realize the new urbanization policy in practice completely. The process of economic growth was interrupted by the insufficient development of urban regions. The backwardness of urbanization became more and more obvious. Therefore, the Government wanted to ensure absolute priority for social aims - such as housing, infrastructure (water, sewer, road network, educational, sanitary institutions) and for the general tasks of urban development. It was not able to achieve these aims because resources were not sufficient for their realization. The underdevelopment of Polish towns became a significant factor of the crisis of recent years.

The schematic system of regional planning as an integral part of national economic planning is as follows. Physical planning is one of the most important means of state policy in the realization of regional policy and the objectives associated with settlements. The framework of the activity was determined by a law approved by the Houses of Parliament in 1961. According to this, the following play types are made: 1) national physical plans as part of the long range national economic plan for the entire territory of the country; 2) regional master and specified plans of the individual voivodships and their sub-regions as part of the long range development plans of the voivodships; and 3) local plans for individual towns or groups of towns, and for the rural regions and recreational areas.

The original concept was based on the fact that the character of physical planning is the same at all levels, only the scale varies in the case of the different plans. In reality, however, planning methods develop in different ways at the different levels. The time horizon of physical plans in harmony with the long range plan is 20 years (that is, at present the period from 1971 until 1990) though certain elements of the plan cover a longer period. National and regional planning is directed by the National Planning Committee, while local planning is directed by the Ministry of Administrative Regional Management and Environmental Preservation.

A regional master plan is made for every voivodship. Specified regional plans are made for such selected regions where large scale investments are planned. Plans of this type are worked out either for a certain part of a voivodship, or neglecting the administrative boundaries, for the neighboring regions of the voivodships.

The regional plans summarize the fundamental socioeconomic regional development problems of the individual regions. Regional plans are not only physical plans, their function is similar to the role which the long range plan fulfills with respect of the whole country. The regional plan is concerned with all socioeconomic activities taking place in the given region irrespective of whether their administration belongs to local or regional authorities, or to the different sectors. The five-year plans of the voivodships are made on the basis of the long range regional plans.

Hungary. In Hungary, the main objective of current regional policy is to promote the exploration of the natural, socioeconomic resources of the regions and to put them into the service of the national economy and to improve the efficiency of social production and simultaneously level living conditions of the population.

In the period following liberation the objectives of regional policy were formulated even more unequivocally. The structure of the country was characterized by districts and regions at different levels of economic devlopment and having different economic structures. In the backward regions, the rate of employment, living standard, the cultural-educational facilities and sanitary supply were low, and the way of life traditionally backward. In 1949, at the end of the post-war reconstruction period, half of all industry was concentrated in Budapest. Of the 19 counties, the number of persons employed in industry was about 100 per 1000 inhabitants in only three counties. In the others it was considerably lower. Thus, the aim of regional policy was the promotion of development of the backward regions by the proper management of industrialization on the one hand and restraints on the capital city. However, efficient industrial development was possible primarily where industry was already located and a great part of the objectives (industrialization of the Great Plain) remained only a declaration for a very long time. Even natural gas and oil discovered in the Great Plain were used and processed in the traditional industrial region. In the fifties and sixties rural industry developed more rapidly in backward areas and new industrial centers came into being in an island-like manner alongside rural traditional industrial centers. Thus, in addition to economic life, the expansion of industry manifested itself also in territorial expansion.

An important regional objective of the 1960s was the infrastructure supply to the population at a higher level. Also connecting smaller settlements to the transport network was realized since this made the utilization of manpower more efficient with migration and commuting. In its entirety, this effort yielded even fewer results than industrial location policy primarily because the proportion of the infrastructure investments (although volume continuously increased) remained below that of productive investments throughout the whole decade. In 1971 the Government adopted three fundamental resolutions which have become the determining factors of regional policy, planning and development activity.

The government resolution containing the guidelines of regional development outlined the aim in the following dual task.

> It should ensure the efficient utilization of the resources of the national economy and the individual regions and the modernization and rationalization of the settlement network and at the same time, by the leveling of employment and productivity levels in the regions and the supply levels of settlements, it should reduce the differences existing in the material and cultural levels of the population of the individual regions.

The government resolution outlining the National Settlement Network Development Concept determined the basic urban center system of the settlement network while the counties established a hierarchy of settlements at a lower level. The government resolution established a system of territorial (regional and settlement) plans.

The government resolutions indicate that by the early 1970s it was possible to harmonize the processes of: 1) the expansive force of regional differences; 2) the load-bearing capacity of the country (in connection with the new system of economic management and with the termination of the socialist transformation of agriculture); 3) the manpower shortage in industry (in the traditional industrial districts); 4) the socioeconomic expansive force of infrastructure shortage; and 5) the general acknowledgement of regional policy and its up-grading to a government level which used incentives and orientations as well as planning.

Regional policy and development - even if they were not free from contradictions - yielded much more spectacular results in the 1970s than earlier. The transformation of industry is indicated by the fact that while in 1949 the number of industrial employees per 1000 inhabitants was 90 to 130 in the three most industrialized counties, in 1981 the proportion of industrial employees was similar in the four least developed counties. In the other counties a considerably higher proportion was recorded. It is characteristic of the rate of leveling that the difference between the most industrialized and least industrialized counties was four-fold in 1970 and only two-fold in 1981. The importance of the capital city in the industry of the country radically decreased: measured in industrial employees, it fell from 50 percent in 1949 to one third by 1970, and to a quarter by 1980.

Regional policy has not been able to handle in every respect the rapid changes taking place. Thus, for example, besides the significant industrial deconcentration and rural industrial location, there was a considerable manpower (population) flow in the opposite direction. Consequently 70 percent of the industrial employees work in the traditionally more industrialized northern and North-Transdanubian regions (as even higher proportion of the value of industrial fixed assets and electric power consumption is concentrated here). Thus, in certain respects, today infrastructure in the industrially more developed regions can be regarded as more backward. Consequently, the contrast exists between the same regions, but since full employment was realized, it is in the other direction. The situation is similar with regard to towns and villages; extensive urban development resulted in overcrowding and now the living conditions in some villages may be considered better than the urban ones.

Another great problem of regional policy is that it has not been able to overcome the problems of the agglomeration ring around Budapest. It has not been able to eliminate the conflicting interests of locally competent councils (for example, the council of Budapest and the council of Pest County), and has not brought about directed and coordinated development.

<u>German Democratic Republic.</u> The GDR, which was torn out of the greater German economy, inherited a poor industrial structure. It was characterized by the lack of

151

raw materials, basic materials, energy and the means of production. On the other hand, agriculture was relatively well developed. Territorially, the southern part of the country could be qualified as sufficiently developed. The industrially underdeveloped northern regions were characterized by a high degree of backwardness. The central part of the country was a transition between the two extreme poles from the point of view of development level.

By the end of the 1960s, a uniform, relatively proportionate industrial structure developed in the GDR. However, the territorial proportions proved less than the ideal, because, in the 1950s and 1960s, the sectoral interests were asserted at the expense of regional policy. Regional policy promoted greater industrial development in the northern part of the country in order to reduce the backwardness and the regional disparities there and to solve the problems created by population concentration in the highly industrialized south.

Regional development, which gained strength in the 1970s on the basis of the county planning offices created in 1965, was organically integrated into the system of national economic planning. Presently, the most characteristic and most peculiar feature of regional planning in the GDR is that its management and administrative system directly determines regional divisions, the regional plan types and the planning organs.

Economic planning directed by the State Plan Committee is closely associated with the administrative system. The Plan Committee has local organs at county and district levels. It is to be noted that the 14 counties formed in 1952 are also economic geographic units, and thus are economic regions. The national economic plan has a regional section which is divided into county plans. The industrial, agricultural plans are only acknowledged by the counties and these are broken down to counties by the national plans. Housing, communal services manpower, food production and building plans are built up from below and the national plan summarizes the county plans. Of course, the sections concerning foreign trade, national income, etc. are not included in the county level plans. Thus, at county level, the national economic plan and the county plan are identical.

County plans are coordinated by the State Planning Committee. Coordination within regional planning is assisted moreover by the settlement network development concept, which starts from the basic principle that the settlement network is nationally an integrated whole.

Development of the settlement system within the individual regions is characterized by the population concentration taking place at a steady rate for decades. Population has increased in towns, and decreased in smaller settlements. However, in the more backward regions, the number of urban inhabitants increases more and more rapidly, and as a result of this process and the proportion of the urban population between the individual parts, the country is gradually leveling. The variation of the regional trend of industrial employees, investments and finally housing is characterized by tendencies in the same direction - leveling between the major regions and concentration within the regions.

On the basis of the processes that have taken place and the experiences gained, the former general regional policy aimed at the industrialization of the North has been modified recently. The strengthening of the urban network is regarded as one of the important means for the reduction of regional differences even today, but the roles and functions of towns are interpreted differently. Thus the significance of the town as the center of material production relatively decreases and the extension and location of productive forces play a more and more subordinate role in further urbanization. At the same time, the cultural, administrative, intellectual-productive function of the towns becomes more and more important and the classical town becomes more and more altered in the agglomeration. In addition, the scarcity of investment funds also induce the regional planner to turn towards agglomerative development. It is believed that the infra-structure costs can be reduced by means of the controlled development of small regions. Thus, they intend to solve development issues by agglomeration in the South and by the intensification of the centers and of the functional relations of the centers and their region in the North.

Rumania. Rumania is a relatively young state in European terms and a significant part of the differences in regional development levels which are observable today are an historical heritage. In Rumania, backward, extensive agriculture was coupled with an extremely underdeveloped and geographically unevenly distributed industrial sector. With the exception of a few centers, entire sections of the country were without manufacturing. Backwardness was especially notable in the regions outside the Carpathians and in Dobrogen.

This regional structure is essentially true even today as the country is divided by a wreath of the Carpathians into two different zones with regard to development levels. The inner regions are the more developed ones whereas in the outer zone, the capital city and the dynamically developing sea coast emerge from a more impoverished background.

In Rumania, the ethnic population distribution resulted in a peculiar situation. The area inhabited by Hungarian and German minorities were more developed and therefore post-war industrialization was especially rapid mainly in

153

the Rumanian regions (primarily in Moldavia).

After liberation, regional leveling was formulated as an objective from the very beginning. Socialist industrialization was regarded as almost the exclusive means to achieve this which meant primarily the creation and development of heavy industry. Rapid economic growth based on exensive development characterized Rumania until the mid-1970s. Development of this type - as verified by international comparative investigations - generally does not favor large-scale regional proportion modifications.

This policy also contributed to the preservation of the regional structure. In Rumania population increase is distributed relatively evenly and purposeful efforts have been made to restrict migration. Population movements are constrained also by nationality composition. Thus, the decisive factor in the initiation of leveling between the major units at the district level was not migration of the population, but the relatively scattered location of production.

It is to be noted that the analysis of the real processes that took place in regional development after liberation is made difficult by the fact that significant changes have taken place in the administrative divisions and thus available data are also limited.

In general, in Rumania the indices characterizing the differences in development levels, although they are not too high, essentially did not change greatly. It must be recorded among the results of decentralized industrial development, however, that the levels of industrialization between regions converged to a significant extent.

There has been a periodically modifying contradiction or discrepancy between the regional development of industry and the sectoral concept of industrial development, frequently to the detriment of the regional point of view. Industrialization of backward agricultural regions took place only in the second half of the 1960s when the development of the processing industry came into prominence.

A significant milestone in the life of the country was the regional reform of 1968, which meant also a change of concept in regional administration. The basic idea was to promote the fulfillment of the program of industrialization and make the settlement network more suitable for the accommodation of industry and, later, to improve service supply to the population at local levels.

Concentrated decentralization became the new regional concept of industrialization. Industrial location outside the traditional industrial regions, that is, in a decentralized manner, and within them into a few select regional centers. The intent was to alter the development then concentrated on one or two centers and distribute it among many centers (40 counties were formed instead of the earlier

16 regions). It may be noted that the slow but progressing deconcentration of industrial development of the backward microregions has started.

In Rumania, the issues of settlement development also received a great emphasis. Rumania inherited one or two large cities from the past, rising out of the rural settlements like islands, very unevenly distributed. South of the Carpathians, only Bucharest was a significant large city.

In Rumania, significant progress was made in the development of an urban network. The importance and role of Bucharest continues to grow and the concentration of non-productive sectors of a higher order is very strong in the capital city. At the same time, the proportion of the population living in rural regions is still relatively high even today in Rumania, and the small and medium sized towns are lacking.

Conclusion

In addition to the profound socioeconomic development which occurred in Eastern European countries during the past decades, great and favorable changes took place in their regional structures as well. A determining role was played in these changes by regional policies which were basically successful. In addition to positive results, undesirable side-effects also manifested themselves and entirely new problems came into prominence. Regional policies were not and are not appropriate to handle these. It has not been possible, despite great efforts made, to solve the problems of backward regions. In several countries, the development of villages and their fate in the long run still remain a serious problem.

The means of planning, despite great improvement are not sufficiently capable even now to provide proper guidance for the development of a social and qualitative type. Methods of economic assessment and analysis of regional changes are not yet sufficient.

The changes that started since the second half of the 1970s will require the formulation of new regional and urban policies - in terms of fundamental content and methodology. The new policies, however, must take into account a few characteristic new elements, such as the present higher development level, lower rates of growth, the increase in importance of qualitative requirements, the rise of the specific cost requirements for infrastructure development, the growing importance of the relations of small regions, the reduction of the proportion of long distance movements and the stabilization of regional structures.

REFERENCES

Berentsen, W. H. (1979) "Regional Planning in the German Democratic Republic: Its Evolution and Goals," International Regional Science Review, 4, 2.

Dolenc, M. and B. Pleskovic (1980) "Postwar Regional Development in Yugoslavia," Regional Science Congress Paper, August

Enache, M. and S. Holtier (1978) "Functional Regions in Rumania: Final Report," Conference Paper, JJASA

Heinzmann, J. (1978) "Structure and Dynamics of the Settlement System in the German Democratic Republic," Conference Paper, JJAAA

Illeris, S. (1980) Research on Changes in the Structure of the Urban Network (Kopenhaven)

Kawashima, T. and P. Korcelli (eds.) (1982) Human Settlement Systems: Spatial Patterns and Trends (JJASA)

Korcelli, P. (1980) "Urban Change: An Overview of Research and Planning Issues," JJASA

Korcelli, P. (1981) "Migration and Urban Change," JJASA

Nyekraszov, N. N. and J. F. Kormnov (1981) "Regionalnije problemi i tyerritorialneje planyirova nyije v. socialistiticseszkih sztrenak Evropi," (Moscow)

Nijkamp, P. and P. Rietveld (eds.) (1981) Cities in Transition: Problems and Policies (Sijthoff and Noordhoff, Alphen san den Rijn)

U. N. Economic Commission for Europe (1980) Report of the Fourth ECE Conference on Urban and Regional Research, July

Van den Berg, L., R. Drewett et al (1979) Urban Europe: A Study of Growth and Decline (Rotterdam, May)

QUANTITATIVE, QUALITATIVE, AND STRUCTURAL VARIABLES IN THE EVALUATION OF REGIONAL DEVELOPMENT POLICIES IN WESTERN EUROPE

Walter Stöhr and Franz Tödtling

On the Evaluation of Regional Development Policies

Although explicit instruments of regional development policy have been applied since the 1950s in most European countries, an evaluation of the success of these measures has received broader attention only in the first half of the 1970s (1). This fact indicates a trend towards the rationalization of regional development policies which may be due to the increasing scarcity of resources available for this purpose on the one hand, and to mounting political pressure of subjectively experienced regional development problems on the other. Although the degree of quantitative interregional disparities has successively decreased in most West European countries (2), the latter has been the case.

During the 1950s and 1960s, a close positive correlation had been implicitly assumed to exist between (objective, quantitative) interregional economic disparities and the degree of political pressure exerted by regional development problems. In other words, it was expected that the regional development problem would disappear automatically with the reduction of interregional disparities in living levels. Most studies evaluating regional development policies were therefore oriented towards such quantitative indicators, as will be shown later. These expectations were frustrated, however, when, in the second half of the 1960s (still a phase characterized by high economic growth rates and predominantly declining interregional economic disparities), a sudden emergence of regionalist movements in many Western countries occurred (3) which could not be explained with the traditional regional development theorems.

The first explanatory approaches traced this fact back to the centralized characteristics of most regional policies aimed at reducing interregional disparities, and particularly to the related pressure for spatial assimilation caused by traditional regional policies along with the penetration of peripheral areas by expanding central regulatory and service functions. These explanatory approaches essentially

157

originated in political science (4).

Other studies undertaken independent of the latter show that important regional economic problems were related not so much to quantitative economic changes but to underlying qualitative and structural transformations stemming from the increasing internationalization of regional and national economies and the new spatial division of labor emerging in this context (5).

Quantitative and Qualitative Transformations Related to the Internationalization of Economies

First one should briefly point to the preconditions under which these transformations took place. They are located on the one hand in the technological-entrepre-neurial sphere, on the other hand in the macroeconomic and international economic sphere.

In the technological-entrepreneurial sphere the preconditions were an increasing division of labor, and the technological possibility for the resolution of production processes into a great number of discrete segments, both horizontally (a sequence of increasingly shorter subproces-ses) and vertically (differentiation between planning, organizing and executing functions) and the entrepreneurial possibility for drawing external and scale economies from these facts (6).

In the macroeconomic and international sphere the preconditions were the widely unhampered possibility of world-wide transfers of commodities, production factors, profits, etc., as well as the increasing integration of most parts of individual countries into a world-wide transport and communications system.

In reaction to this situation, both private and public functional institutions started to organize across territor-ial borders: the first in the form of multiregional and multinational enterprises, the latter in the form of interregional and international development and financing institutions. Both make use of increased factor mobility and increased market and/or influence areas for realizing their specific objective(s), be it maximizing profit, minimizing or compensating risk, increasing the efficiency of their inputs and/or increasing their stability and power (7).

Increased market and influence areas, the increased divisibility and mobility of functions, as well as the ease of overcoming distance have facilitated the transfer of functions and subfunctions over space for both public and private organizations according to their intra-organiza-tional objectives (8) which may not necessarily coincide with the objectives of the territorial units (regions, countries, etc.) involved.

Gyllstrom (9) like others before him including Hymer

(10), distinguishes various hierarchical levels of entrepreneurial functions for multinational firms. For example,
at the highest (world-wide) level one finds entrepreneurial
decision-making, medium and long-term planning, interplant
production and resource allocation, research and development
functions; at the second (continental) level are market and
financial analysis, advertising, etc.; and at lower (e.g.
national or regional) levels are purchasing and sales,
service functions, etc. Routine production processes will
frequently take place at still lower hierarchical levels and
usually in peripheral locations. A similar spatial division
of labor, although with less vertical differentiation, can
also be found in multiregional enterprises within states
(11).

Although the spatial reorganization of specialized
functions within multiregional and multinational enterprises has become easy and is taking place at a large scale
(12), this fact has been widely ignored so far in terms of
explicit regional policy. Such a spatial reorganization of
entrepreneurial functions frequently causes rapid changes in
the pattern of spatial supply and service relations, in the
use of regional natural and human (labor market) resources
(13). However, there are also direct repercussions upon
the level and quality of regional economic activities,
employment, environmental quality, etc., of the respective
territorial units.

In the economic sphere this leads to changes in
regional multipliers, patterns of capital flow, technology,
and innovation, changes in dependency relationships of
individual plants as well as their degree of stability; in
the sphere of labor markets they lead to changes in the
qualitative structure of employment, the degree of diversity
and stability of jobs, and to the formation of spatially
segmented labor markets (14). All these characteristics,
however, are of considerable importance for the medium and
long term development potential of individual regional
communities.

Border-crossing activities of transregional or transnational private or public organizations often manifest
themselves in the transfer of private capital or public
finance which, in the recipient regions, usually leads to an
increase in productive capacity and thereby to a rise in the
usual quantitative indicators of development such as regional product, per capita income, and balance of trade. This
frequently also leads to the statistical reduction in interregional economic disparities mentioned (15). If less
developed areas are promoted by capital incentives and
public transfers as is the case in most West-European
countries (16), the standard evaluations of regional
development policy (see note 25 below), which only deal with
quantitative indicators, will in all likelihood yield a

formally positive result (17). The qualitative and structural transformations mentioned above and their medium and
long-term consequences upon regional development however,
will not appear in these analyses.

During the 1950s and 1960s, the negative effects of
these transformations were concentrated upon <u>peripheral</u>
areas (18). They are no longer restricted to the latter;
an acceleration in changes in the international division of
labor, and an increasing spatial division of labor also
within larger metropolitan areas (between their respective
centers, intermediate and peripheral zones) have major
repercussions also on core-regions and particularly the old
industrial areas.

In the public sector these structural transformations
in most countries have led to spatial incentives and
redistributive measures which, in view of the world-wide
origin of these transformations, became established mainly
at the central, national level, thereby leading to an
increased centralization of governmental policy even in
federal states (19).

The results in most countries were increasing demands
upon central governments (in Europe: national or EEC
funds), an increasing centralization of effectively
disposable resources at the national level, increased
redistributive requirements and an increasing distance
between effective public decision-making and the individual
citizen. In a self-reinforcing process this has led to
further concentration of entrepreneurial decision-making
functions around the locations of central government (20)
and consequently, in most cases, to a parallel shift in
subcontracting, mostly to the detriment of regional
multiplier effects in less developed areas.

In previous rapid growth periods these structural
transformations had been temporarily superseded in
quantitative terms by spatial spill-overs generated via the
market process or by public transfers. In the present slow
growth or stagnation period, however, they become visible
directly and in the short run.

In evaluating strategies and instruments of regional
development policy it will therefore be important to include
consequences of such qualitative and structural transformations. Methodologically this is still a research frontier
but it seems clear that the methods of traditional economic
analysis will not be sufficient and will have to be complemented by theoretical concepts and analytical methods of
other social sciences.

On the Formulation of Regional Policy Objectives

In most countries, explicit objectives of regional
policy are related to the reduction in regional disparities
of living levels. This is the case in the FRG, in France,

Great Britain, Italy, Austria, and in Switzerland (21).

In some countries the terms <u>regional disparities</u> and <u>levels of living</u> are defined only vaguely and lack specification. This is the case in France, Great Britain and Switzerland (22).

In some other countries at least a few specific objectives are specified, such as sufficient employment opportunities in quantitative and qualitative terms, sufficient supply of social, commercial and cultural services, or the preservation of a <u>good</u> environment (FRG, Sweden, Austria) (23). These objectives, however, are usually not operationalized and quantified, nor are there relative weights attached to them.

Although in some countries non-economic (service provision, social, cultural, environmental) objectives concerning regional economic structure are stated at least in general terms, at the level of concrete regional programs and strategies clear priority is given to aggregate economic goals (e.g. number of jobs created, increase in per capita income, in overall productivity, etc.) (24). This is also true of most studies evaluating regional policies.

Quantitative, Qualitative and Structural Variables in Regional Policy and Its Evaluation

By <u>quantitative variables</u> we here mean (usually regionally) aggregate or average measures of economic or social variables such as regional product, total employment, rate of unemployment, total investment, per capita income, net migration, etc. By <u>qualitative variables</u> we here mean the internal distribution or qualitative characteristics of aggregate quantitative variables and their varying implications for the development process (25). In the present context this refers for example to differences in the qualitative composition of the work force and of jobs, in the age of the capital stock and its flexibility, in the innovative character of products, etc. By <u>structural variables</u> we here refer to information about functional interrelations in the sense of a "net of interrelations of parts that form the social system and their functions in maintaining the system (26)." In the present context these concern mainly organizational and institutional relationships between plants and/or territorial units (e.g. regions) and the resulting symmetrical interdependencies or asymmetrical dependencies. Examples of these three groups of variables are given in Table 3.9.

Regional policy as well as analyses to evaluate it have until now mainly dealt with aggregate quantitative (growth) variables (see Table 3.9). Most of these analyses have focused on uncontroversial and easily measurable aggregate quantitative economic and social variables such as regional product, per capita income, aggregate employment, net

Table 3.9: Examples of Quantitative, Qualitative and Structural Variables of Regional Development

	Aggregate Quantitative Variables	Qualitative Variables	Structural Variables
Economy (Production)	-Number of plants/jobs. -Regional product. -Volume of investment.	-Sectoral structure (growth characteristics). -Distribution of entrepreneurial functions (information processing, decision-making, R+D, planning, financing and distribution, routine product, processes). -Distribution by stage in product cycle. -Innovation Capacity (e.g. rate of R+D expenditures, number of product and process innovations applied). -Degree of external "exposure" of economic functions. -Share of regional supply, service, and sales relations. -Rate of fluctuation (openings, closures, transfers, etc.) of plants or entrepreneurial functions.	-Vertical division of labor between regions. -Degree of external functional dependence of branch plants.

Table 3.9 (cont'd)

	Aggregate Quantitative Variables	Qualitative Variables	Structural Variables
Labor Market	-Number of employed.	-Sectoral diversification of regional employment. -Distribution of employment by level of qualification. -Job fluctuation. -Migration by level of qualification.	-Regionally segmented labor markets. -Degree of external organizational dependence of regional employment.
Public Finance and Administration	-Financial capacity of territorial administrative units. -Amount of public investment in region. -Per capita supply of public facilities and infrastructure.	-Distribution of public receipts/expenditure by administrative level. -Degree of concentration of tax receipts upon specific sources (by types of income, sectors, enterprises, etc.). -Intra-regional multipliers of public investment. -Spatial incidence of public contracts. -Degree of adaptation of public services and infrasturcture facilities to regional requirements.	-Degree of centralization of public expenditures. -Regional dependence upon external fiscal transfers.

163

Table 3.9 (cont'd)

Aggregate Quantitative Variables	Qualitative Variables	Structural Variables
Environment	-Rate of conservation of renewable and non-renewable natural resources. -Degree of environmental pollution. -Degree of maintenance of a harmonious man-made environment and of an integrated natural environment (closed feedback loops).	

164

migration, quantity of service provision, etc. (27). Very often these evaluation approaches showed positive results of regional policy measures (28).

Regional policy and its evaluations, however, have with few exceptions (29), hardly considered the question of whether a positive change in the above variables did actually lead to an increase in the development potential of the respective region, or whether it only represented the quantitative aspect of a spatial reorganization of functions within multiregional organizations, the qualitative and structural consequences of which were important but escaped explicit evaluation. In most cases capital imports or increases in gross skilled product or employment have been accompanied by a lowering of labor requirements (increased social downward mobility) for employment and by an increase in the extraregional dependency of jobs (by the establishment of branch plants) (30). This lowering of skill requirements of the regional labor force has, together with a regionally uncoordinated educational policy, in many cases increased the negative selectivity of outmigration still further (IIR forthcoming) instead of reducing it. Both processes would, without doubt, in the medium and long run lead to a decrease in the regional development potential which is determined in large measure by qualitative and structural characteristics - although there may have occurred a positive change of aggregate quantitative variables in the short run (31).

Differentiated qualitative or distributional variables (changes of interpersonal regional disparities, of disparities in income, employment, migration or service provision by educational level or job qualification) as well as specific structural variables (financial, organizational and ownership dependencies) and their related functional and technological changes in space have hardly been systematically analyzed in evaluations of regional policy, in spite of the fact that they have become increasingly important in the 1970s in connection with the increasing internationalization of economic organizations.

Some analyses which attempted to consider explicitly qualitative and structural factors (of entrepreneurial and employment structure), have done so either in a descriptive and unsystematic way (32) or with only an implicit relationship to regional policy instruments (33).

Methodological Aspects of the Evaluation of Regional Policies

Evaluation studies of regional policy (see Figure 3.1) either aim at measuring to what extent regional policy objectives have been met (goal achievement control) and/or to which degree changes in regional conditions have been caused by regional policy instruments (impact-control). In

165

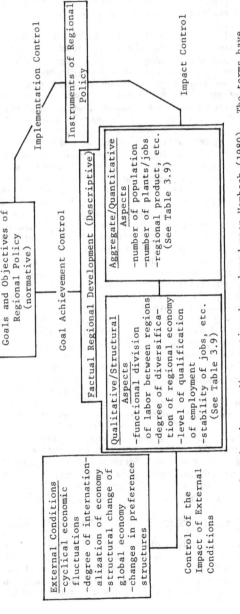

Figure 3.1: Types of Evaluation Studies of Regional Policy (Schematic Representation)*

166

*The major types of evaluation studies mentioned are based upon Hembach (1980). The terms have been translated by the present authors and adapted to terminology used in English.

some cases what might also be called implementation control studies were undertaken in which the orientation and implementation of specific programs with regard to states' objectives were analyzed (34). Studies of this kind and especially impact-control studies involve a number of problems. Usually there are no operational and weighted objectives given and data on important structural and non-economic (social, cultural and political) variables are lacking. One must keep in mind, however, that the availability of statistical data is very often determined by the consciousness of scientists and politicians of certain problems and causal relationships.

In the context of the more narrow impact-control situation one encounters considerable methodological problems trying to isolate the effects of specific regional policy instruments (35). Such an isolation and quantification of effects of specific instruments is, in principle, of course, desirable and could bring valuable insights as to the kinds and magnitudes of policy instruments to be used. In reality, however, such an isolation of the effects of specific instruments has in view of the above stated methodological problems and the required data (long time-series, cross-sectional data) up to now been possible only for highly aggregated variables and indicators. Examples of this latter kind of analysis are the reference-approaches and regression analyses for Great Britain (36) or for the FRG (37). Among the variables included in these analyses were total number of jobs, number of newly established plants, jobs created therein, etc. or the amount of regional investment.

Because of the difficulties mentioned above, structural and qualitative variables have not been included in these quantitative assessments of the impact of regional policies. There seems to exist a "trade off" between the degree of methodological rigor in quantifying specific effects of policy instruments on the one hand, and the actual relevance and explanatory power for regional development of the variables investigated on the other hand. We have tried to show above that the success of regional policy instruments – which in a narrow quantitative sense may be very effective – has often been unsatisfactory due to qualitative and structural transformations related to changes in external conditions. Those qualitative and structural characteristics, however, have hardly been dealt with explicitly. In other words, evaluations have usually analyzed only a small segment of a much more complex set of relationships in regional development. They have especially neglected the qualitative and structural transformations related to the recent internationalization of the economy which have assumed increasing importance for medium and long-range effects on regional development.

167

Such was the case in part because these transformations have attracted attention only within the last few
years, partly because of difficulties in operationalizing
such qualitative and structural variables and because of the
traditional bias of regional analyses and regional policy
work towards the concepts and methods of neoclassical
economics. There are, however, as noted above, also
problems related to the availability of data and methods.
The required differentiated data, which are very often
difficult to operationalize and quantify, are rarely
available from official data sources; also the required
methods of analysis are usually complex and little tested.
On the other hand it must be noted that the selection of
data collected and the choice of methods used, depends on
the problems and questions which are posed systematically
and pursued by decision-makers and scientists. It therefore
seems particularly important to draw attention to these new
problems and the functional interrelations underlying them.
It is important that in future regional analyses and
regional policy evaluations that more emphasis be placed on
qualitative and structural transformations, even if the
impact of specific regional policy instruments on these
changes (impact-control in the narrow sense) cannot be
precisely quantified.

The effects of regional policy instruments on these
qualitative and structural changes might be tentatively
estimated by theoretical and empirical analyses at
micro-levels of investigation (analysis of the importance of
specific regional policy instruments for spatial decisions
of specific types of firms/households) and by a systematic
analysis of the implications of specific regional policy
instruments on changes of qualitative and institutional
regional conditions of regional economics, regional labor
markets public administration and the natural and man-made
environment (see Table 3.9).

NOTES

1. See B. Moore and J. Rhodes, "Evaluating the Effect
of British Regional Economic Policy," *Economic Journal*, 83
(1973), pp. 87-110; D. Fürst and K. Zimmerman, <u>Standortwahl
Industrieller Unternehmen: Ergebnisse Einer</u> Unternehmens-
<u>befragung</u> (Gesellschaft fur Strukturentwicklung, Koln,
1973); F. Wolf "Effizienz und Erfolgskontrolle der
Regionalen Wirtschaftsforderung: Ergebnisse einer
Untersuchung in Hessen," (Hessische Landesentwicklungs und
Treuhandgesellschaft, Wiesbaden, 1974); H. Spehl, K. Topfer
and P. Topfer, <u>Folgenwirkungen von Industrieansiedlungen</u>
(Gesellschaft fur Regionale Strukturentwicklung, Bonn,

Quantitative, Qualitative and Structural Variables

1975); H. Kohler and L. Reyher, "Zu den Auswirkungen von Forderungsmabnahmen auf den Arbeitsmarkt des Regierungsbezirkes Niederbayern nach kreisfreien Stadten, Landkreisen und Arbeitsamtsbezirken," (Beitrage der Arbeitsmarkt und Berufsforschung 6, Institut fur Arbeitsmarkt und Berufsforschung der Bundesanstalt fur Arbeit, Nurnbert, 1975); H. M. Bölting, <u>Wirkungsanalyse der Regionalen Wirtschaftspolitik</u> (Institut fur Siedlungs und Wohnungswesen, Munster, 1976); OECD (ed.), <u>Methods of Measuring the Effects of Regional Policies</u> (OECD, Paris, 1977); C. P. A. Bartels, W. R. Nicol and J. J. Van Duijn, "Estimating Impacts of Regional Policies: A REview of Applied Research Methods," (Working Paper 81-59, International Institute for Applied Systems Analysis, Laxenburg, 1981); B. Ashcroft, "The Measurement of the Impact of Regional Policies in Europe: A Survey and Critique," <u>Regional Studies</u>, 16, 4 (1982), pp. 287-305; W. R. Nicol, "Estimating the Effects of Regional Policy: A Critique of the European Experience," <u>Regional Studies</u>, 16, 3 (1982), pp. 199-210.

2. This study covers the period 1950-1970, although a similar trend seems to have lasted at least until the middle of the 1970s. See W. Molle et al, <u>Regional Disparity and Economic Development in the European Community</u> (Saxon House, Farnborough, 1980).

3. J. Milton Esman, <u>Ethnic Conflict in the Western World</u> (Cornell University Press, London, 1977).

4. Ibid; S. Tarrow, P. J. Katzenstein and L. Graziano (eds.) <u>Territorial Policies in Industrial Nations</u> (Praeger, New York,1978).

5. J. Westaway, "The Spatial Hierarchy of Business Organizations and its Implications for the British Urban System," <u>Regional Studies</u>, 8, 2 (1974), pp. 145-55; A. Liepitz, <u>Le Capital et son Espace</u> (Maspero, Paris, 1977); W. Stöhr and F. Tödtling, "An Evaluation of Regional Policies - Experiences in Market and Mixed Economies," in N. Hansen (ed.) <u>Human Settlement Systems: International Perspectives on Structure, Change and Public Policy</u> (Ballinger, Cambridge, MA, 1978); F. J. Bade, "Funktionale Aspekte der Regionalen Wirtschaftsstruktur," (Internationales Institut fur Management und Verwaltung, IIM-dp 79/91, Berlin, 1979); B. E. Mettler-Meibom, <u>Internationalisierung der Produktion und Regionalentwicklung: Elsab und Lothringen als Beispiele</u> (Campus Verlag, Frankfurt/New York, 1979); D. Massey, "In What Sense a Regional Problem?" <u>Regional Studies</u>, 13 (1979), pp. 233-243; K. Müller, <u>Wirtschaftlicher Strukturwandel und raumliche Entwicklung. Fallstudien-Ergebnisse zum Ausmab sowie zu den Ursachen und Wirkungen funktionaler Konzentration in der Schweiz</u> (Haupt-Verlag, Bern 1981); N. J. Glickman and E. McLean Petras, "International Capital and International Labor Flows: Implications for Public Policy,"

169

paper read at a Conference on Structural Economi Analysis in Time and Space at Umea, Sweden, June 1981.

6. G. E. Törnqvist, "Contact Requirements and Travel Facilities - Contact Models of Sweden and Regional Development Alternatives in the Future," in A. Pred and G. Tornqvist <u>Systems of Cities and Information Flows</u> (Lund Studies in Geography, No. 38, 1973); F. Fröbel, J. Heinrichs and O. Dreye, <u>The New International Division of Labour: Structural Unemployment in Industrialized Countries and Industrialization in Developing Countries</u> (Cambridge University Press, London, 1980).

7. One third of the total world trade already takes place within multinational enterprises. See Independent Commission on International Development Issues (ICIDI), <u>North-South: A Programme for Survival</u> (Pan Books, London, 1980).

8. H. J. Ewers, R. Wettmann, J. Kleine, H. Krist and F. J. Bade, "Innovationsorientierte Regionalpolitik," (Schriftenreihe 'Raumordnung' d.Bundesministers fur Raumordnung, Bauwesen und Stadtebau, 6.042, Bad Bodesberg, 1980).

9. B. Gyllström, "International Integration, Transnational Corporations and Developing Countries," Discussion Paper for the Symposium on Division of Labour, Specialization and Technical Development in Linkoping, Sweden, 1982.

10. St. Hymer, "The Multinational Corporation and the Law of Uneven Development," in J. N. Bhagwati (ed.) <u>Economics and World Order</u> (The MacMillan Company, New York, 1972); St. Hymer, <u>The International Operation of National Firms</u> (MIT Press, Cambridge, MA, 1976).

11. See F. Bade (1979), op. cit.; D. Massey (1979), op. cit.; K. Müller (1981), op. cit.; F. Tödtling, "Multiregional Firms and Spatial Division of Labour in Austria," (Wissenschaftszentrum Berlin, Internationales Institut fur Management (IIM), Discussion Paper IIM/1982-13).

12. R. Leigh and D. J. North, "Regional Aspects of Acquisition Activity in British Manufacturing Industry," <u>Regional Studies</u>, 12 (1978), pp. 227-246; D. Massey and R. A. Meegan, "The Geography of Industrial Reorganisation," <u>Progress in Planning</u>, 10, 8 (Pergamon Press, Oxford, 1979); and K. Müller (1981), op. cit.

13. J. N. H. Britton, "Environmental Adaption of Industrial Plants: Service Linkages, Locational Environment and Organization," in I. F. E. Hamilton (ed.) <u>Spatial Perspectives on Industrial Organization and Decision Making</u> (John Wiley and Sons, London, 1974); H. Spehl et al (1975), op. cit.; J. N. Marshall, "Corporate Organization and Regional Office Employment," (Centre for Urban and Regional Development Studies of the University of Newcastle upon

Tyne, Discussion Paper No. 20, 1978); J. N. Marshall, "Ownership, Organization and Industrial Linkage," (Centre for Urban and Regional Development Studies of the University of Newcastle upon Tyne, Discussion Paper No. 22, 1978).
14. K. Gerlach and P. Liepmann, "Konjunkturelle Aspekte der Industrialisierung peripherer Regionen - Dargestellt am Beispiel des ostbayrischen Regierungsbezirkes Oberpfalz," Jahrbuch f. Nationalokonomie und Statistik, (Bd. 187, S 1-21, Stuttgart, 1972); F. Buttler, K. Gerlach and P. Liepmann, Grundlagen der Regionalokonomie (Reinbeck b.Hamburg, Rowohlt, 1977); B. E. Mettler-Meibom (1979), op. cit.
15. For example, see W. Molle et al (1980), op. cit.
16. D. Yuill, K. Allen and C. Hull (eds.) Regional Policy in the European Community - The Role of Regional Incentives (Croom Helm, London, 1980).
17. For example, see B. Ashcroft (1982), op. cit.
18. These are defined as areas with the least accessibility potential to national resources, market, innovation and decision-making centers. See W. Stöhr, "Alternative Strategien fur die integrierte Entwicklung Peripherer Gebiete bei Adgeschwachtem Wachstum," DISP, 61 (Eidgenossische Technische Hochschule, Zurich, 1981).
19. G. Krumme, "Corporate Organization and Regional Development in the American Federal System: Theory and Policy Perspectives," in G. W. Hoffman (ed.) Federalism and Regional Development (University of Texas Press, Austin, 1981).
20. I. F. E. Hamilton, "Multinational Enterprise and the European Economic Community," Tijdschrift voor Econ. en Soc. Geografie,67,5 (1976), pp. 258-278; A. Pred, City Systems in Advanced Economies (Hutchinson, London, 1977).
21. M. Sant, Regional Policy and Planning for Europe, (Lexington, Westmead, 1974); N. Hansen (ed.) Public Policy and Regional Economic Development (Ballinger Publishing Company, Cambridge, MA, 1974); W. Stöhr and F. Tödtling, "Spatial Equity - Some Antitheses to Current Regional Development Doctrine," in Papers of the Regional Science Association, 38 (1977), pp. 33-53; W. Hess, Regional und Raumordnungspolitische Ziele und Mabnahmen von Bund und Kantonen (Hauptverlag, Bern, 1979); H. Hollenstein and R. Löertscher, Sie Struktur und Regionalpolitik des Bundes. Kritische Wurdingung und Skizze einer Neuorientierung (Verlag Ruegger, Diessenhofen, 1980); N. Vanhove and L. Klaassen, Regional Policy - A European Approach (Saxon House, Westmead, 1980); ÖROK, Osterreichisches Raumordnungskonzept - Entwurf (Wien, 1981).
22. M. Sant (1974), op. cit.; N. Hansen (1974), op. cit.; W. Hess (1979), op. cit.
23. See W. Stöhr and F. Tödtling (1978), op. cit. and ÖROK (1981), op. cit.

24. See Vanhove and Klaassen (1980), op. cit.; Yuill, Allen and Hull (1980), op. cit.; K. Hemback, <u>Der Stellenwert von Wirkungsanalysen fur die Regionalpolitik</u> (Main, Frankfurt, 1980).

25. We are aware of the fact that this definition of qualitative variables differs from that used by other authors (for example see P. Batey, "Information for Long-Term Planning of Regional Development," paper presented at the International Workshop on Information Systems for Integrated Regional Development, held at the International Institute for Applied Systems Analysis (IIASA), Laxenburg, Austria, December 1982; and E. Hinloopen and P. Hijkamp, "Information Systems in an Uncertain Planning Environment - Some Methods," paper presented at the International Workshop on Information Systems for Integrated Regional Development, held at the International Institute for Applied Systems Analysis, Laxenburg, Austria, December, 1982) but we consider it more useful in the present context.

26. This definition of structuralism begins with Radcliffe-Brown, <u>The New Encyclopaedia Britannica</u>, Vol. IX (Micropaedia, 1978), p. 620.

27. See H. Nuppnau, <u>Wirkungen der Zonenrandforderung</u> (Hamburg, 1974); H. Bölting (1976), op. cit.; B. Moore and J. Rhodes, "Evaluating the Economic Effects of Regional Policy," <u>OECD</u> (OECD, Paris, 1977); E. Recker, "Erfolgskontrolle Regionaler Aktionsprogramme durch Indikatoren," <u>Forschungen zur Raumentwicklung</u> (Bd. 6, Bonn, 1977); B. Ashcroft, "The Evaluation of Regional Economic Policy: The Case of the United Kingdom," (Studies in Public Policy 12, University of Strathclyde, 1978); B. Ashcroft and J. Taylor, "The Effect of Regional Policy on the Movement of Industry in Great Britain," in Maclennan and Parr (eds.) <u>Regional Policy in Britain</u> (Martin Robertson, Oxford, 1978); K. Henbach (1980), op. cit.; and B. Ashcroft (1982), op. cit.

28. B. Ashcroft (1982), op. cit.

29. For example, see M. Frost and N. Spence, "Unemployment, Stuctural Economic Change and Public Policy in British Regions," <u>Progress in Planning</u>, 15, 1 (Pergamon Press, Oxford, 1981), pp. 1-103.

30. See F. Tödtling (1981), op. cit.

31. Frost and Spence (1981), op. cit. state that ". . . A large part of the apparent convergence (of unemployment rates for different areas of the country over the last 15 years). . . can be accounted for by patterns of response to particular cyclical events" . . . and . . . "government policies have had insufficient effect to transform the nature of the balance of demand for and supply of labour in their areas." (p. 99). "Such evidence only emphasizes the self-perpetuating nature of regional problems, with relatively low skill, high risk, institutionally peripheral

jobs being replaced by new jobs with the same
characteristics and the same problems" (p. 101).

32. For example, see Wolf (1974), op. cit.; Kohler and
Reyher (1975), op. cit.; J. Stark, <u>Regionalpolitik im
landlichen Raum</u> (Stuttgart, 1978); L. Ohlsson, "Assessing
Swedish Regional Policy," <u>OECD</u> (ed.) (OECD, Paris, 1977).

33. J. Westaway (1974), op. cit.; Spehl et al (1975),
op. cit.; Marshall (1978), op. cit.; I. J. Smith, "Ownership
Status and Employment Changes in Northern Region
Manufacturing Industry 1963-1973," (Centre for Urban and
Regional Development Studies, University of Newcastle upon
Tyne, Discussion Paper No. 7, 1978); B. E. Mettler-Meibom
(1979), op. cit.; K. Müller (1981), op. cit.; F. Tödtling
(1981), op. cit.

34. See W. Jann and E. Kronenwett, "Handlungsspiel-
raume und Entscheidungsfahigkeit des politisch-administra-
tiven Systems der Bundesrepublik Deutschland," (untersucht
am Beispiel strukturschwacher Raume, Speyrer Forschungs-
berichte 9).

35. Regional policy instruments have direct effects,
but also indirect effects and side effects which are
difficult to operationalize. There always exists
considerable time-lags which should be taken into account.

36. B. Moore and J. Rhodes (1977), op. cit.; B.
Ashcroft and J. Taylor (1978), op. cit.; B. Ashcroft (1978),
op. cit.

37. H. Bölting (1976), op. cit.; R. Thoss,
"Identification and Measurement of the Effects of Regional
Policy in the Federal Republic of Germany," <u>OECD</u> (OECD,
1977); E. Recker (1977), op. cit.

PART IV: NATIONAL CASE STUDIES IN REGIONAL DEVELOPMENT

RECENT DEVELOPMENTS AND PROPOSED CHANGES IN ITALIAN REGIONAL
POLICY: THEIR IMPACT AND POTENTIAL IMPLICATIONS

Allan Rodgers

Introduction

This paper is concerned with recent developments in
Italian regional policy, proposed changes and implications.
As has been noted so often, the Mezzogiorno (1) is a classic
area of subnational underdevelopment whose problems are
replicated in many other segments of the developed world.
However, in the Italian case, we are treating a region with
a relatively long history of regional planning exceeded only
by the British regional planning experience. Since the
1950s, it has been estimated that billions of dollars have
been spent by the Italian government in attempts to narrow
the socioeconomic gap between southern Italy and the far
more prosperous Center and North (2).

The per capita income maps for 1951 and 1971 (Figures
4.2 and 4.3), the figure demonstrating the absolute changes
in manufacturing employment, by province, during that
two-decade interval (Figure 4.4), and Table 4.1, all
illustrate the results of these efforts. Put simply,
although progress has been made, its magnitude has been very
limited. Nor has the gap between the North and the South
been significantly reduced. Certainly, not enough to match
the hopes and one might add the dreams of most
meridionalisti (Southerners). Poverty still persists, and
some areas, such as the Appenine spine (the osso), with
continuing out-migration have, in fact, retrogressed.
Rural-urban differentials are still great and gross
intra-urban inequities continue. Although the general tenor
of life in the Mezzogiorno is now far better than it was in
the early fifties, most southerners still lament what they
view as the failure of the development efforts in the South
to achieve a standard of living approaching levels common in
most areas of northern and central Italy. The most eloquent
among these southern advocates argue convincingly that their
region has failed to receive what they conceive of as an
equitable share of the nation's socioeconomic product!

174

Table 4.1: Changes in Manufacturing Employment in Italy from 1951 to 1971

Region Years	Industrial Employment (000)			Absolute Change (000)			Relative Change percent			Share Industrial Employment	
	1951	1961*	1971	1951-61	1961-71	1951-71	1951-61	61-71	51-71	1951	1971
North	2925	3844	4513	919	669	1588	31.4	17.4	54.3	83.6	85.4
South	574	649	774	75	125	200	13.1	19.3	34.9	16.4	14.6
Italy	3499	4493	5287	994	794	1788	28.4	17.7	51.1	100.0	100.0

*Data for 1961 derived from the IV Censimento Generale dell'Industria e del'Commercio, 1961, Volume 1 (Rome 1962), various pages.

Figure 4.1: The Mezzogiorno

Figure 4.2: Per Capita Income, in Constant 1971 Prices,
Italy by Province, 1951

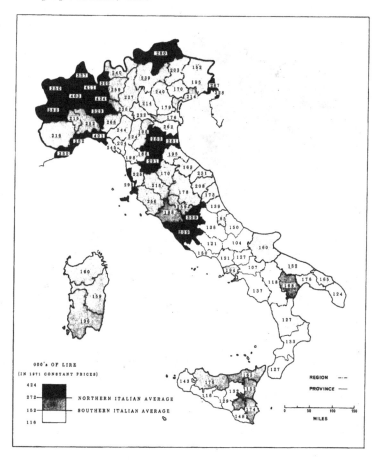

Figure 4.3: Per Capita Income, Italy by Province, 1971

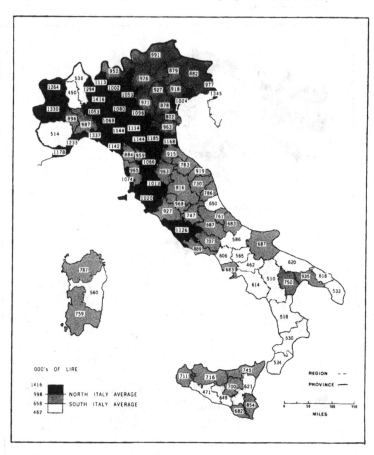

Figure 4.4: Absolute Change in Manufacturing Employment in Southern Italy, By Province, 1951-1971

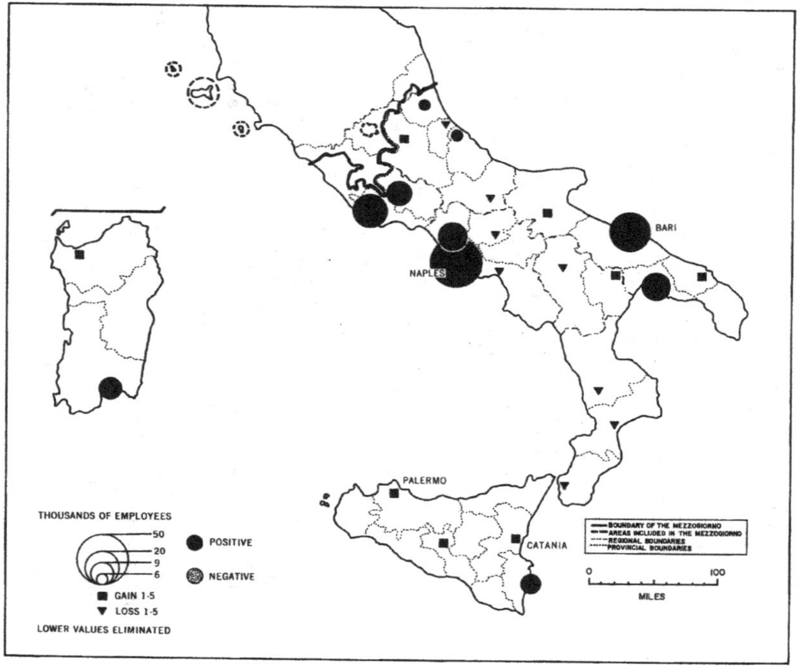

Regional Policy in the 1970s

A decade has passed since the census of 1971. These years have witnessed marked economic, social and political change in Italy. While these developments have affected the nation as a whole, their influence has been felt most notably in the Mezzogiorno. This has been an era of significant reductions in industrial investment in southern Italy (3), but contemporaneously there have been significant alterations in the development program itself.

There have been many shifts in the development legislation since 1970. A major modification of the development policy was approved in October of 1971 (No. 853), and this new law was subsequently amended in May of 1976 (No. 183). Given the fact that these two legislative acts have been thoroughly discussed in the Italian and English literature, only a summary of key innovations at this point is given. Since the two laws are so highly interrelated, they will be referred to here collectively as the new legislation or the new program.

In broad terms, the new legislation supports and strengthens the role of planning in southern economic development. Investment in the Mezzogiorno <u>must</u> now take place within the overall framework of <u>national</u> social and economic goals. Thus, the role of C.I.P.E. (the Interministerial Committee for Economic Planning) in the determination of the direction of the development program has been sharply increased. However, at the same time much more power has been delegated to the <u>regioni</u> or regional governments. Thus these two elements of the new program could conceivably run counter to each other. It should be added that the role of the Cassa per il Mezzogiorno (Agency for the South) has been markedly reduced and, as we shall see, it is scheduled for elimination or drastically reduced responsibilities.

More specifically, the following are the chief elements of the new program as defined in the 1971 and 1976 legislation.

1) Private firms whose assets are over five billion lire (roughly four million dollars at current exchange rates) and all state enterprises in Italy <u>must</u> submit their planned investment programs to the Ministry of the Budget. It was now obligatory for firms proposing to construct new industrial plants or expand existing ones, where the investment exceeded seven billion lire, to submit their proposals to the same authority. C.I.P.E., working closely with this Ministry, may issue a negative decision if such a project would contribute to further congestion or if the new plant was not located in an area of significant unemployment. Firms which ignored such negative assessments are subject to severe fiscal penalties. I have, however, no personal knowledge of the enforcement of such fines. In

contrast, all state organizations <u>must</u> adhere to C.I.P.E. decisions. Such entities <u>must</u> also submit five year plans for investment in the South to the central planning authorities.

2) State-owned or controlled industries <u>must</u> now devote at least eighty percent of their new investments and sixty percent of overall investments to the Mezzogiorno (as opposed to sixty and forty percent in the 1960s). In addition, forty percent of the investments programmed by public administrations and thirty percent of the value of all contracts involving purchase of industrial products <u>must</u> be allocated to the South. Both provisions were to be far more strictly enforced by C.I.P.E. than in the past.

3) The support of industrial growth was sharply increased at the expense of agriculture. Infrastructure, however, remained a relatively high priority, particularly in what were termed the <u>Special</u> <u>Projects</u> (such as the decontamination of the Bay of Naples).

4) The loan and grant program was restructured so as to give greater priority to small and medium sized firms. Grants increasingly became a major feature of the investment program. Their size could range from as high as forty percent for investments up to 1.6 million dollars (two billion lire) down to fifteen percent for investments as high as twelve million dollars (fifteen billion lire). In addition, firms planning to invest in the South could continue to get low interest (four to six percent) - long term (ten to fifteen years) loans as in the past. The normal upper limit for both forms of aid was seventy percent, but could be raised to as much as eighty-six percent if the projects were located in particularly depressed areas that had suffered severe depopulation and if the proposed industry was in a <u>priority</u> <u>sector</u>. In the latter instance, the move was away from the support of basic industries like primary petro-chemicals and steel (which received the lion's share of financing earlier so often with minimal multiplier effects) to industries that, because of market conditions and technological efficiency, were needed in the South (4). These were the so-called growth sectors like machinery, metal fabrication, electronics and a host of secondary chemical products. As in the past, the <u>traditional</u> industries were not encouraged except where a major technological innovation was envisaged. First order industries in those sectors considered to be saturated (with respect to market potential) were to be actively discouraged. Similarly, as noted above, proposed new plants in the congested areas of southern Italy were to be curbed. However, despite continued discussion of the possible adoption of an <u>Industrial</u> <u>Development</u> <u>Certificate</u> program, similar to that in Britain, this method was not adopted for the heavily industrialized areas of the Po Valley.

Proposals for aid for large plants (with investments over
fifteen billion lire) were now to be approved by C.I.P.E.
Another change was the greater emphasis on labor-intensive
industries. Establishments with low investments per worker
were to receive the highest priority.

   5) Leasing was to be encouraged and facilitated, but
this feature, common to programs in western Europe and the
U.S., still did not attract prospective investors in
southern Italy.

   6) Rebates on social insurance, which had been
designed to reduce labor costs in the Mezzogiorno, were
strengthened; not all such charges were waived for a minimum
of five years, and the terminal date is now indefinite.

   7) The most perturbing part of the new legislation was
the essential elimination of the locational advantages of
the agglomerati (Industrial zones) of the areas and nuclei
of industrial development. The program as defined by this
legislation, appears to be even more diffusive in character
than the previous policy of the 1950s and 1960s. The focus
on the most depressed regions which had suffered severe
out-migration appeared to be another response to political
pressure. It was clearly not an economically rational
approach, given the continued scarcity of investment funds.
The other disturbing element of the new program was the
decentralization of the development efforts which reduced
the power of the Cassa and transferred many of its
reponsibilities to the regioni.

Economic Performance in the 1970s

   The years since 1971 have been an era of erratic
economic growth in Italy, punctuated by intervals of minimal
increase and one year of modest decline. Studies by Moore
and Klein (5) have demonstrated that Italy's economic
performance during this epoch lagged behind that of its
partners in the European Economic Community; in fact, the
nation has yet to surmount these recurring economic crises.
The 1970s were also an era of severe unemployment,
particularly in the South, coupled with inordinately high
inflation (an annual rate averaging more than twenty
percent) (6). Though the current level is still far too
great, there has been a very modest reduction.

   This history of erratic growth could be illustrated by
a variety of temporal indicators such as: gross domestic
product, value added, investment, unemployment, etc.
Several of these measures are used here to document these
trends. Table 4.2 illustrates the growth of gross domestic
product from 1971 to 1980, at constant 1970 prices, for the
two Italies both per inhabitant and per worker.

   Economic fluctuations in the Mezzogiorno were
apparently not as drastic as those in the North. This
differential regional economic growth would appear to

Table 4.2: Changes in Gross Domestic Product per Inhabitant and per Worker from 1971 to 1980*
in thousands of lire
(at constant 1970 prices)

Region	1971	Index 1971	1972	1973	1974	1975	1976	1977	1978	1979	1980	Index 1980
Per Inhabitant												
Northern Italy	1383	117	1423	1506	1559	1480	1577	1597	1640	1706	1775	118
Southern Italy**	812	69	820	875	895	878	891	907	915	974	1000	67
Italy	1184	100	1212	1286	1327	1269	1335	1354	1384	1446	1499	100
Per Worker												
Northern Italy	3561	109	3737	3953	4051	3860	4115	4174	4529	4421	4541	109
Southern Italy**	2619	80	2673	2871	2935	2900	2922	2974	3025	3131	3269	79
Italy	3278	100	3416	3628	3718	3574	3755	3810	3884	4031	4157	100

*Annuario di Contabilita Nazionale 1980-81, Volume X, Tomo II, Parte B (Anni 1971-1980) (Instituto Centrale di Statistica, Rome, 1982), page 3.
**Southern Italy here does not include southern Lazio.

indicate that in the short run, at least, southern Italy's economic performance may have been somewhat more stable than its northern counterpart. Podgielski (7) has argued that this variance could, however, reflect the structural backwardness of the Mezzogiorno with its greater dependence on the production of consumer goods and agricultural products for local consumption. This she argues would have made it far less sensitive to national and international economic fluctuations than northern Italy with its far greater emphasis on the production of producer goods. Nevertheless, the relative growth demonstrated in this table indicates that the South fell somewhat further behind northern Italy when measured by these two indicators (at least in a relative sense) during this period.

From a more positive perspective, industrial employment in the Mezzogiorno grew at a faster pace than was true in the North (see Table 4.3). These data are not directly comparable with those published in the 1971 Industrial Census, because of the sampling methodology employed in their computation (8); however, they do indicate that the growth in manufacturing employment in the South was roughly fifteen percent in eight years, compared to only one percent in the same era for northern Italy. Using net shift analysis (9), the highest inward movements were in Abruzzi e Molise and in Puglia, while Sicily had a strikingly high level of missing jobs (10). In absolute terms industrial employment grew by over one hundred thousand workers in the Mezzogiorno with the bulk of the growth concentrated in Campania and Puglia. The gap, measured in this fashion, had narrowed, but again not appreciably.

In Table 4.4, which shows the data on value added by manufacturing per worker by region, despite some relative and absolute improvement, southern Italy's lag is clearly discernable. However, the regional patterns within the South were quite different from those in Table 4.3. These obviously reflect the industrial structure of both areas. For example, note the high values for Sicily and Sardinia with such high value added industries as chemicals as opposed to Campania and Calabria with their labor intensive industrial plants and low value added by manufacture.

The per capita incomes (at constant prices) demonstrated in Figure 4.5 should be compared with those in Figure 4.2. Incomes in the Mezzogiorno had sharply increased but still remained at roughly half the level of those in the North. Provincial patterns did demonstrate higher averages than the southern mean for Latina and Frosinone in Lazio, Taranto in Puglia, Matera in Basilicata. As for the islands, Syracuse in Sicily and Sassari and Cagliari in Sardinia exceeded the average for the South.

Table 4.5 shifts to a sectoral focus in manufacturing. Two indicators were used, employment and product. Although

184

Table 4.3: Estimated Changes in Industrial Employment, by Region, in the Mezzogiorno During the 1970s* (in Thousands)

Regions	1971	1972	1973	1974	1975	1976	1977	1978	1979	1980	Absolute Change (1971–1980)	Net Shift (1971–1980)
Abruzzi and Molise	64	65	73	81	82	82	83	81	83	82	18	+8
Campania	251	253	266	278	276	283	287	285	289	287	36	-4
Puglia	154	159	166	175	178	181	184	181	184	185	31	+7
Basilicata	19	19	19	21	22	22	22	22	22	21	2	-1
Calabria	36	34	35	36	37	38	38	38	39	39	3	-3
Sicily	152	150	152	155	156	158	159	158	159	160	8	-16
Sardinia	41	42	44	48	48	49	50	51	50	55	14	+8
Southern Italy** (absolute)	717	723	755	792	800	814	825	817	828	830	113	
Share Industrial Employment %	15.2	15.4	15.8	16.1	16.3	16.6	16.8	16.8	16.9	17.0		
Northern & Central Italy(absolute)	4007	3966	4035	4120	4094	4092	4086	4043	4056	4065	58	

Table 4.3 (cont'd)

Regions	1971	1972	1973	1974	1975	1976	1977	1978	1979	1980	Absolute Change (1971-1980)	Net Shift (1971-1980)
Share Industrial Employment %	84.8	84.6	84.2	83.9	83.7	83.4	83.2	83.2	83.1	83.0		
Italy (absolute)	4724	4690	4790	4912	4893	4906	4910	4860	4883	4894	170	
Share of Industrial Employment %	100.0	100.0	100.0	100.0	100.0	100.0	100.0	100.0	100.0	100.0		

*Occupati per Attivita Economica e Regione, 1970-1980, Istituto Centrale di Statistica, Collana d'Informazioni, Vol. 5, No. 4 (Rome, 1981), various pages. These values are estimates rather than a true census, but they are considered reasonably reliable. The classification code for industry is based on standard E.E.C. categories. These values are solely for "dipendenti" (employees) and are more readily comparable with those in the 1971 Census. The relative increase between 1971 and 1980 for southern Italy was nearly sixteen percent, while that for the North was roughly one percent for the same period.

**Net shift values based upon the average employment growth rate for Southern Italy during this period.

Table 4.4: Estimated Changes in the Value Added by Manufacture per Worker, by Region, from 1971 Through 1979* (thousands of lire, at constant 1970 prices)**

Regions	1971	1972	1973	1974	1975	1976	1977	1978	1979	Absolute Change 000 (1971-1979)	Relative Change %
Abruzzi	2134	2237	2323	2186	2279	2599	2808	3013	3304	1170	55
Molise	1749	1776	1992	1959	2118	2568	2196	2696	2801	1052	60
Campania	2711	2652	2860	2641	2606	2744	2760	2854	3194	483	18
Puglia	2707	2851	3061	2803	2802	2882	2625	2929	3345	638	24
Basilicata	2718	2704	3026	2617	2427	2754	2813	3299	8745	1027	38
Calabria	2350	2495	2449	2292	3305	2524	2427	2203	2428	78	03
Sicily	2249	2475	2691	2491	2574	2536	2546	2625	3060	811	36
Sardinia	3095	3162	3546	3547	3282	3722	3673	4101	4549	1454	44
Southern Italy	2550	2632	2831	2628	2623	2730	2721	2891	3255	705***	28
Northern and Central Italy	3248	3541	3783	3416	3461	3715	3772	3908	4276	1028	32
Italy	3218	3386	3618	3277	3312	3544	3581	3723	4089	871	27

*Annuario di Contabilita Nazionale 1980-1981, Tomo II, Parte B (Istat, Rome, 1982), various pages.
**Constant prices in this table were computed from the wholesale price index as given in Il Valore della Lira dal 1861 al 1979, (Istat, Rome, 1980), page 23.
***The relative share (value added per worker) in the South was 79 percent of that in northern Italy in 1971 and only 76 percent of that value eight years later!

Figure 4.5: Per Capita Income, In Constant 1971 Prices,
Italy by Province, 1979

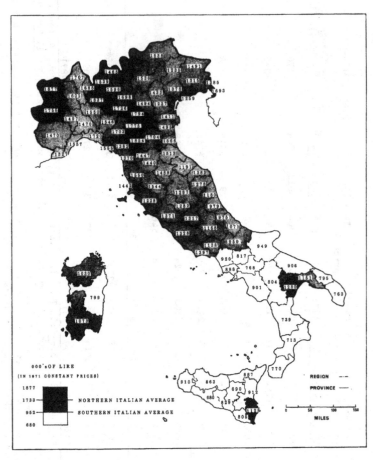

Table 4.5: Manufacturing Employment and Product in the Two Italies from 1971-1980*

Branches	Employment South %	Employment Center-North %	Product South %	Product Center-North %	Employment South %	Employment Center-North %	Product South %	Product Center-North %
1. Ferrous and Non-Ferrous Metal Products	5.9	4.9	8.1	6.2	8.3	5.4	9.3	5.1
2. Non-Metallic Mineral Products	12.9	7.1	11.1	7.0	10.6	6.8	11.2	7.3
3. Chemical Products	5.7	6.0	8.9	8.7	6.3	5.7	8.5	6.7
4. Metal Fabrication and Machinery	14.9	26.4	10.9	26.1	13.5	28.1	13.0	26.7
5. Transport Equipment	5.2	7.4	5.9	7.7	7.7	8.1	7.9	7.1
6. Food, Beverage and Tobacco Products	14.9	6.8	18.6	9.9	13.1	6.8	15.4	9.5
7. Textiles, Clothing, Leather and Shoes	29.9	24.3	19.8	17.3	26.8	21.2	18.9	18.4
8. Wood and Paper Products and Printing	2.7	5.0	3.9	6.1	2.4	5.4	3.1	5.9
9. Other Manufacturing Industries	12.3	12.1	12.7	11.1	11.3	12.5	12.7	13.3
Total (in percent)	100.0	100.0	99.9	100.1	100.0	100.0	100.0	100.1
Absolute Total (in Thousands of employees and Billions of Lire)*	717	4007	2198	13,917	830	4065	3531	20,882

*Annuario di Contabilita Nazionale 1980-1981, Vol. X, Tomo II, Parts A and B (Istat, Rome, 1981-82), various pages, monetary data revised to constant 1970 prices.

**Branches based on newest EEC categories and are not directly comparable to previous Italian classi-fications of manufacturing as defined in their census volumes.

detail is quite limited, certain patterns emerge. First, the absolute percentage shifts were minimal during the eight year interval. The variations ranged from one to three percent, and within that range they were less variable in the North than in the South. Although there were percentage differences from sector to sector, the average change was roughly the same for both employment and product.

Regarding investment by sector and by region from 1971 to 1980, there was a sharp decline in relative and absolute terms of fixed investment in industry. Its impact, however, will only be felt in the early 1980s. However, one cannot argue that 1980 was an isolated phenomenon, for investment in industry had declined steadily from 1971 through 1980. Then too, the share of the South compared with northern Italy in industrial investment showed a notable widening of the so-called gap. If these reductions are portents of impending economic events, then the future of the Mezzogiorno does indeed appear quite bleak.

Proposed Changes in the Regional Development Legislation for the South (11)

Many of the key features of the current development program are scheduled to end as of June 30th, 1982, for that is the terminal date of law No. 183 of 1976 for the Mezzogiorno. However, efforts are now underway to salvage much of this legislation under the so-called Capria Law. But even if this bill were passed, considering all of the amendments added to it since it was first proposed, the face of the development program would be vastly altered.

Nicola Capria, the former Minister for the Mezzogiorno, has long since been replaced by Claudio Signorile, but both are Socialists and members of the current shaky Spadolini coalition. The main instrumentality that would cease operations at the end of June would be the Cassa per il Mezzogiorno, the chief development agency for the South. Contrary to the demands of the Communist party, which has called for the complete elimination of the Cassa, the amended law would liquidate that organization and at the same time create two new entities: the first is termed a Fondo or a monetary agency responsible for planning and financing the development program, while the Azienda, its technical counterpart, would be an agency responsible for the territorial reequilibrium of the South and its development. Undoubtedly, even in toto, what was an admittedly huge bureaucratic apparatus would now be far smaller than its predecessor with much of its power diluted and dispersed to the individual regions of southern Italy.

Some scholar-politicians like Professors Saraceno (12) (the chief architect of the southern development program) and Compagna (13), one of the deputies from Naples, and at the same time geographer-editor of Nord e Sud, are strongly opposed to this dismemberment of the Cassa, but they are clearly in the minority.

As for the immediate changes suggested for the program by the new legislative proposals, they are numerous and far reaching. The main elements of the bill are summarized here and these, of course, are still subject to amendment. However, its passage now appears probable, unless the current coalition falls in the interval.

1) As noted earlier, the chief change, if approved, would divide the Cassa into two new agencies. However, even in combination, it appears that both organizations would be far smaller and more limited in power than the current Cassa.

2) Loans which were designed to provide long term-low interest credit (far below current market levels) and now require a double approval by the Cassa and by the appropriate credit institute <u>would be abolished</u>. In their place, there would be a significant increase in the size of the capital grants with only a <u>single</u> agency approval required. There would be new rules that, on one hand, <u>promise</u> transparency (openness), comparative automaticity, and rapid disbursement; and on the other, it would penalize entrepreneurs who now often file false unsubstantiated loan requests.

3) Contributions or direct grants would be increased to compensate, at least in part, for the elimination of the loan program. Except under special circumstances, grants shall be confined to firms whose investments for new construction, expansion or modernization of facilities is less than 60 billion lire (roughly forty-three million dollars at currect exchange rates), with priorities favoring small and medium sized establishments. There would be a somewhat higher subsidy for Basilicata and Calabria, the most depressed areas in the South. At the same time, there would be a lower assistance level for those parts of southern Lazio, Marche and Toscana previously eligible for full subsidies. With some exceptions, these areas no longer fit the depressed category.

4) Labor incentives that would provide temporary subsidies (for up to two years) to enterprises that give jobs to unemployed youngsters and would provide them with occupational and professional training. The payments would apparently be forty percent of overall labor costs for a maximum of fifteen percent of the total number of employees of any subsidized plant. Also included is an employment premium similar to the British case, but, unlike the latter, as a share of labor costs rather than as a fixed sum per employee. However, reports indicate that some students of the development problems of the Mezzogiorno view this subsidy as a type of handout which would, they believe, discourage the technological evolution of southern firms.

191

5) Although the original Capria bill provided that government ministries would have to place at least forty percent of their purchase orders with southern firms, that level would <u>remain</u> at the current thirty percent value.

6) Greater emphasis is to be placed on the improvement of urban infrastructure in the South, especially in the metropolitan areas of Palermo and Naples where problems of congestion and urbanization diseconomies have multiplied at an accelerated level.

7) Contributions to support a more effective commercial structure, coupled with greater tax, tariff and freight rate incentives would be instituted.

8) From a geographical perspective, there is no evidence in the original Capria law nor in its amended version of any coherent locational design. If the so-called growth pole policy is to be preserved, given all of its limitations, there is no hint of that fact in the literature. Perhaps, the formulators of the amended legislation take for granted the continuance of that long-term policy.

Over time, as a result of the development process, the largest share of the loans and grants have been disbursed to the areas closest to the Center and some coastal zones thus aggravating disequilibria within the Mezzogiorno. These suggest the necessity for a gradual contraction of the limits of that development region and the introduction of a quasi-automatic diversity in the level of incentives within the <u>New South</u> in favor of the most backward areas which previously had been largely excluded from the development process. The new legislation does take some modest steps in that direction.

9) In all, there is to be a provision of ninety billion lire for the Mezzogiorno to be spent by 1990, a modest <u>decrease</u> in the annual level of subsidies over those expended in the 1976-1980 period.

Venturini (14), in her recent article in <u>Mondo Economico</u> talks about the problems that still face the parliament before the June 30th deadline and the arguments in process between the various interest groups about the proposed new legislation and its implications. To one who has worked with the previous development policy, with its delays and complexities and the problem termed <u>clientilismo</u> (the favoring of special friends and interests), the lags in the passage of this legislation could be debilitating for the South. Compagna (15) has also warned that there may be lengthy delays with grave consequences for the Mezzogiorno. He cites the experience of the 1971 and 1976 laws which resulted in a two year lag between passage and implementation of the newer legislation.

According to Venturini, again, Professor Saraceno, despite the new amendments, strongly opposes, as noted earlier, the planned breakup of the Cassa and the abolition of the loan program (16). In addition, the chief credit agencies for the Mezzogiorno-Isveimer (Institute for the Economic Development of Southern Italy), Irfis (Regional Institute for the Financing of Industry in Sicily), and Cis (Sardinian Industrial Trust) - argue, with some justice, that small enterprises in the South do not have the wherewithal for self-financing, therefore, they reason that some type of loan program must be retained at least for the gestation period to preserve the economic vitality of such enterprises. Above all they hold that the grant program must, at least, operate with minimal delays in fund disbursement if it is to be effective.

Implications of the Proposed New Development Legislation

It is, of course, premature to forecast with any surety the presumed effects of the new development law before legislation passage. Whatever its ultimate form, there is no doubt in the minds of those concerned with southern problems that either a new bill will be passed or the current law will be extended. There appears to be absolutely no sympathy on the part of any of the contending parties for the <u>abolition</u> of the development program. However, further amendments are possible, if not probable, before passage.

If the proposed law, as reviewed, is passed with only minor modification, changes are envisaged. First and perhaps foremost is the contraction of the limits of the areas eligible for subsidy to the <u>truly</u> impoverished areas of the South with varying levels of incentives graded according, hopefully, to more meaningful criteria than were used in the past. Unquestionably, the main focus of attention will be on those small and medium sized enterprises that are labor rather than capital-intensive. The Cassa, in its present form, will undoubtedly be eliminated and much of its power dispersed to the "regioni." The priority industries will be in the so-called growth sectors, particularly those that are minimally energy dependent. Such industries may include electronics, telecommunications, information systems, and activities linked to research and development (assuming that such industries truly desire to locate in the Mezzogiorno which is questionable). Then too, the available data still indicate a rapidly growing population in southern Italy of which a far smaller portion than in the past will emigrate to the North and abroad. The South has an extraordinarily high percentage of unemployed youth, for whom employment opportunities seem minimal. The employment provisions of the Capria Law could provide meaningful incentives for entrepreneurs to hire a significant portion of this group given improved economic circumstances.

Table 4.6: Gross Fixed Investment, by Major Economic Sector, and Region, from 1971 to 1980*
(Billions of Lire at constant 1970 prices)

Sector	1971		1972		1973		1974	
	South	Center-North	South	Center-North	South	Center-North	South	Center-North
Agriculture	9.8	5.3	9.6	5.7	9.9	4.7	10.3	4.4
Industry **	30.5	29.4	31.9	27.3	30.7	29.9	30.9	31.0
Services	59.7	65.3	58.5	68.0	59.4	65.4	58.8	64.6
Total (%)	100.0	100.0	100.0	100.0	100.0	100.0	100.0	100.0
Total (absolute)	4291.5	8709.5	4355.0	8766.0	4489.9	9644.1	4613.1	9993.9
Share of Investment (%)	33.0	67.0	33.2	66.8	31.8	68.2	31.6	68.4

*Annuario di Contabilita Nazionale, 1980-1981, Vol. X, Tomo II, Parte B (Istat, Rome, 1982), page 29.
**Industry here includes manufacturing plus mining, utilities and construction.

194

Table 4.6 (cont'd)

Sector	1975 South	1975 Center-North	1976 South	1976 Center-North	1977 South	1977 Center-North	1978 South	1978 Center-North
Agriculture	12.4	5.1		5.7		5.8		6.0
Industry		28.3		28.2		28.8		28.7
Services		66.6		66.1		65.4		65.3
Total (%)	100.0	100.0	100.0	100.0	100.0	100.0	100.0	100.0
Total (absolute)	4101.8	8643.2	4179.1	8864.9	4021.7	8976.3	3881.7	9103.3
Share of Investment (%)	32.2	67.8	32.0	68.0	30.9	69.1	29.9	70.1

Table 4.6 (cont'd)

Sector	1979		1980	
	South	Center-North	South	Center-North
Agriculture		5.6	12.5	4.8
Industry		31.1	19.5	32.6
Services		63.3	68.0	62.6
Total (%)	100.0	100.0	100.0	100.0
Total (absolute)	4143.0	9599.0	4452.5	10658.5
Share of Investment (%)	30.1	69.9	29.5	70.5

Regarding the negative features of the new legislation, the focus on areas that have suffered severe depopulation and the seemingly deliberate omission of any growth pole strategy are mistakes that development planners may regret in the coming decade. Then too, the elimination of the loan program appears to be a gross error that will hurt <u>most</u> of the small entrepreneurs that the program deems its highest priority.

In sum, legislation is under consideration in Rome which may have both positive and deliterious effects on the Mezzogiorno. The outcome is still in question!

NOTES

1.   Figure 4.1 demonstrates the limits of the Mezzogiorno and its regional divisions.
2.   There are many books, monographs, and articles on regional   economic   development   in   the   Italian   South. However,   in   my   view,   from   the   Geographer-Regional Economist-Regional Planner's context the best in Kevin Allen and M. C. Maclennon, <u>Regional Problems and Policies in Italy and France</u>, University of Glasgow, Social and Economic Studies, No. 19 (London, 1970). The Italian facet of this study was covered by Dr. Allen. He also co-authored with Andrew Stevenson a volume entitled: <u>An Introduction to the Italian Economy</u>, Glasgow Social and Economic Research Studies, No. 1 (London, Robertson, 1974).   Also noteworthy and of great value for its perceptive critique of the development effort is G. Podbielski, <u>Twenty-Five Years of Special Action for the Development of Southern Italy</u>, SVIMEZ (Milan, Rome, 1978); note in particular its extensive bibliography covering the Italian literature.   The most recent Italian study was that by the economist Vera Cao-Pinna, (ed.) <u>Le Regioni del Mezziogiorno</u> (Il Mulino, Bologna, 1979).
3.   A. Rodgers, <u>Economic Development in Retrospect</u> (Winston-Wiley, Washington, 1979) when measured in constant prices.
4.   The reference to markets refers to rising demand in the   South,   itself   for   the   improvement   in   transport connectivity between the Mezzogiorno and the North has opened the region to a flood of cheap manufactured goods moving   in   by   truck.   With   regard   to   technological efficiency, later in the paper a reference is made to those industries which because of technological innovation have been identified in the development legislation as high priority industries and should, if possible, be centered in the South.
5.   J. Moore and P. Klein, <u>International Economic</u>

Indicators (New York, National Bureau of Economic Research, 1978).

6. See various *Rapporti sul Mezzogiorno* published by SVIMEZ in Rome and annual reports of ISTAT (Instituto Centrale di Statatistica) also in Rome.

7. G. Podbielski, *Twenty-Five Years of Special Action for the Development of Southern Italy* (Milan-Rome, SVIMEZ, 1978).

8. The differences are explained in the various volumes of the *Industrial Census of 1971* and the annual issues of the *Annuario di Statistiche del Lavoro* all published by ISTAT. The former is presumably a true count, while the latter is a restricted stratified sample that is particularly weak in its regional coverage.

9. The most commonly cited early papers are Lowell Ashby, "The Geographical Redistribution of Employment: An Examination of the Elements of Change," *Survey of Current Business*, Vol. 44 (1964), pp. 13-20, and Edgar Dunn, "A Statistical and Analytical Technique for Regional Analysis," *Papers and Proceedings of the Regional Science Association*, Vol. 6 (1960), pp. 98-112. Considerable criticism has been leveled at the utility of this tool, particularly at its value in studying projected changes in the composition of employment; see David Houston, "Shift-Share Analysis of Regional Growth: A Critique," *Southern Economic Journal*, Vol. 33 (1967), pp. 577-581. This criticism has not gone unchallenged; see Lowell Ashby, "The Shift and Share Analysis, A Reply," *Southern Economic Journal*, Vol. 34 (1968), pp. 423-425; and F. J. B. Stilwell, "Further Thoughts on the Shift and Share Approach," *Regional Studies*, Vol. 4 (1970), pp. 451-458.

10. Missing jobs are defined in shift-share analysis as fewer or deficit jobs than might be expected from, in this case, the growth anticipated based on southern Italian growth rates.

11. These materials have been drawn mainly from Camera die Deputati, *Disegno di Legge N. 2276, Intervento Straordinario nel Mezzogiorno per il Decennio* (Rome, January 23, 1981) or the so-called Capria Law.

This summary was derived mainly from materials originally distributed to the Chamber of Deputies and kindly provided to me by Dott. Zerilli of I.A.S.M. in Rome in June of 1982. Additional materials came from Maria Venturini, "Mezzogiorno, Senza Soldi e con Due Casse," *Mondo Economico*, 1982, p. 11.

12. This is confirmed by Saraceno's testimony before the Chamber of Deputies as reported in *Informazione SVIMEZ*, New Series, Vol. 34 (November-December, 1981), pp. 475-480.

13. Francesco Compagna, "Abolire la Cassa o Farne Du 1," *Il Tempo* (March 30, 1982). Although Compagna and Saraceno are opposed to that provision of the Capria law

which would divide the Cassa into two agencies, there is sufficient opposition to the present structure of the Cassa that this provision of the new law has the necessary votes to be approved. It had become, many argue, an enormous cumbersome bureaucracy. In fact, the view of the minority Comunist party is that it should be eliminated completely and its powers transferred to the regional governments where they have relatively more power than they do in Rome. In contrast, both Saraceno and Compagna were against the breakup of the Cassa as proved in the Capria law because they envisaged a period of at least two years between time of passage and implementation. This delay they argued would stifle the development of the Mezzogiorno at what they deemed was a critical period in its economic development.

14. M. Venturini, "Mezzogiorno, Senza Soldi 1 con Due Casse," Mondo Economico (1982), p. 11.

15. F. Compagna, "Abolire la Cassa o Farne Due," Il Tempo (March 30, 1982).

16. On July 4th of 1982 the Council of Ministers extended the life of the legislation for the South to the End of that year and allocated 980 billion lire for southern development (IASM Notizie, Vol. XV, No. 27-28, July 19, 1982, p. 1).

REGIONAL DEVELOPMENT ISSUES IN FRANCE

Michel Savy

Introduction
From the post-war period until today, both the French economy and geography have greatly changed. Economic activities have experienced a general shift with industrial and tertiary sector expansion, and regional productive structures have been thoroughly realigned. During most of the period here considered, various public policies have been developed to try to coordinate economic and geographic tendencies in seeking a better territorial equilibrium. These policies are generally designated by the phrase, amenagement du territoire (this phrase will be translated as regional management (ed.)). Here are briefly described regional economic changes and corresponding regional management policies, so as to analyze their meaning and assess their effectiveness.

In the recent past there may be discerned three homogeneous periods concluding with today's situation, problems and prospects (1).

Reconstruction and National Growth: The First Regional Management Initiatives
At the end of the 1940s, France was still a very differentiated country with some regions already intensively urbanized and industrially developed and others still rural and agriculturally oriented. By 1946, 33 percent of the total working population was still employed in agriculture.

The reconstruction period appeared first in the form of the redevelopment of the previous industrial activities and regions, the restoration of basic infrastructure, the attempted restoration of the entire economy with the nationalization of banks and selected industries. There was also developed an original planning process. Therefore, until the 1950s, the evolution of the traditional French regional economic structure was not noticeable. Heavy industry was still - and more than ever - concentrated in four main regions: Nord-Pas de Calais, Ile de France (Paris built-up area), Lorraine, and Rhone-Alpes, together with

Figure 4.6:   Regional Employment Evolution, France, 1954-1962

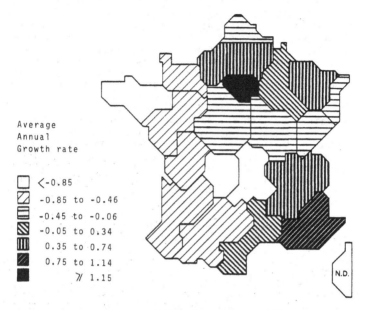

Average
Annual
Growth rate

☐ <-0.85
▧ -0.85 to -0.46
☰ -0.45 to -0.06
▨ -0.05 to 0.34
▥ 0.35 to 0.74
▨ 0.75 to 1.14
■ $\geqslant 1.15$

National average +0.14%

other but more isolated traditional locations throughout the country.

Although the industrial apparatus was modernized, the basic industries (steel, coal and energy, chemicals, transport, building materials) stimulated the development of machinery industries both for productive and private purposes (aircraft, automobiles, etc.). Simultaneously, strong rural out-migration and urbanization processes appeared. Paris continued to attract a growing proportion of the national population and wealth.

At the time of the 1954 census, regional contrasts remained very sharp, as shown in Figure 4.8 for the 22 French regions. Each region is represented by a point, according to the proportions in which primary, secondary and tertiary sectors are represented in the total regional employment. In 1954, the gap is still very large between rural and non-rural regions. One observes the very singular position of Ile de France (Paris region), as regards both the secondary and tertiary sectors.

In the late 1950s, the danger of the polarization trend was noted and concern arose regarding diseconomies of scale overtaking agglomerative benefits. In the search for cheaper industrial parks and manpower, Paris industries tended to deconcentrate toward the ring of medium-sized towns surrounding Paris.

The first corresponding public policies appeared with equipment subsidies in critical zones in 1954 (particularly for the coal industry areas in the North and Massif Central), the Industrial Decentralisation Subsidies, and the Approbation Procedure (any new industrial move was submitted for the approval of a special administrative committee tending to limit industrial investments in the Paris area).

Economic Growth and International Relationships: The Development of Territoral Management Policies

The creation of the EEC in 1957 opened a long period (up to the depression in 1974) of fifteen years of uninter-rupted growth in captial accumulation and production. The industrial change that had begun in the previous period was now fully underway (2). Investments increased and were focused in some quickly growing and highly profitable industries, profiting by labor productivity increases due to the new industrial work organization and to the enlargement of demand for industrial and household equipment.

The French economy opened itself to international investment and trade as intra-European exchanges grew in importance. Capital concentration and centralization increased and firms merged and reassigned their various activities in the face of foreign competition.

The State supported these various trends, financing infrastructure growth (e.g. maritime industrial areas and

Figure 4.7: The Evolution of Regional Industrial Employment, France, 1954-1962, 1962-1968, 1968-1975, 1975-1978

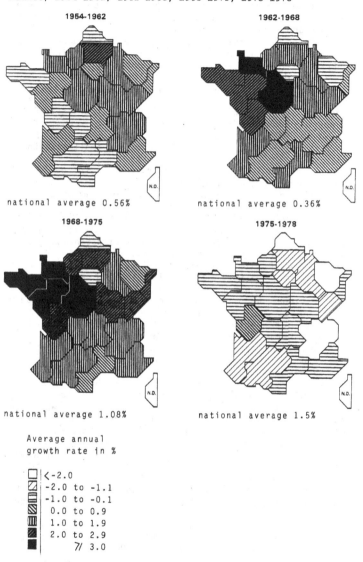

1954-1962

national average 0.56%

1962-1968

national average 0.36%

1968-1975

national average 1.08%

1975-1978

national average 1.5%

Average annual growth rate in %

☐	<-2.0
▨	-2.0 to -1.1
▤	-1.0 to -0.1
▨	0.0 to 0.9
▥	1.0 to 1.9
▨	2.0 to 2.9
■	7/ 3.0

203

highway construction) and other public facilities necessary
for new production and urbanization (the urban population
proportion changed from 53 percent to 73 percent between
1946 and 1975), and supported new industries (aircraft,
nuclear and computer industries).

Three industrial sectors played a major part in the
movement: the automotive, machine and electrical industries. These three industries were able to reorganize
their production processes so as to lower their tred-
itionally highly skilled manpower requirements. Unskilled
manpower availability then appeared to be one of the main
industrial location criterion. Instead of attracting
migrating manpower to ever-growing urban areas, firms
located their new plants in the rural exodus regions,
particularly in the vicinity of medium and small size towns
(3).

From 1962 to 1968, there was a tendency for employment
in the traditional industrial regions to decline and a
simultaneous industrial growth in the regions surrounding
the Paris area. Later, from 1968 to 1975, this trend
shifted toward the rural, western regions. These shifts
corresponded to the extensive development goals of industry,
although its achievement required the simultaneous accom-
paniment, enlargement and regulation of policies by the
State. DATAR (the Commission for Territorial Development
and Regional Policy) was created in 1963 as an interministerial national agency for regional planning.

Regional development doctrine was then more thoroughly
elaborated, with three main targets: to promote more
balance between the development of Paris and the other
regions, between the production structures of agricultural
and industrial regions, and to promote conversion of the
obsolete 19th century industrial areas (4).

Regional development policy was both pragmatic and
global: pragmatic in that it was carried out through many
trial and error operations; global in that it referred to a
general conception of development, according to which an
action affecting industries had to be accompanied by
simultaneous action in towns, transport, administration and
services, etc.

The two main policy tools were disuasion (the agreement
procedure deterring additional investments in the Parisian
area) and incentives (investment subsidies in the West,
Southwest, Massif Central agricultural areas and in the
Northeastern areas where older industries were concentrated
(5).

This subsidy system has yielded unquestionable quantitative results, as shown in Table 4.7 of manufacturing
employment change between 1968 and 1975. For the sake of
simplicity the 22 French regions have here been arranged
into 8 zones. By the end of this period of expansion, the

Table 4.7: Employment Subsidy and Creation, France: 1968-1975

Region	Subsidized Jobs PDR* (1968-1974) (000)	Manufacturing Jobs (1975) (000)	Industry Jobs Change (1968-1975) (000)	Subsidized Jobs/Total Employment %	Subsidized Jobs / Job Creation %
Ile de France	0	1288	-48	0	0
Bassin Parisien	30	1218	196	2.5	15
Nord	50	509	34	9.8	147
Est	40	732	73	5.5	55
Ouest	88	610	115	14.2	76
Sud Ouest	57	455	44	12.5	129
Centre Est	22	838	68	2.6	32
Mediterranee	9	338	29	2.7	31
FRANCE	296	5981	511	4.9	58

*PDR: Prime de Developpement Regional, for industrial activities only.

structure of regional activities can no longer be analyzed by distinguishing strictly rural and industrial-urbanized regions.

Figure 4.8 depicts sectoral employment by region in 1979. Does this indicate that a convergence phenomenon has taken place with wage level differences between regions having decreased through the shift of industrial investment location and a more even assignment of activities throughout the regions? In terms of jobs and earnings, the answer is positive. But, if one considers labor skills and the production function each region represented in the multi-regional segmented organization of production, the answer is more ambiguous. Indeed, the new proximity of regional structures corresponds to a new type of spatial division of labor, a functional specialization of regions replacing the traditional sectoral specialization.

Regions neither follow, with various lags, similar growth patterns (according to stage theories) nor do they constitute development poles structuring regional activities. Rather, they specialize, in a similar general process, in segmented and related activities. Some regions (mainly Paris) specialize in management activities, research and highly skilled activities; traditional industrial regions specialize in skilled industrial production (depending on outside headquarters); newly industrialized regions specialize in unskilled activities.

The largest firms create a multiregional plant network, in which each regional plant occupies a place according to its hierarchic position (6), in terms of labor skills and production functions.

Economic Crisis and New Territorial Questions

The economic crisis that began in 1973 following the crisis of the international monetary system, the rise of inflation and of unemployment and the decline of capital productivity at the end of the 1960s revealed the weaknesses of some regional economies (7). A significant economic redistribution began. It concerned production structures concentration trends continued. For example, French auto industry mergers resulted in only two firms. Technological modernization (new energy types, electronics and telecommunications, biotechniques), and new relationships between manufacturing industry and services tended to form new complexes where hardware and software activities were necessary complements to one another.

Trends towards structural differentiation increased. The polarization scheme was off-set by large multi-plant firms organizing their own multiregional exchange network for semi-finished products, skilled manpower, information, technology and finance, to smaller firms largely dependent on their regional environment. The competitiveness of the

Figure 4.8: Regional Employment Distribution in Three Sectors, France, 1954 and 1979

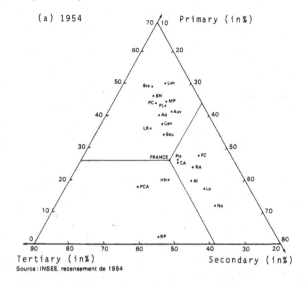

(a) 1954

Source : INSEE, recensement de 1954

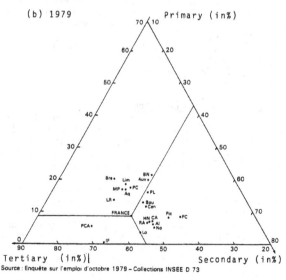

(b) 1979

Source : Enquête sur l'emploi d'octobre 1979 – Collections INSEE D 73

large firms requires an ability to indirectly control the smaller ones through sub-contracting and other unequal relationships (8).

Unemployment rose in the whole country, but its effects were very unequal from one region to another. One observed that the job decline was particularly sharp in the most industrialized regions. Therefore, the happy coincidence of industrializing rural regions and job creation where the employment needs were great (due to rural exodus) - a coincidence that motivated regional development action during the expansion period - no longer existed.

After 1975, a certain transitory period began when, at the same time, the traditional objectives of regional development policies were still valid, and a pause occurred in day to day practical policy measures. On the one hand, the explosion of unemployment in some mono-industry areas required specific and powerful means of intervention so as to subsidize quickly generated new jobs. On the other hand, the previous subsidy system in the other regions proved less efficient than before, following the decrease in investment.

These two divergent processes explain why, at the end of the 1970s, most of the jobs created with the help of regional development interventions are located in industrial crisis-stricken regions: Nord-Pas de Calais and Lorraine (steel industry, coal, textiles), in Saint-Etienne, and in the Loire estuary (shipbuilding). And, simultaneously new approaches were sought so as to strengthen the general regional economic dynamism, through services to companies, industrial training, technological and commercial information diffusion, etc.

These forms of regional enlivening, however, are limited by the general economic recession, and by the strict framework defining local authorities' responsibilities in a traditionally centralized country.

Regional Development and Decentralization

Those difficult problems did not disappear at once, of course, with the political changes that occurred in France in 1981. The effects of an industrial speed-up, attempts to recapture the home market, the stimulation expected from an enlarged public sector - all require some time to be perceptible.

In the medium term, political decentralization, with significant devolution of resources and responsibilities to local authorities, and particularly to regions, will call for a new type of planning. Starting in 1984 planning will be simultaneously conceived on the national and regional levels, and contracts between the State and the regions will identify planning targets (9). In the interim, however, some change has already taken place with a new subsidies system. The Prime d'Amenagement du Territoire deals with

Regional Development Issues in France

Figure 4.9: The 22 French Regions

projects involving more than 30 jobs. Within some limits projects are initiated by the regions themselves, apart from national level large projects supported by large enterprises that remain in the jurisdiction of State authorities. And, smaller projects are entirely dealt with by the regions themselves, at their own expense and located in the area of their own territory which they choose.

This policy evolution corresponds to political as well as economic trends: at the time of rapid growth, centralized procedures to locate industrial plants in rural manpower areas were, in spite of the drawbacks we have examined, effective. The situation is different when development no longer depends on extra-regional inputs, but on bringing into play existing local resources. This requires that local economic and political decision-makers take an active part in the process.

The idea, of course, is not to abandon any type of large scale projects, but, rather, to combine large and small, public or private structures, the large ones contributing to the development of the smaller ones, through a positive use of the polarization of the industrial pattern. Thus a new doctrine and a new practice of regional development, decentralized planning and territorial management will progressively emerge, together with the economic, political and institutional changes that will develop in France.

The French regional development case appears particularly interesting from two main points of view: 1) the evolution of the location of industries and the theoretical explanation that can be related to it and 2) the particular role of the State and its potential ability to influence the spatial behavior of private economic agents.

Activity location has undoubtedly exhibited great change during the past 30 years. In spite of a strong reassignment of industrial and tertiary sectors throughout the country, the thesis of convergence cannot, in our opinion, be retained. A redistributing of economic activities has simultaneously been accompanied by stronger polarization of decision-making capacities. New discrepancies have taken the place of former ones. The gaps in labor skills, regional research, technology, commercial information, and services to companies, which are the very result of the new functional division of labor that has replaced the previous sectoral division among regions, set the various territorial areas in uneven positions to face today's crises. The new territorial imbalances are not related to raw materials, heavy infrastructure or unskilled manpower availability as before. Now they are more the result of industrial training capacity, regional ability to use new information networks efficiently, attractions of the regional environments, and of the large urban centers which

Figure 4.10: Industrial Projects Aided by DATAR in 1979

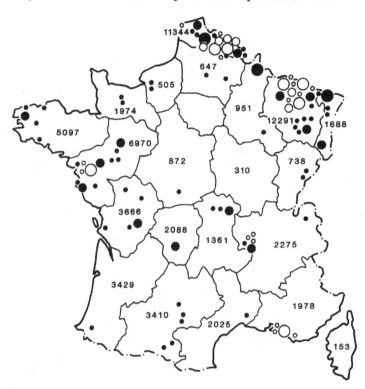

Principal Aided Projects

●   **PDR**   ●   From 100 to 200 employees

○   **FSAI**   ●   From 201 to 500 employees

                                        ●   More than 500 employees

1361   Number of employees per region

Source: La Lettre de la DATAR, no. 48, mars 1980.

Figure 4.11: Map of Areas Nominated for Industrial Projects, France

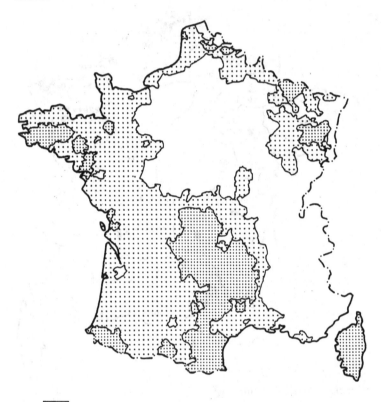

::::: Nominated areas

▦ Nominated areas with maximum rates

can attract research services and skilled productive activities. The role of the State has not been negligible in this evolution. Long lasting procedures and policies have played a main part in the emergence of a new economic geography. However, in spite of their vigor, they have never been completely <u>voluntarist</u>, endogenous to spontaneous economic movement, but rather appear as a specific and necessary regulation of it.

These two aspects are still valid in the present situation, when the aim of an industrial and economic restructuring is indistinguishable from its spatial aspects.

NOTES

1. For these various topics, I am largely indebted to my colleague Jean BOUCHET, and the collective works of SESAME, the research and long range studies team of DATAR.

2. INSEE, "Fresque Historique du Système Productif," (INSEE, Paris, 1975).

3. P. Aydallot, <u>Dynamique spatiale et Développement Inégal</u> (Economica, Paris, 1976).

4. J. Monod and P. Castelbajac, <u>L'aménagement du Territoire</u> (PUF, Paris, 1980).

5. P. Durand, <u>Industries et Régions</u> (Documentation Francaise, Paris, 1974).

6. A. Lipietz, <u>Le Capital et Son Espace</u> (Maspero, Paris, 1977).

7. B. Guibert et al, <u>La Mutation Industrielle de la France</u> (INSEE, Paris, 1976).

8. "Bipolarisation Industrielle et Développement Régional," in <u>Redéploiement et Espace Economique</u> (Collection Travaux et Recherches de Prospective no. 85, Documentation Francaise, Paris, 1982).

9. <u>Plan Intérimaire 1982-1983</u> (Documentation Francaise, Paris, 1981).

REGIONAL DEVELOPMENT ISSUES IN POLAND

Andrzej Wróbel

Regional Development Disparities in Poland: Character of the Problem and its Historical Background

The regional differentiation of levels of development in Poland has been expressed with numerous economic and demographic characteristics. The present paper starts from the assumption that the most important and, at the same time, the most meaningful analytically is a regional differentiation determined by two intercorrelated factors: location of economic development near the European core area and the historical conditions of economic growth in the crucial period in the several decades preceding World War I. The present territory of Poland formed at that time the marginal provinces of three foreign powers, the economies of which differed quite considerably.

It should be remembered that - according to estimates of W. Rostow (1) - Germany entered into the stage of self-sustained growth in the period 1850-73, Russia in the period 1890-1914, while Austria remained in the stage of preconditions of growth on the eve of World War I. These historical circumstances determined the basic pattern in levels of economic development which can be characterized as dividing the country into two parts: the developed western area and the eastern, undeveloped section.

Use of the term basic refers to the variables most significant in determining the advancement of the development process including the currect results of this process (i.e. per capita incomes, fixed assets, and social and technical infrastructure).

These basic features are associated with the underlying structural characteristics of the economy. The association, however, is not neccesarily the same at the scale of individual regions.   Indeed, in the case of Poland, the structural characteristics were not uniform either in the less developed part of the country or in the more developed area. In both sections, the level of industrialization was more advanced in the south than in the north, reflecting the pattern of natural resource distribution which favored the south. As a result, some northern provinces in western Poland were less industrialized than the southern provinces of eastern Poland which did not make them less developed.

The outline above permits a more meaningful analysis of some important aspects of the regional development processes in Poland, particularly when compared to many studies which use one or a number of development indices and rely on various measures of concentration or coefficients of variation (2).

In the present paper, attention will be concentrated on the less developed area of the country and the policies aiming to raise the relative development levels. Two indices of development will be taken particularly into account: per capita personal income and the occupational structure of regions. The choice of personal income instead of value-added or similar measures was dictated not only by theoretical considerations (the importance of looking at the problem from the point of view of the final results of the economic process) but also as a recognition of the difficulties of measuring economic efficiency correctly given the distorted price system and high degree of arbitrariness in the allocation of resources.

Characteristics of the Data

Data on population and its occupational structure have been taken from the censuses for the period 1950-1978. Data on income were accessible only for a shorter period and refer to the years 1961 and 1973. These data, elaborated on the basis on regional income estimates by the Central Statistical Office, and presented in a previous study (3) constitute the only available estimates of personal income per capita which might be meaningfully compared for different time periods and the same set of areal units.

These estimates have been achieved in the following way. From regional income statistics for provinces data were extracted on personal income from economic activities, namely: wages in the public sector and farmers' income derived from agricultural production. These income figures have been classified according to four sectors of the economy: a) private agriculture, b) socialized agriculture and forestry, c) industry, and d) other activities. To the last category have been added estimated figures for income derived from non-material services (education, health care, public administration, etc.) which are not included in the Polish income statistics. Employment data have been classified according to the same four sectors (figures on occupation in private agriculture were interpolated or extrapolated on the basis on the census data).

Thus, a comparable set of income and employment tables for the years 1961 and 1973 were obtained comprising, not

all, but most of the economic activities and the bulk of the
personal income. These tables allowed calculation of
various per-capita income figures, meaning "personal nominal
income from economic activities per one working person."
        The income data and most of the population census data
used in the paper refer to the highest-order administrative
units (voivodeships) called here provinces, according to the
previous administrative division of the country into 17
provinces and the five largest cities. This division was
replaced in June 1975 by a new one of 49 smaller units.
This makes comparison of 1978 census data with the set of
data from previous censuses for individual provinces
impossible. However, for the sake of macroregional comparison 1978 census data were grouped into two classes
corresponding, with relatively minor deviations, to the
grouping of the previous provinces into developed and less
developed areas. Since the 1970 data were recalculated by
the Central Statistical Office for the new administrative
divisions, the 1970 data are presented in the tables in two
columns corresponding to the old and new grouping of
provinces.
        It is evident that the degree of areal and topical
generalization applied in the paper is indeed very high.
Certainly, it diminishes the descriptive detail and weakens
the precision of the conclusions. On the other hand, it
brings to light some basic dimensions of the problem and
helps in an attempt to evaluate generally regional development policy in Poland.

The Less Developed Area - Initial Conditions and Problems
Challenging Development Policy
        The approach presented in the introductory section of
the paper permits distinguishing a large compact area which,
defined in terms of the grouping of provinces, comprised in
1950 nearly one half (48 percent) of national territory and
over a half (51 percent) of national population. For the
sake of convenience we shall refer to this area as the East
and to the more developed part of the country as the West.
        The East was a predominantly agricultural area with
about 64 percent of the labor force engaged in 1960 in the
agricultural sector. This was almost exclusively composed
of small private farms (until now, state and collective
farms are an insignificant percentage of the total agricultural land). The productivity of these farms was low,
whereas agricultural density of population high - the
provincial averages exceeding 70 persons working in agriculture per 100 hectares of agricultural land in the South
(the provinces of Rzeszow and Cracow), to about 40 persons
in the Northern provinces of Warsaw and Bialystok (high
density figures were associated with a high percentage of
farms of below two hectares which was a farm-size insuf-

ficient to provide a livelihood for a family).

The average share of industry in the occupational structure was 13 percent; in some provinces (Bialystok, Lublin) the share was as low as 5 percent, which means that industry hardly existed there at all, with the exception of handicrafts. The general level of infrastructure of all kinds was very low.

This predominantly agricultural and poorly urbanized area, contrasted sharply with the three biggest Polish cities located there: Warsaw, Cracow and Lodz (the latter being an important industrial center). The contrast might be considered one of the typical characteristics of an underdeveloped country. With the exception of these three big cities, all provinces in the East were markedly differentiated from the West in terms of per capita income. In the year 1961, after more than a decade of a policy of diminishing interregional levels of development, the average personal income in the East was about 35 percent lower than in the West and not much more than a half of the level of the highest income areas (the province of Katowice and the city of Warsaw).

This macroregional pattern of income differentiation was due primarily to differentiation of per capita income in the agricultural sector; in the East, they were about half as high as in the West. This meant, of course, also a great difference in the renumeration for work between agricultural and non-agricultural activities in the former area.

Comparison of. the corresponding set of figures for the year 1961 reveals the striking but not unexpected fact that sharp differences in the remuneration for work between the two types of activities were characteristic only for the regions classified as underdeveloped which seems to be another typical characteristic of underdeveloped countries. Although the average industrial wage in those regions was generally lower than in the more developed part of the country, due to a different industrial structure (a lower share of high wage industries), the ratio between the industrial wage and per capita income in agricuture was here generally around 1.7, and reaching in some provinces values exceeding 2 (in most regions of the West, this ratio was close to 1).

In conclusion, it may be stated that the relatively low level of income per capita in the East resulted mainly from two characteristics of this area: 1) lower incomes in agriculture as compared with the West, and 2) the high share of agriculture in the total volume of employment.

In this situation, the relatively high average per capita income in the East might have been achieved in three different ways: 1) the transfer of a part of the labor force from low productivity agriculture to other activities, 2) a similar transfer associated with out-migration to other more developed regions, and 3) an increase in productivity in the agricultural sector. There were, in fact, various interconnections between these three processes (it was impossible to raise per capita income in agriculture without a transfer of some of the redundant labor force from this sector).

All three processes were operative in the Polish case and, it should be pointed out that because of the size and relative importance of the East, they all implied structural changes in the national economy. The problem was further aggravated by the relatively high rate of natural increase, reaching about 2 percent per year in the 1950s.

The role of regional development policy in the sense of specific regionally oriented measures of state policy directed to raise the economically backward regions was limited mostly to the first process, that is the promotion of new income generating activities and, to a lesser extent, some measures which contributed to the increase in agricultural productivity. In the present paper, an attempt is made to evaluate the significance of such regional development policies in raising the relative level of development of these regions and changing their economic structure, in the context of the impact of the general structural changes of national economy and of national economic policies.

Regional Development Policies and Facts

Overcoming the regional inequalities inherited from the past became one of the aims of the economic and social policy of the socialist state after the initial period of postwar reconstruction and population resettlement in the late 1940s. The economic system gave the central authorities considerable opportunity in this respect, since capital accumulation of the production units was redistributed via the state budget. An important consequence for the regional economy is that regional growth is less dependent on regional economic performance and equity goals might be pursued more freely (although only to a certain degree) under the constraint of economic efficiency. Moreover, the type of regional development policy was obviously constrained by the character of general economic policy.

The model of economic growth accepted as the strategic guideline was that of accelerated industrialization based on the expansion of heavy industry. Accordingly, industry became nationally the privileged sector which, during the postwar period, received well over 40 percent of the total investment funds. Moreover, to the industrial investment figures one should add also the accompanying outlays, that is, the supplementary outlays in other sectors connected with industrial projects. In this situation it was obvious that the surest way to foster economic growth of regions was industrialization, and the most important instrument of such a policy was an industrial location policy exercised by the State Planning Commission.

The institutional forms in which regional development plans were elaborated and executed, as well as the conceptual framework of these plans, changed over time. In the 1970s, the conceptual framework of spatial planning assumed the primary importance of the development of the most efficient urban system, and the promotion of controlled growth of large urban agglomerations with belts of infrastructure linking them (4). The implementation of such a conceptual framework accepted in 1974, was, however, hindered by the actual course of economic policy and later by a deep economic crisis. It should be pointed out that in the 1970s the share of industry in the national investment total increased again compared to the 1960s and even the 1950s and industrial investments remained the most important instrument for the promotion of growth in less developed regions (5).

Changes in the Distribution of Industry

There exist a number of studies presenting and analyzing various aspects of Polish policy and its results. All of them describe the spread of industrial growth to the regions weakly industrialized before and the rise of a number of new industrial centers and districts.

As the most general measure of the degree to which location policies affected the accelerated industrial development of the East, one may use the value of the positive employment shift towards this area (the value exceeding the hypothetical employment growth resulting from the national growth rate). The value of this shift for the whole area of the East in the period 1950-78 was equal to about 300,000 persons. For the sum of three big cities in the area, the value of the shift was negative (mainly due to the high negative shift in the textile center of Lodz), so that the relative gain of the remaining area was equal to about 0.5 million employed or about 28 percent of the actual total growth of industrial employment in the area.

One may add that the negative shift for the West originated almost exclusively in the province of Katowice containing the largest Polish industrial agglomeration of Upper Silesia. In fact, the negative shift for this region was greater than for the West as a whole, which means that in this developed part of the country there was occurring a process of industrial deconcentration - mainly towards the Northern provinces.

The question may be raised whether the positive value of industrial employment shift represents the results of government location policy. It seems, however, that in case of the regions of the East there is little doubt about this since the area as a whole offered (with obvious exception of the extractive industries) less favorable conditions for industrial location than the more developed West so that, in the absence of a deliberate location policy, the value of the shift might well have been negative.

How were industrial location policies related to the changes in agriculture, population size and its occupational structure, and per capita income? An attempt to answer these questions is presented below.

Changes in Agriculture

The rapid increase in employment in industry and in other non-agricultural activities was accompanied by a decline of the economically active population in agriculture, both in relative as well as in absolute terms. Although this process was of particular importance for the underdeveloped East, burdened with overemployment in the agricultural sector, it was not limited to this area. In the twenty year period between 1950 and 1970 the active population in agriculture declined in Poland by 14.5 percent; in the East the decline was equal to 16.4 percent and in the West it amounted to 10.8 percent. The process was intensified markely in the 1970s largely as a result of aging of the agricultural labor force because of the selective character of the previous rural-urban migration. The difference in its intensity between East and West decreased; in the intercensal period 1970-78, the national rate of decline was 20.1 percent, in the East, 21.0 percent and in the West 18.4 percent.

While employment in agriculture declined, the value of production as well as per capita productivity and incomes increased. Although the numerically dominant private agricultural sector was underprivileged in accessibility to material inputs, credits, etc., the productive reserves hidden in the sector combined with hard work of the farmers and the growing demand of a rapidly growing urban population resulted in the fact that after 1956 (after the government abandoned the collectivization policy) incomes in agriculture were raising in Poland at the rate similar or even slightly higher than the average wage in non-agricultural activities. This was demonstrated in the study by the author (6) presenting the estimates for per capita income changes in the period 1961-73. According to this study, the indices of growth of personal incomes of those working in the non-socialized sector of agriculture were highly differentiated regionally. In the underdeveloped regions there was discovered high negative correlation of these indices with the differentiation of the ratio of the number of persons working in agriculture per 100 hectares of agricultural land.

Thus, the lowest income increase in agriculture occurred in the southern provinces of the East. Although at the same time they were characterized by the most intensive outflow of labor from agriculture, the growth of per capita income remained also the lowest in the underdeveloped part of the country. This suggests that the decisive factor of the rise of labor productivity in agriculture was the size-structure of the farms, representing the ability of farmers to react to the rise of national demand and to the opportunities created by national economic progress for improving farming techniques (by the growing availability of fertilizers, electrification, agricultural services, investment materials, etc.).

The agricultural development programs implemented by the authorities on the scale of individual regions, although of importance, were certainly of secondary or supplementary significance in comparison with the impact of national economic policies.

Changes in Population and Occupation Structure

The demographic and economic growth processes were accompanied by changes in the occupational structure both on the national and regional scales. The regional differentiation of these changes was determined firstly by the diversified situation of individual regions at the beginning, and secondly by the different growth rates of individual sectors of the economy. In the underdeveloped East these changes were particularly drastic, since, in the beginning, two thirds of the economically active population was engaged in agriculture which then suffered from overemployment (or hidden unemployment) and where the employment situation was becoming critical in view of the high post-war rate of natural population increase. On the other hand, it was to this area that the effort to develop non-agricultural activities was directed, with the results described above. Thus, after twenty eight years the occupational structure was changed here much more radically than in the more developed part of the country (see Table 4.8). It was stated above, as a result of a simple shift analysis, that the total shift of industrial employment towards this area was equal to about 300,000 persons. The total shift for all non-agricultural activities was equal to about 380,000 persons, indicating a relatively more modest share of tertiary activities in this eastward trend (although the social, cultural and, in the long, run, economic effects of the development of the functions like education, health care etc., certainly exceeded the significance of this additional employment).

The shift in agricultural employment was negative for the East, equal to about 100,000 persons, an insignificant figure compared with the absolute decline in agricultural employment in this area by about 1.5 million. Yet, the negative structural effect of the great share of declining

221

Table 4.8: Employment Structure in East and West Poland

Sector	East				West			
	1950		1978		1950		1978	
	(000)	%	(000)	%	(000)	%	(000)	%
Total economically active population	6825	100	8808	100	5579	100	8757	100
Agriculture	4530	66.4	3017	34.3	2486	44.6	1856	21.2
Industry	879	12.9	2359	26.8	1449	26.0	3045	34.8
Other Activities	1416	20.7	3432	39.0	1644	29.5	3856	44.0

agricultural employment in the East's economy was so great that the total shift of economically active population for this area was heavily negative, equal to about 740,000 persons (about twice as high as the positive total shift of non-agricultural employment).

This negative shift of non-agricultural employment was reflected in the negative value of the shift of the total population, equal to about 1.2 million people. It must be noted that this shift occurred not only via interregional migration but also as a result of the difference in the rate of the natural increase of population influenced by past migration (the resettlement of Western and Northern Territories in the period 1946-50).

The simple calculations presented above permit an important conclusion notwithstanding the fact that the East contained the national capital, which was one on the important in-migration centers in the country, as well as several rapidly expanding new industrial centers, the problem of surplus agricultural population in this area was solved in greater part by migration outside of the area to the more developed part of the country. This does not denigrate the significance of the high industrial dynamics directed by locational policies for the development of this area. It simply points out the occurrence of a case in which the solution to the employment problem in the timespan of one generation is impossible without out-migration.

Changes in Per Capita Income

The combined effect of migratory movements of population accelerated industrial growth in the East, as well as the rise of agricultural productivity resulted in the rise of per capita income in the East compared with the West. As the data for the years 1961 and 1973 demonstrate, all provinces of the East experienced in that period a per capita income growth faster than the national growth. Thus, regional income per capita disparities had in fact diminished: while in 1961 the income per capita in the East (excluding the big cities) was about 35 percent lower than in the West, after 13 years it was lower by about 20 to 30 percent. The latter figure indicates that the rise of incomes in the East was not regionally uniform. In the southern provinces (Rzeszow, Cracow) the rate of growth was only slightly higher than the national rate and the northern provinces experienced a markedly faster growth.

These differentiated rates of income growth were the outcome of two main tendencies - the intensity of industrialization processes (the expansion of high income activities) and the growth of agricultural incomes. The southern provinces of the East experienced a high rate of industrialization but the agricultural income increases were relatively insignificant due to unfavorable conditions (a

223

high share of very small farms). The northern provinces, where agriculture developed much more rapidly, experienced the highest rate of average per capita income growth. This comparison brings to light the compensatory effect of industrialization on raising the income level in an area of very high agricultural population density where, due to the size-structure of the farms, conditions for substantial growth of agricultural production were not favorable.

A special case existed in the large cities which, independent of their location in the country, experienced higher income per capita growth than the nation as a whole.

An Evaluation

In the previous section the indisputable effects of the policy of diminishing the interregional disparities in the level of economic development were described. The presentation of effects, however, does not constitute an evaluation which would require the comparison of costs and benefits, which, in the context of regional development, is often referred to as the question of trade-offs between equity and efficiency. The question is a very difficult one to answer for several reasons. One of them is the general difficulty of measuring efficiency in the type of economy existing in Poland where prices are fixed by state authorities and in many instances are rather remote from equilibrium prices and do not reflect supply and demand relations.

The difficulty is, however, also more complex. Regional policy has been conducted in the context of certain general economic policies and certain general conditions in the social, political and economic system. Therefore, analyzing the performance of a given regional system, it is difficult to distinguish the role of the spatial pattern from the role of the general principles of the functioning of the economy and society. Perhaps, the very idea of an objective evaluation of the results of regional development policies shall remain utopian. Yet, an attempt to weigh the positive and negative impacts of regional development is certainly not meaningless. Some comments on issues relevant to such an attempt in the Polish case are made here.

Transportation Costs and Location

The set of price policy measures combined with the neglect of expenditures on transport infrastructure were responsible for the generally low freight rates in Poland. These, in turn, had an effect in the apparent diminishing of the friction of distance and naturally favored the development of areas located peripherally to the existing concentrations of population and economic acitivity. In agriculture, this resulted in production reacting mainly to changes in national demand and national agricultural policies, neglecting specialization of production according to the location towards the market.

In industry, it caused the neglect of the issue of the distance to the suppliers and/or customers both in the phase of location planning of new plants as well as in the operation of existing plants. The latter case became more and more marked as the imbalances in the supply–demand relations in the national economy grew, creating difficulties in obtaining necessary inputs by individual plants.

As a result, the general level of cargo transport was high and tended to increase rapidly. An illustration of this tendency may be provided by comparing the Polish and French transport system. In the year 1960 the total volume of domestic transport (defined as the sum of shipments in railway, truck and inland water-transportation, in terms of ton kilometers) was in Poland equal to about 80 percent of the French figure. By the late 1970s the Polish figure was already about 20 percent higher than the corresponding figure for France; however, the latter country exceeded Poland by over 50 percent in terms of population and territory, to say nothing about the evident superiority of France in terms of gross national product.

Of course, as stated above, the diminished friction of distance in Polish economic space has been more apparent than real since a large part of the transport costs was covered by the national economy indirectly – by subsidies to transport enterprises and to the prices of fuels, or by neglect of necessary investments in the transport system which resulted in the deterioration of the performance of this system as well as accumulation of enormous investment needs by the late 1970s.

The Sectoral Bias of Economic Planning and the Role of Industrial Location Policy

The highly centralized socialist planned economy existing in Poland gives to the central planning body a vast power of disposition of national capital accumulation. It was this power which made possible the interregional transfer of resources and deliberate changes in the spatial structure of the national economy. The same power has been widely used also to transfer resources between activities and sectors of the economy which had indirect but important consequences for regional development.

The favoring of one sector – in this case industry – meant, however, neglect and relatively slower growth of other sectors, and particularly of technical and social infrastructure. Initially, this had the character of a deliberate strategy of concentrating investment efforts in the sectors considered to be of primary importance for the accelerated growth of the economy – while postponing

temporarily other investment needs. However, the intersectoral balance has never been fully restored, especially
considering that the difficulties in the fulfillment of
investment plans usually involved cuts in the expenditures
in infrastructure in the plan execution stage.

This type of economic policy constituted the context of
regional development planning and imposed definite
constraints on the range of solutions which could be
implemented. In this context, regional development planning
had to use industrial location policy as its main tool.
With all the loss of efficiency this might have involved,
this policy was an indispensable factor in the regionally
balanced growth of the urban system and the whole spatial
structure of the national economy.

The existing sectoral bias in economic development
combined with the eventual absence of an industrial location
policy favoring the less developed regions would have
probably resulted in a degree of spatial concentration of
growth at the scale more serious than that in many market
economies.

The Urbanization Gap

The sectoral bias referred to above considerably
affected the urbanization processes accompanying regional
development in post-war Poland. Several Polish authors
pointed out the phenomenon of an urbanization gap or urban
infrastructure gap. The most evident manifestation of this
was an inability of the economic system to provide enough
housing in towns for migrants from rural areas - although
industrial and other activities developed in the urban
centers required manpower. As a result of tremendous
housing shortages the phenomenon of journey-to-work became
inflated and some authors even denoted it pathological in
view of the amount of time and energy lost by the commuters
(7).

Among various consequences of this urbanization gap was
the slackening of urbanization effects in terms of
attitudes, professional qualifications and general
adaptation to living in a modern society; this in turn
influenced unfavorably the performance of the whole economic
system. Particularly, it relates to the less developed
areas of the country where urbanization processes were rapid
and the existing urban network very poor.

Relative scarcity of resources for housing construction
has been responsible also for otherwise unjustified areal
extension of rapidly growing cities. In the conditions of
the pressure of the housing shortage, new living quarters
had to be constructed in a short time and were frequently
developed quite far from the city center. It was
technically simpler and cheaper (at least in terms of
construction costs) than reconstruction of the inner city.

Table 4.9: Share of the East in National Population and Employment (in percent; national totals in thousands)

Area	1950	1960	1970 old division	1970 new division	1978
Population					
Poland	25035	29795	32658	32658	35061
East	51.3	49.3	48.4	48.4	48.0
3 big cities	7.2	7.9	8.2	8.2	8.9
Remainder	44.1	41.4	40.2	40.2	39.1
Economically Active Population					
Poland	12404	13197	16442	16442	17565
East	54.9	53.5	51.6	50.9	50.1
3 big cities	7.0	7.7	8.2	8.2	9.1
Remainder	47.9	45.8	43.4	42.6	41.0
Industrial Employment					
Poland	2328	3238	4610	4576	5404
East	37.7	40.6	42.5	41.8	43.6
3 big cities	13.9	13.1	11.4	11.5	10.2
Remainder	23.8	27.5	31.1	30.3	33.4

Figure 4.12: Differences in Regional Income, Poland, 1961

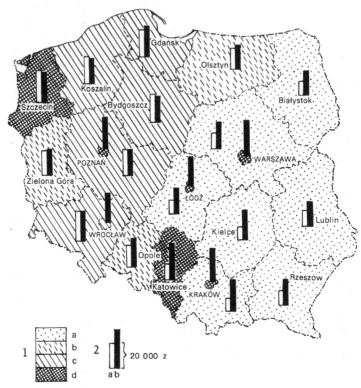

1. Income per Capita (Polish zlotys)

   a - 13-14.5
   b - 18-19.5
   c - 20-21.9
   d - >22

2. Income per Capita

   a - Private agriculture
   b - Industry

The ensuing extended journeys to work (commuting) in the conditions of overcrowded public transport constitute a repetition on the urban scale of the suburban commuting patterns described above. Moreover, the services in the new residential districts were most frequently limited to the barest essentials; hence, the very high concentration of service activities in the CBD and long shopping trips (8).

It should be pointed out that the less favorable features of the past processes of regional development were only partly related in a direct way with the basic characteristics of the socialist economy as such. It seems that they resulted mainly from specific economic policies and the institutional context was indirectly involved, as it permitted the distribution of resources to diverge from social demand. The economic reform which is to be introduced in Poland will undoubtedly have serious consequences for the course of regional devlopment processes in the country.

NOTES

1. W. W. Rostow, <u>The Stages of Economic Growth</u> (Cambridge University Press, Cambridge, 1960).

2. For example, see I. S. Koropechyj, "Equalization of Regional development in Socialist Countries: An Empirical Study," <u>Economic Development and Cultural Change</u>, 21, 1, pp. 68-86; H. Zimon, "Regional Inequalities in Poland: 1960-1975," <u>Economic Geography</u>, 55, 3 (1979), pp. 242-252; and S. Misztal and W. Kaczorowski, "Spatial Problems of Poland's Post-War Industrialization, 1945-1975," <u>Geographia Polonica</u>, 43 (1980), pp. 199-222.

3. A. Wrobel, "Industrialization as a Factor of Regional Development in Poland," <u>Geographia Polonica</u>, 43 (1980), pp. 187-197.

4. See K. Dziewoński, "Population Problems in Polish Regional Planning," in H. L. Kostanick (ed.), <u>Population and Migration Trends in Eastern Europe</u> (Westview Press, Boulder, CO, 1977), pp. 81-97.

5. A. Wróbel, "Industrialization and Regional Development Policy: Polish Experiences," in A. L. Mabogunje and R. P. Misra (eds.), <u>Regional Development Alternatives: International Perspectives</u> (Maruzensia and U.N. Centre for Regional Development, Nagoya, 1981), pp. 159-169.

6. Wróbel (1980), op. cit.

7. A. Stasiak, "Historical Development of the Suburban Zone of Warsaw," <u>Geographia Slovenica</u>, 11, pp. 209-233.

8. I. Chudzyńska, "Locational Specialization of Retail Trade Functions in Warsaw," <u>Environment and Planning A</u>, 13 (1981), pp. 929-949.

REGIONAL DEVELOPMENT ISSUES IN SPAIN

J. R. Lasuen

The Limits of Regional Policy

Regional policy has been and still is basically used worldwide for three broad purposes. In the Anglo-Saxon and Northern European countries, it is employed as a complement to demand policies, to wipe out geographic pockets of unemployment resistent to standard income redistribution measures. In Eastern and Western Europe, it is a complement to industrialization policies, to fill in voids due to unbalanced concentrations of physical and social activities. In Southern Europe and the developing countries, it is a complement to national development policies, to accelerate the <u>trickling down</u> process from advanced to underdeveloped regions and to minimize the <u>backwash</u> effects on most of the territory which results from national policies aimed at increasing profits and concentrating them in productive investments in developed areas.

These three main purposes, however divergent, have one common characteristic that is worth stressing. Namely, that in all three cases regional policy is conceived as a minor, corrective, <u>subsidiary</u> instrument of national policies. The basic subsidiary design of customary regional policy obviously but essentially implies target regions accept that the national policies which discomfort them are worth pursuing no matter what minor relief is obtained as compensation. Regional policy as practiced should therefore be addressed only to nations whose regions unequivocally accept that national goals should prevail over regional ones. Since there are many such nations in the world, the relevance of conventional regional policy is evident.

There are, however, many nations whose regions do not subordinate their goals to those of the nation, at least not in the same manner. For those nations, regional policy and theory, as known, are of little avail, if not clearly counterproductive.

This author maintains that, first, conventional (subsidiary) regional policy of any of the three above mentioned varieties should not be applied without appropriate corrections to nations where regions are less well-integrated into the nation. Secondly, that for those countries, a <u>new</u> regional policy is worth pursuing in which regional policy clearly should not be a minor corrective device but a center piece in the design of national policy, precisely with the object of solving the <u>real</u> regional problem which is the unstable integration of the regions within the nation.

According to P. Vilar, the regional issue has been one of Spain's four main problems (1). The cultural, the religious and the socioeconomic have been the other three for the last two centuries. Today the regional problem is certainly the most critical. The Spanish experience may be easily generalized to very many other countries, less aware of their basic regional instability.

The Real Regional Issue

It is my opinion that since the middle of the 18th century most Spanish historic failures resulted from its critical regional problem. Its system of regions is structured and operated in such a way that only during long-term national booms do the regions accept the priority of national costs and benefits over their own. Consequently, only during those times can the nation develop without disintegrating tensions. In long-term depressions regions put at least some of their own goals above the nation's and civil strife of all sorts tends to occur.

The main traits of Spain's modern history (i.e. regional and cultural diversity, social conflict, slow growth, political instability) are strongly related to the recurrent wide civil strife resulting from its unstable regional structure, have been identified since the 18th century by both national and foreign experts. But they have been attributed to: a) the special characteristics of the Spaniards (by the culturists, among others: M. Unamuno, J. Ortega, A. Castro, C. Sanchez Alborniz, Sanchez Drago); b) to the country's special geographic, social, demographic or cultural structures (by the positivists, among others: P. Braudel, V. Vives, Nadal, Dominguez); c) to the special characteristics of its social structure (by marxists, among others: Tunon de Lara and Fontana).

Consequently, all sorts of hypotheses, geographical, anthropological, social, cultural and political have been put forward to explain those characteristics as abnormal behavioral patterns. Corresponding partial rectifying solutions have been proposed and applied to modernize Spain with little success. As Carr (2) and the other Anglo-Saxon historians of contemporary Spain have pointed out, those problems could not be solved unless the country overcomes its underdevelopment which is, and was, a cause of them all (3).

The repeated failure of all those partial solutions, which cover from right to left the Western socio-political catalogue has not been conducive, however, to questioning the validity of the basic hypothesis which all those approaches have in common. How was development to take place? Through a real working democracy, as they recommended? How then, can we explain why democracy did not take root in Spain when, as Herr acknowledges, it started earlier on its own than in most other countries? Is this due again to special cultural, social factors (4)?

There are two sets of facts which clearly refute present-day hypotheses. Namely: 1) Spaniards of all sorts, northern, southern, Catholic, atheists, workers, artists, entrepreneurs, scientists, etc., do better abroad than at home; and 2) foreigners of all sorts, too, from businessmen to football players do better in their respective homes than in Spain. In short, the topic "Spain is different" has always been interpreted literarily, never literally. There are enough reasons to think the contrary. It is not the contents, the Spaniards and their circumstances, that are different, but the container, the Spanish State.

Research on whether the regional structure of Spain is similar or different from that of the Western model - why this is so and what are its effects - has been totally absent in Spain's socio-political and economic analysis and in other countries of similar problems. Given the failure of the conventional approaches, it may be time to begin to analyze hypothetically the basic structure of the Spanish State and how it forces the behavior of its citizens in Western abnormal ways, how it can be corrected, and whether those traits are generalizable.

The aim of this paper is to show in broad terms, first, that Spain's regional structure is basically different from those prevailing in the Western world. Secondly, that this basic fact explains why Western measures, which are designed for opposite types of national structures, fail in Spain. Thirdly, that, consequently, <u>the solution for the Spanish</u> <u>regional issue is not subsidiary - but central in the design</u> <u>not only of short term national economic policy but of</u> <u>national long-term economic and political development</u>. Fourthly, how can that be achieved, economically and politically?

I can achieve this aim only by implication of the abstract reflection I have had to develop to think out those questions in an organized manner. The results of that reflection are presented as a rough, initial, behavioral model of the multi-regional state, and its <u>normal</u> and inverted types, which I have built on notions developed from 1) the new Theory of the State; 2) the Center-Periphery approach used in History, Geography and the Social Sciences;

3) historical relations abstracted from Spain's Modern History; and 4) my own previous ideas on regional development theory. Thus, I aim to describe, tentatively, the normal and abnormal forms of structure and function of a multi-regional state and how they can be modified, using as a reference Spain's past, present and future.

Also, such questions, more than the answers, may attract attention in developed countries for I believe they may not be exempt forever from the multi-regional state perverse dynamics. Regional structures may invert themselves, and whenever that happens countries change from long term stable expansion to long term unstable stagnation. In fact, from the 15th to the 17th century Spain's regional structure developed and was operated alongside the "normal" multi-regional pattern which was later followed by the western world and was instrumental in Spain's growth. Its 17th century regional structure <u>inversion</u> can be shown to be related to its decline. The main factors that caused the regional inversion are well known, and can be generalized.

Nations and Regions

It seems appropiate to start establishing clearly the relationship between the units of analysis: the nation and the regions. With the exception of the so-called newly settled areas, the rest of the world's nations are made up of regions which, as in Spain, were previously independent nations and later were incorporated into the present nations.

Few of these regions have lost their identity or personality. Physical, economic, social and cultural interaction with the other regions within the new nation throughout history have not totally erased their original differences. Regions are not physically heterogeneous geographical areas of the nations which are homogeneous in other dimensions (economic, social and cultural) as is basically assumed in the conventional, contractual Theory of the State.

Regions in a multi-regional state are also heterogeneous in social dimensions and not in the accidental, exceptional and correctible way which is tacitly hypothesized. Regions seem to be historically permanent entities with variable territorial limits and political powers, which many join and/or leave larger political units. They seen to behave as if they exercised certain self-preservation rights. A legacy of those rights which their citizens once transferred to them when they became states and yet have not transferred entirely to the multi-regional nation into which they have integrated.

These regional self-preservation rights, which are critical, have been forgotten practically and theoretically and need to be taken seriously into consideration. They

233

have been forgotten in the legal processes of multi-regional
national building of the Modern Age, but this oblivion has
not erased them.

Multiple monarchies of the Spanish confederated type,
of the Austrian dynastic class or of the British legislative
union form, German-type federations, Swiss-type confederations and French-type centralizing republics, have been used
to build unified nations from old regional states with
varying success (5). But none has been able to erase the
identity of their constituent regions.

Breaking away from the Greek confederated tradition of
international defense leagues represented by Bodin and
Grotius, and following the Jewish federal model of national
integration of loosely related tribes developed further by
Althusius (6), all these new state forms attempted to bypass
the regions, relating the new nation's government directly
to the old regions' citizens. Whenever they allocated power
to their constituent regions, it was always done with
pragmatic criteria, never on the theoretical recognition of
the regions' identity. On the contrary, since all justified
the multi-regional nation on the Contractual Theory of the
State, which was conceived as a base for the birth of
regional states out of the feudal ones (not the multi-
regional out of the regional), it was believed to be
achieved when the constituent regions' citizens exercised
their self-preservation rights to enter a multi-regional
political association for their mutual advantage. Thus,
they in theory pre-empted the possibility for the regions to
remain mini-states and, hence, potentially capable of
recuperating their previous independence.

Not only were the regions' self-preservation rights
forgotten but also denied. But they do exist, and the
denial has always been flagrantly contradictory to the
Contractual Theory of the State which was used as the legal
basis. For the constituent regions, themselves states,
could not disappear as implied unless by consent of their
citizens, which did not take place.

The Multi-regional States

Can a state dissolve? The classical theorists of the
Contractual State, for whom the state was created by the
explicit consent of mutual advantage-seeking individuals,
gave contradictory or unrealistic responses to this
question.

At one extreme, Hobbes (7) and Rousseau (8), for whom
the individuals transferred to the new state <u>all</u> their
personal rights, came out with the opposing views that: 1)
the state could not be dissolved in any case (Hobbes); and
2) by its founders whenever it overstepped the procedures
consented to in administering the mutual advantage pact, and
in all cases by their descendants (Rousseau). Hobbes'

larger historical realism was marred by his logical incoherence, for contracts, even statehood contracts cannot be conceived to be irrevocable, so that Rousseau's coherence, though blurred by his historical unrealism, prevailed.

At the other end, Locke (9), for whom the individuals transferred only _some_ of their rights to the state, was not much better than Hobbes on logical grounds. In effect though, in his view, the state founders could dissent when the state impinged on the personal rights they had reserved for themselves, its descendants (who did not consent) could not yet dissent except on the same grounds as their ancestors, and collective dissent (secession) was not conceived to be logically possible for it implied an abnormal state which, instead of serving the interest of mutual advantage, purposely stepped on its founders toes. But he was the most realistic.

History, later, has solved the classical dissent-consent problem by siding with Locke's realism against Rousseau's logic. Individual dissent has been defended worldwide, generational dissent or collective dissent (secession) has been forcefully resisted by the states affected and rarely defended by the rest. But the fact that History has negated the consequences of Rousseau's coherence (since contracts are revocable), has upheld the more important proposition that the state cannot be the fruit of contract.

How have the multi-regional states been able then to subsist based on a deficient theoretical foundation? The multi-regional nation builders, unaware of that falsehood, used the contractual Theory of the State very imaginatively, profiting from the dissent-consent vacuum, and anticipated many new theoretical developments. They began to gradually fill in the new modern age confederations of regional states (of various political forms) with centralizing political structures based on the Contractual Theory of the State, on the basic and novel assumption that the permanence of the confederations in the presence of a growing transfer of power from the old regions to the new nations implied, at the same time, a generalized dissent towards the old states and a generalized consent to the new. We know now that implicit consent is certainly as valid a base for the state as explicit consent. In this respect, the multi-regional builders were breaking new theoretical ground which has only been recognized lately. But implicit consent brings in unexpected theoretical effects which have not been fully appreciated.

To start with, an implicit consent Theory of the State is a Natural Law Theory and not a Contractual Theory and, consequently, it requires a different explanation. First, how can it come about?

235

Not by design as in Locke, certainly. It can only come about as a result of unplanned social evolution. Once it appears and its virtues are recognized, however, it can be adopted as in Contractual Theory if the unexpected new state works to the benefit of all its future citizens who consequently want to retain it.

The implicit consent state can come about, in other words, by means of A. Smith's <u>invisible hand</u> type processes. In Nozick's case (10), which is very attractive, it results from the need for dominant self-protective associations to use power to guarantee that just procedures will be applied in the administration of justice to all persons in a continuous territory - irrespective of whether they are members of the association. Acknowledgement of the benefit of procedural justice as the highest public good by the area population creates the implicit consent for the transformation of that agency into a state.

As different as its origin are the consequences of the Implicit Consent State. In contrast to an explicit consent state, an implicit consent one can be conceived neither to be created by a mutual-advantage contract nor anulled by a better statehood recontract. An implicit consent state can neither be traded nor retraded, because its existence is determined by its provision of the statehood's founding public good and public goods are neither contractable nor sellable (11).

It is precisely because public goods, in opposition to private goods, cannot be traded that markets have to be complemented with states in order to guarantee their provision (12). Thus, once created, an implicit consent state becomes itself a <u>seminal</u> public good, a quality which if fulfilled ensures its continious existence. The multi-regional nation builders were right, therefore, in their basic intuition. The various types of modern-age regional-state confederations were originally conceived as self-protective agencies of regional states, against other regional state threats, but they developed into multi-regional states by invisible-hand means, precisely through the standardization of the procedural rules in the exercise of their power. As the multi-regional nation-builders rightly thought, the recognition of the higher public goods the new nations provided gradually created the multi-regional national conscience among the citizens of the old regions.

They were wrong in assuming that, at the same time, the old regional states would disappear, for, like the multi-regional national states themselves, the regional states once created - could not disappear unless the new multi-regional state produced all the public goods they previously provided, for that was the justification for their existence. Now, since as we shall see later, only certain

236

types of multi-regional states would come close to providing
all public goods, in all other cases the regional states
could be subordinated to the new multi-regional states only
in the proportion that people demanded the public goods they
respectively were to provide.

As a result of this error, they structured those
multi-regional states on the basic misconception that the
old regional states were not only subdued by the new, which
they were, but also anulled, which they were not (because
the public goods provided by the multi-regional and regional
states were both desired).

In consequence, the different sorts of political
skeleta they built to organize the new nations (federal
systems, legislative unions and the like) were not designed
to carry on the policies needed to balance out the
inevitable tensions within the new multi-regional states,
between its central region and the old peripheral regional
states, concerning who had the responsibility and the power
to produce which public good. They were set up for achieving the contradictory goal of minimizing the short-run
resistance of the old regions to a complete centralized and
homogenous union, by means of letting them participate, as
much as possible, in the formation of common national
policies, for it was assumed that it would facilitate their
inescapable convergence towards unification and centralized
provision of public goods.

From this perspective, it is easy to see why the constitutional historians have considered legislative unions,
monarchies and federal republics almost as sufficient conditions for effective unification of multi-regional nations
(12). In fact, the larger the decentralization schemes used
in the process of unification, the more difficult it is for
the dominant region of a nation to try to impose too rapid a
complete incorporation of the other regions and hence create
a basic conflict among the two levels of states within the
polity. Or more directly, the more decentralized the power
the easier it is to achieve a regional balance closer to the
natural when no one knows which one is necessary.

It is also easy to see, however, that the sufficient
conditions provided by the decentralized apparata are not
enough to guarantee a good administration of a multi-regional state. The necessary conditions for the balance of
regional power have not been specified and, in consequence,
only by chance have some decentralized apparata been able to
put them in practice. Some have not, and have exploded,
shattering their decentralized organs. Multi-regional
states lacking both conditions have naturally failed
earlier. But many centralized systems which have not put
sufficient conditions into practice yet, by chance, have
fulfilled the necessary conditions of regional balance, and
worked almost as well as decentralized and balanced systems.

237

This means that the smooth functioning of multi-regional states, whatever their political or constitutional structure, requires a strict fulfillment of the necessary conditions for their dynamic stability, i.e. a specific dynamic, regional balance.

One way to attempt to determine which is the normal interregional balance in a multi-regional state is to find out empirically its origins. Then, to try to abstract from it, checking (again empirically) if deviations from the abstracted norm have created (historically) abnormal regional tensions and whether a return to its normal pattern eased the conflicts.

The Spanish Case

The Original Constitution. In Spain, the initial confederation of the previously independent regional states was consumated at the beginning of the 16th century. It took the form of a multiple confederated monarchy, establishing a pattern later followed directly or indirectly by other European nations (14).

It should be established from the beginning that it was an event contrary to the previous geopolitical trends of the five Spanish Kingdoms. Hillgarth (15) has stated that the Spanish confederation would probably not have taken place without the failure of the previous (12th century) Catalano-Aragonian Confederated Monarchy. In effect, the Catalonian-Aragonian attempt to create a Mediterranean mercantile confederated empire, which was the most successful experiment of the five Spanish Kingdoms up to the 14th century (more so if one takes into consideration its small population), was blocked by the conflicting interests of France in the 14th century, and Turkey in the 15th century. Only after this did the Catalano-Aragonian state turn itself inland and looked towards Castille. A similar argument could be developed for Castille's failure to unite with Portugal for an Atlantic expansion.

Second, as Suarez (16) from Castille's viewpoint, and Vicens (17) from Aragon's have remarked, the Spanish confederation was facilitated by the fact that the demographic, economic and military rise of 15th century Castille coincided with Aragon's decline.

Third, most modern historians agree that it was not the product of any kingdom's design, for when it was presented prematurely in that way (14th century) it was forcefully resisted, but with the result of the expanding idea through all the kingdoms (including the Italian) that the union was beneficial to all in most dimensions.

Basically it was rightly felt that it would help to avoid the common threat of the French (to the Castillians in the Gulf of Biscay and to the Catalonian-Aragonians in the Gulf of Leon and in Italy). But apart from that, as Braudel

(18) stressed it attracted also the merchants' interest for it had the positive side-effect of linking the Catalano-Aragonian Mediterranean with the Castillian Atlantic. Thirdly, culturally it was also agreeable to the Church, for it allowed homogenization of the Christian traits of the northern kingdoms and so imposed them over the Jewish and Muslim components in the south.

It was, in short, at the origin, a mutual-advantage association of threatened weak and blocked states. But there were limitations, for in order to guarantee the political, judicial and economic autonomy of the constituent Kingdoms (for all other purposes than defense) the union adopted the old Catalano-Aragonian confederated scheme (19).

The Spanish Confederated Monarchy lasted two centuries almost unchanged until the Sucession war (which was also a secession war) and the replacement of the Hapsburg by the Bourbon dynasty in 1714. During those two centuries, the initially dominant regional state, Castille became, thanks first to her wool trade and then to the American treasure, the world's largest economic and military power (20). But this did not make her the confederation's undisputed leader. Castille used her great power in a continuous imperial war against the French, British, Dutch, Germans and Turks, until it eventually collapsed. However, Castille never tried to exercise her power fully over her weaker partners.

Castille was absorbed in her imperial adventure which was strictly her own in terms of ideas, men and money. The other Spanish Kingdoms did not participate with the exception of the French and the Turkish wars. Castille, with few exceptions, respected scrupulously the confederation's rules, although becoming the leading kingdom in the Peninsula.

But this curious behaviour was pregnant with important consequences for the future. To maintain her imperial foreign policy on her own, Castille had to reorganize itself and act in a manner which later became incompatible with the confederation. Castille had to homogenize and centralize itself erasing heterogenous and decentralized feudal traits, and initiate mercantilist policies as a complement to heavy internal taxation, in order to organize and finance the heavy administration and military professional machinery which would later become standard in Europe.

The other kingdoms, which went happily along with Castille's unexpected world leadership (including the newcomer Portugal which up to then had resisted joining) because it was a free ride, did not restructure themselves accordingly. They grew on their old feudal bones. Certainly, they benefited from Castille's adventure. Direct benefits were the exclusive reserve of Castille, but at no cost at all, Castille's new self-financed role as world power was, in fact, an added plus to their unchanged structures within their untouched self-protective covenant. They grew by themselves with stability during the long peace brought about by Castille's armies, profiting from the spillovers of her power while Castille first boomed and then hemorraged in men and wealth.

At the end of the period, Castille, as a consequence of a taxation rate twenty times larger than the other kingdoms and of the war halving her population, was no longer the leading economic region and was reduced in its relative political and military power over the other kingdoms. However, she had become the most modern though impoverished state and the leading political unit in the confederation.

The historical sketch above shows clearly that the implicit acceptance by the other kingdoms of Castille's weak dominance of the confederation during these two centuries, not envisaged in its constitution, was, in short economic free riding in exchange for passive but costless subordination. Would the confederation hold if that implicit consent was broken? It was soon put to the test.

In 1640, when Castille was exhausted and declining, Olivares tried to extend to the other kingdoms Castillian oversized administration, taxation and drafting, in order to be able to continue her perpetual wars. Portugal, Catalonia, Aragon, Navarra and Andalucia rebelled. Portugal seceeded and the other regions were difficult to control until Olivares was removed and the old confederated pact reinstated. Historically, Olivares' test has been enormously relevant. The same pattern re-emerged in the centuries after, more or less acutely, when similar situations arose.

The first lesson for Confederated Spain was therefore clear: Castille could only rule outside of Spain if she was ready to pay the bill for power herself and not if it had to be shared by the other kingdoms. It remained to be tested under which conditions it could be admitted to rule within Spain.

The first incomplete test of the second question did not wait long. When, in 1700, at the death of heirless Carlos II, Castille opted for the French alliance instead of the British (by choosing the Bourbon Felipe V as successor), Catalunya, Aragon and Valencia rebelled once again because their political and economic interests conflicted with those of France. Euskadi and Navarra backed the Castillians because their interests were complementary.

Centralized Spain. Throughout Bourbon Spain, however, the conditions for Castille's internal dominance were totally defined. The first century of the new dynasty showed that Castille could rule within Spain, even altering her original confederated scheme, provided that her policies were beneficial to the economic growth of the peripheral

240

regions. The second century showed that, on the contrary, the system would explode if they were inimical to the peripheral regions' economic growth.

The positive first part of the process was curiously activated by the loss of the Low countries, the Rhine corridor and Northern Italy in the 18th century. Castille, faced with loss of its classical North-South European axis, took the critical geopolitical decision of turning her back on Europe and addressing herself to her southern apex, from the Mediterranean to Latin America. This benefited her economic growth considerably because it permitted her to dedicate to internal investment most of the extravagant administrative and military resources of the two centuries before (21).

This strategic external turnaround was accompanied by a change in internal policy no less dramatic. Castille, through the Bourbons, did what she couldn't through Olivares: she broke the old confederated scheme and imposed a policy of homogenization, centralization and modernization on the other kingdoms (though it left ground for some regional autonomy especially in Euskadi and Navarra, the regions that had sided with her in the secession war). The French dynasty started in fact the <u>castillianization of Spain</u>, applying to all the other kingdoms the administrative patterns and policies directly developed in Castille two centuries earlier plus some of the innovations which the Bourbons had introduced in them. Surprisingly, the constitutional coup meant the process of centralization was not resisted, but actually welcomed. Historians agree that it was precisely in this century that the national conscience, which would consolidate in the Napoleonic wars, was first created.

This happened because the homogenization of the kingdoms was not an added cost or without extra benefit, as earlier. Without planning for it, the new American-induced growth benefited most peripheral regions which, in fact, traded more subordination for faster growth.

With the data available for the 19th century, I have shown (22) that the orientation towards America and the opening of the peripheral regions to that trade, which, until then were restricted, favored them over Castille because their <u>competitive effect</u> was greater than Castille's (the "industry-mix" effect was small in both, though larger in Castille). Something similar must have happened and in higher relative terms in the 18th century, because then the periphery's economic and demographic growth relative to Castille's was very large. As the census figures show, at the end of the century, the periphery had become the dominant economic center of the peninsula and the relative demographic advantage of Castille was further reduced.

In short, the old confederated scheme was watered down

and Castille's direct rule over all ancient kingdoms was initially, though yet slightly, established through the Bourbon Absolute Monarchy, because its 18th century policies resulted in peace and prosperity for the periphery, as Vazquez de Prada recognizes (23).

The condition then for Castille's undisputed leadership over the other kingdoms was peace and prosperity for the peripheral regions. The revealed natural interregional balance that assured the stability of centralized multi-regional Spain was the trade-off of peripheral, political subordination for Castille's promotion of growth in peace.

As in the case earlier of Confederated Spain, the negative confirming test did not last long. It came a century later, in the 19th century. The Napoleonic war had the positive effect of strengthening the national conscience against the foreign aggressor, but it also had the very negative effect of generating the independence of the American territories (except the Philippines and Caribbean Islands), on whose trade Spain's 18th century growth was based.

The loss of that late external source of growth, which was not replaced by an effective internal one until the loss of the last islands launched two of the gravest processes of 19th century Spain. In effect: 1) Spain initiated her process of underdevelopment, extending her external income per capita gap relative to Europe (24); 2) she also registered an increase in her internal inequality gap which reinforced the shift of the economic center from Castille to the periphery initiated in the 17th century, for the peripheral regions continued to grow faster than Castille on the reduced American trade (the Caribbean trade), thanks to their greater competitive advantage (25).

Castille's vacillating response to the new situation was not novel. It attempted to transform her previous model of centralized externally-led growth into an even more centralized but autarkic model of internally-led growth.

The Bourbon Parliamentary Monarchy of the 19th century and its backbone, the liberal party, intensified the drive towards homogenization, centralization and protected industrialization of the whole country, which the Bourbon Absolute Monarchy and her ilustrados had applied less vigorously and more mercantilistically to the periphery in the previous century, and the Hapsburg Confederated Monarchy and its arbitristas only to Castille in the 17th century.

But this time, the project was not only unwelcome but strongly resisted. Both the right wing Carlist and the left wing democrats in the peripheral regions rebelled, because the project of unification was inimical to all peripheral interests (26). It set up a continuous process of confrontation, which was peaceful in the periods when international booms induced some internal growth, and produced revolutions

242

or civil wars in the periods when international depressions accelerated the long-term structural decline (27).

By the end of the 19th century, therefore, all the positive and negative tests needed to determine which was the necessary condition to maintain the stability of multi-regional Spain, under confederated, centralized, absolute or democratic formulas were completed. It was clear that multi-regional Spain could only be peacefully viable if her double constitution trade-off 1) centralization with growth or 2) autonomy with stagnation, was met.

Spain's 20th century history reflects, in fact, that Castille finally perceived the critical importance of Spain's basic constitutional trade-off and behaved accordingly. Authentic reqenerationists and superficial regenerationists (mediocrats) have all attempted to modernize 20th century Spain through more centralization in order to achieve faster growth and thus maintain Castille's power. The regenerationists proposed a homogeneous, centralized, progressive and democratic state which would develop the country, but were never able to set it up. The mediocrats established two dictatorships (Primo de Rivera's and Franco's) which aimed autocratically and conservatively at the same goals. Both succeeded while the international booms of the 1920s, 1950s and 1960s propped the Spanish economy but both failed when the international crises of the 1930s and 1970s occured. Their respective successions, the second Republic and the present Parliamentary Monarchy, submerged in stagnation, have had to back up to the other alternative of the constitutional trade-off – autonomy with stagnation (28).

The Espana Integral and the Espana de las Auto-nomias of the 1931 and 1978 Constitutions are, in fact, clear recognition of the last worse-balance condition, with the difference that in 1931 the political structure proposed was more congruent to the Spanish tradition. It was a diluted form of the old Confederate Monarchy. In 1979, an alien form of diluted federalism has been built into the Parliamentary Monarchy.

Centralization with Growth. The Spanish multi-regional constitutional trade-off, however, requires further qualification for, one of the alternatives, centralization with qrowth, has historically been far more durable than the other, autonomy with stagnation, as already indicated above. In fact, the autonomy with stagnation solution has only worked peacefully for relatively long periods (decades) at the beginning of the 16th century and at the end of the 18th century (in periods when global, external, defense was more important than any other goal, national or regional). In the 19th century, without equivalent foreign threats, it lasted only a few years. The reason is that stagnation without foreign threats breeds demand for autonomy in the periphery in the hope that it will permit the peripheral regions to start growth processes of their own, and substitute for lacking centrally-generated growth. When these autonomy demands failed, it resulted in revolutionary processes in the periphery, which demanded forced Castillian interventions.

If the only durable constitutional principle of multi-regional Spain, and possibly of other multi-regional countries, is dominion (of the political center) with growth (of the political periphery), how can that relationship be guaranteed in the long run? It seems necessary, first, to mark Spain's Modern History and, with regard to the state's role in the western world.

Concerning the first point, I agree with Carr and the other Anglo-Saxon authors that Spain's (rather, Castille's) basic failure in the contemporary period was her lack of understanding that no superstructural solution would work until the country was developed. I disagree with the idea that the basic condition for development was the establishment of a real democracy, for I don't think any real democracy could have been or can be established until the 17th century _inversion_ of Spain's regional balance is righted. A basic restructuring of the Spanish state was and still is the basic prerequisite for development, democracy, and modernization.

Secondly, it is my belief that modern-age multi-regional states grew around the higher order public goods that some nucleating regional states provided. Since public goods normally show increasing returns to scale (29), technological change favored a trend towards their increased centralized provision which, therefore, led to growing centralization of those states. Further, since, as Denison (30) suggests, most of the causes of productivity growth have been related to public goods, that increment determined that the centralization of those states fostered their economic growth. Growth itself became some sort of synthetical public good. Thus, lack of growth meant a threat to the integrity of states which, like Spain, did not provide it and yet tried to impose an artificial centralization.

This centralization trend also has a limit. As states tend to overcentralize and overregulate in order to favor not only the provision of the positive aspects of public goods but to impede some of their negative effects, they threaten growth itself because they slow productivity growth, as Denison has also shown (31). Centralization, in other words, is bounded by the territoral structure of public goods supply and demand. Economic policy effects on public goods, as on income assignments (32) can effect the stability of the states by affecting the regional or the individual status-quo. This general case is even more critical in states whose political structure, though formally similar, has shallower roots because it has not been the outgrowth of the same process of centralizing growth supported by growing public goods provision. How, then, can <u>centralized growth</u> be provided on a long term basis in those countries?

    <u>The Multi-regional Balance.</u> Spanish history shows that Castille achieved the growth her periphery desired when she had her own internal source of growth (the 15th century wool trade) or when she was able to control external sources of growth. Since external sources of growth are naturally shorter, the only long-term condition to guarantee the stability of multi-regional states, not refutable by Spanish experience is, therefore, that the political center of the country be at the same time its autonomous, dynamic, economic growth center.

    This coincidence of the economic with the political center, a fact which is implicitly assumed as universally valid based on analysis of western countries which met that condition, is what led the constitutionalists to propose as <u>necessary</u> the constitutional conditions for stability. In reality they are only sufficient conditions, for though decentralized democracies facilitate a situation in which the economic centers are the engines of national growth, they cannot create them. Democracy (centralized or decentralized) in Spain has not solved the <u>real</u> regional problem because it has not caused Castille to become her economic center.

    The correspondence of the political and economic centers is not, and has not been, a frequent trait among multi-regional nations. For many reasons the political and the economic center may be two different regions. More critical, from our perspective, even a <u>normally</u> structured multi-regional nation, i.e. one where the political center is also the economic center, can <u>invert</u> itself if that center decays economically and yet, as is most probable, maintains the political power (as Castille did from the 17th century onwards) (33).

    It is intuitively obvious that in nations where the political center is the economic periphery, i.e. in <u>inverted</u> multi-regional nations, the policies needed to achieve the same goals as in the <u>normal</u> nations cannot be exactly the same. Western types of constitutional policies are likely to fail because the necessary economic growth conditions are not present. Similarly, Western type growth policies are prone to fail also because the democratic politically sufficient conditions cannot be maintained.

    The explicit absence of the necessary conditions in the modern application of constitutional theory has prevented many modern multi-regional nations in Africa, America and Asia from achieving stability. Without growth, democracy has not stayed long. Secondly, the additional unfulfillment of the sufficient condition has threatened the physical integration of those countries. Dictatorial power without growth has normally ended in revolutions.

The solution to this fundamental problem, however, does not forcefully require anti-Western political or economic methods, as sometimes thought in the Third World. The same Western institutions and policies can be used, if they are well designed, economically and politically, to achieve the basic interregional balance condition - centralization with growth. How can this be done?

Center-Periphery Relations

The Center-Periphery approach has been used by authors of different ideologies to explain why economic growth does not spread homogeneously over international or interregional space, as mainstream economic analysis concludes it should. The basic argument is that the economic center controls growth spread and limits it for its own benefit through political means. In all those arguments, therefore, there is an identification of the economic with the political center of the areas analyzed.

I have called those Center-Periphery cases "normal," no matter whether their analyses are liberal, social-democratic, Marxian or Marxist, in order to differentiate them from all the other, most frequent cases, where the political center is not the economic center of the country, which I have termed inverted Center-Periphery cases (34). The normal Center-Periphery relation is relatively strong in the short run. Space friction, transport breakpoints, market complementarities of inputs and outputs on the demand and supply side (internal and external) at the production, exchange or consumption levels, which are the conventional brakes of the economic centers spread effects are reinforced by polarizing technological, organizational and sociological discontinuities which characterize every stage of economic development. The backwash effects induced by income and profit differentials between the center and the periphery cannot be easily scaled down to equilibrate the reduced spread flows.

In the medium run, however, I believe that the normal Center-Periphery relations are weaker because the two effects are more balanced. It has been proved everywhere that in healthy economic centers old activities are replaced by new ones and expelled to their periphery, for it is no longer necessary and advantageous for the center to hold on to them (but only in that new activities are mostly financed from profits from the old, internally or externally to the firm). The investment resources for the new activities, which are largely drawn from the periphery to the center through the pricing process (as backwashed profits), must precede and equal roughly the <u>spread</u> return of the investments in older activities transferred from the center to the periphery.

Over the longer run, growing divergence of income per capita levels between the center and the periphery cannot last, in the normal case, for the centers cannot hold both the new and the old activities, since they cannot keep financing new investments from growing old losses. The only two possible outcomes in the long run seem to be 1) a permanence of the Center-Periphery differential over a strong center-induced growth path; or 2) a growing convergence of the Center-Periphery differential over a relatively stagnating path set up by a weakening center. These two outcomes are the logical result of the fact that, over the long-run, <u>backwash</u> and <u>spread</u> effects must balance out even more than in the medium run, once the economic center has acquired the maturity needed to pull its periphery at a competitive world pace. Initially, in order to reach that size and composition, the economic center has to <u>backwash</u> more. Once at its worldwide competitive structure, if it <u>backwashes</u> less than it <u>spreads</u>, its loses relative strength and can decay, gradually <u>inverting</u> the Center-Periphery relations and becoming an economic periphery and a political center, as 18th century Castille.

This conceptual framework is based on the following economic notions that I have developed earlier.

1) National economic development is primarily induced internationally; the most a nation can do is to profit from international trends by adapting to incoming activities faster than its competitors (35).

2) Incoming and outgoing activities follow closely fixed specialized technological and organizational channels and, as a consequence of their geographical fixity, result in geographically stable patterns of diffusion and adoption, from the first worldwide originating center to the last adaptor (36).

3) In consequence, the rate of national development is basically determined by the relative speed with which its national economic center adopts the newer activities relative to other nations' central regions and transfers the older activities to its periphery (37).

4) The political and economic center has a larger, acquisitive but nationalistic bourgeoisie and a competent, contesting but cooperating proletariat. Both understand clearly that their well-being depends on how fast the center adopts to new innovations in order to keep up in the world competitive race and, therefore, they set up their own claims on the growth benefits at levels compatible with that common goal (38).

5) The political economic periphery has a smaller, less ambitious but also less nationalistic bourgeoisie who

feels itself incapable of competing alone in the world-race of continuous technological change. Its proletariat feels rightly that its <u>depending</u> bourgeoisie does not use its power to increase the well-being of the two classes but that it caters parasitically only to its own (39).

6) As a consequence, the convergence of interests of the two classes in the center permits their stable democratic rotation in power to be fully consistent with the maintenance of the center's <u>backwash-spread</u> sequence with its periphery. On the other hand, in the economic periphery democracy is unstable; there is a constant potential threat of revolution which can only be averted by the growth benefits resulting from the investment of the center's bourgeosie. While the periphery's proletariat is not so eager to accept the same dependent alliance with the center's proletariat, because the latter's accomodating attitude conflicts with its own revolutionary attitudes, it is also forced to accept it for there is no other way out. It cannot rebel against its own bourgeosie for it is supported by the two classes in the center. The <u>dependent</u> status-quo is very stable. It can only be broken by an unlikely nationalistic revolution in the periphery of the proletariat allied to the bourgeoisie against the center, which can be put down by an equivalent interclass alliance in the center. Given, in fact, the objective convergence of interests between the bourgeoisie and the proletariat of the economic center, the best the two peripheral classes can obtain for themselves is through political dependent associations with respective classes in the Center. Therefore, the polity is organized in country-wide class-parties dominated by their economic center sections.

The Inverted Center-Periphery Case

Whenever the economic center is not the political center, which is largely the case in countries where economic development has not yet matured or where underdevelopment has set in (for then the underdeveloped regions are demographically dominant) the economic and socio-political behavior of the economic and political centers and peripheries are the same as above. Their interaction results are contradictory to the normal case because the economic inefficiency and political instability of the economic periphery are no longer stably compensated and controlled by the efficiency and stability of the economic center. On the contrary, the economic inefficiency and political instability of the economic periphery slows down efficiency and erodes the stability of the economic center because it dominates it politically. As a consequence, instead of progressive and stable, an inverted Center-Periphery nation tends to be necessarily regressive and unstable.

It tends to be regressive because the peripheral economic centers can only adopt the new technologies and diffuse the old and therefore induce national growth at the rate which the politically dominant economic peripheries allow the <u>backwash-spread</u> mechanism to operate on themselves. Normally this is at a low rate in order to impede a greater antagonism of their own bourgeoisie and proletariat.

It tends to be unstable because, unless growth comes from outside sources, the political center cannot guarantee the basic <u>centralization with growth</u> condition, unless it lets itself be exploited by the politically weak economic center. Since it cannot let itself be so exploited, the resulting unfulfillment of the basic growth conditions generates nationalistic alliances among the convergent peripheral bourgeoisie and proletariat which, even if not violent, make peaceful national government difficult.

Since both the acquisition of external sources of growth through territorial imperialism and internal growth through self-permitted exploitation are easier to attain under autocratic centralized systems than under democratic decentralized ones, it is clear that inverted multi-regional states must be more prone than normal multi-regional states to imperialistic territorial acquisitions when they are demographically strong. They must also be, in all cases, but more so when they are weaker, more inclined to autocratic centralized governments.

Since these two logical consequences seem to be common traits of all inverted multi-regional states in the past and present, we can proceed to analyze the final and most striking consequence of the interregional balance condition of <u>inverted</u> multi-regional states. Why do their political centers seem to prefer exploitation from their dominated peripheries rather than to permit their autonomy? It is in fact compulsory to analyze that behavior, bacause only by revealing the hidden factors which maintain the durable multi-regional <u>inversion</u> will we be able to understand how to bring about normalcy.

Let us start with the central question implied in the trade-off described above. Why, in the first place, do people seem to prefer power over wealth in the political center and wealth over power in the economic center, and why at certain times, do they seem to change their choices? Since I do not accept that those abnormal and incoherent preferences are due to the different beliefs, attitudes, motives, etc. of their citizens as conventionally hypothesized, the central question becomes - what are the structural reasons among those stated before which, due to the inversion of the units in the <u>normal</u> Center-Periphery case, that cause such unusual behavior?

In the economic center, the issue of coherent goals seems to be less important over time than in the political center. The economic center appears to choose wealth over power most of the time. When it demands power over wealth, as pointed out before, it is only to achieve that wealth that the political center does not procure externally or does not permit the economic center to generate internally. Why does it prefer the power to wealth goal? The answer is clear and functional - in order to maintain the social cooperation of its classes which is a fundamental condition to keep on being a dynamic, progressive, though politically dependent economic center.

Are there any exceptions? The only time an economic center seems to be willing to sacrifice wealth is in those periods of revolt from their normally cooperative proletariats, when they try to become almost autonomous to guarantee growth and social cooperation and fail. Then, they demand protection from the political center and are willing to pay for it, not only with subordination, but with wealth transfers.

But is this an exception? Hardly. The situation is not desired and would not be chosen if known in advance, though it could be predicted because in a dependent center without a periphery there cannot be class cooperation but rather unmitigated class structure. Secondly, even in that unexpected situation, there is not goal inversion but submission to a higher, hidden goal - regional social peace and regional self-preservation.

In the political center, over time, the choices of inverted Center-Periphery political centers seem to be more abnormal and incoherent than those of their economic centers. At certain times they act as if they are willing to sacrifice wealth for power. But once certain limits of economic loss are reached, they are willing to give away power to minimize losses.

The fundamental reason for the preference of power over wealth in the political centers is the same that determines the preference of wealth over power in the economic centers, only less obvious. For reasons advanced in the normal case, the socio-political structure of the inverted political center, which is an economic periphery, is very unstable because of its deep class antagonism. It can only be maintained in a stable form, democratically or autocratically, with the inter-class help of its economic center (its political periphery). And this support can best be achieved through the political dominance of the periphery for it permits the political center to carry on easier the swift shifts in policies more conducive to that support. In short, political centers prefer power over wealth because it is a better guarantee of regional self-preservation.

Wealth transfers, from the rich or from the poor in the political center to the periphery, depending on the class in power, can again be justified (as power transfers in the

250

case of the economic center) as a means to obtain the higher
goal of multi-regional social peace and self-preservation.

Wealth transfers are stopped and power instead is
transferred, from the political center to the economic
center (as power demands are stopped and protection is
demanded by the economic centers), when those decisions
effect even more directly the political center own's
regional social peace. If wealth transfers to the periphery
are bound to generate immediate social conflict in the
political center they are stopped, even if that action
increases the nationalist alliances of the peripheral
bourgeoisie and proletariat which, later, will threaten
(through their separatist tendencies) the multi-regional
security and finally the political center's self-preservation.

Political and Economic Solutions for Unstable Multi-regional States

History shows that what a declining inverted multi-
regional nation can best expect is that international booms
may push it up from time to time and thus slow its secular
decay (which is first economic and then becomes territorial
when peripheral economic centers finally are forced to break
away). It also shows that, for the reasons advanced above,
the separated regions undergo revolutionary processes which,
though initially nationalistic, may become social.

How can an inverted multi-regional nation be trans-
formed into a normal one? The immediate answer is to use
the power of the political center to develop it above the
economic center. This has been the purpose of Spanish
arbitristas, ilustrados and mediocratas and of Third World
modernizers. They have proposed to do it autocratically
through inter-regional balancing measures because the
strategy cannot be totally detrimental but compatible with
the economic center's interests. It has always failed
because it takes too long a period of implementation and
many events intervene.

The second answer is the transfer of political power to
the economic center. It sounds more difficult to initiate
but it seems faster to accomplish. This is one of the
procedures used to build monarchic regional states out of
feudal ones, through dynastic marriages during the Middle
Ages.

How can that be done in multi-regional democratic
states today? The problem is not so much economic as
political. Normally, economic policies are favorable to the
solution of the problem because they work towards the
strengthening of the existing economic centers. Economic
development policy proponents on the whole maintain that, to
reduce a nation's international gap, it is necessary to
concentrate investment in its developed regions where

251

infrastructure and the market already exist. At least half
the regional development authors would also agree that,
although the reduction of the international gap initially
increases the interregional gap, it eventually also closes
it if the policy of minimizing infrastructure investment is
strictly maintained for productive investment automatically
moves southward as the northern infrastructure is exhausted
(40).

Politics, especially politics of the distributive-
justice type which still dominate, are clearly against the
idea of strengthening, not only economically but also
politically, the existing economic centers. Distributive
politics favor economic redistribution (sectoral,
functional, personal and geographical) but through the
centralization of power.

For a time the impact of Distributive Justice,
especially a-la-Rawls (41) has been so intense that it
affected not only politics but economics. By justifying
welfare policies, the enlargement of centralized government
has been promoted. Demand oriented policies have been
favored over supply side ones, even in less developed
countries where they later are essential. Today this impact
is being overcome. Its effect is likely to remain
restricted to politics where it will also be diminished as
new and opposing schools of thought in distributive justice,
like Nozick's (42), appear.

Political obstacles to the transfer of political power
to economic centers will remain, although on more managable
terms, for it is not only a matter of doctrine but also of
structure. In effect, comparative political analyses (43)
show that, independent of constitutional type and electoral
laws, political parties of multi-regional states tend to be
<u>territorially</u> <u>aligned</u> <u>and</u> <u>not</u> <u>class</u> <u>aligned</u>. In the
inverted cases, additionally, regional self-preservation
rights eventually impose upon the existence of nationalistic
interclass parties or alliances at least in the political
peripheries, i.e. in the economic centers.

This fact, clearly determined by the pre-existing
multi-regional state structure and thus difficult to
overcome, hinders the smooth transfer of power to the
peripheral economic centers through the integration of
nationalist bourgeoise and proletariat groups in
country-wide class parties. Thus, the possibility of
replicating, in the inverse case, the political procedure
prevalent in the <u>normal</u> multi-regional case is excluded.
Because power cannot be transferred through the internal
channels of country-wide parties, power transfers from the
political to the economic centers have to be made through
other procedures.

At worst, it must be done from national to regional
governments (controlled by class parties in the center and

nationalistic parties in the peripheries, respectively), through unpopular piecemeal reversible pacts in atomized national parliaments which are necessarily ineffectual and divisible, instead of efficient and cohesive.

A different and more efficient procedure consists of establishing majority national government alliances of the political center - class parties with the peripheral nationalists. Transfers within the secrecy of government can be arranged.

Thus, peripheral nationalisms are necessarily dominated by their bourgeoisie groups and there are only two possible types of majority alliances. One, the alliance of the political center bourgeoisie with the peripheral nationalists; two, the alliance of the political center proletariat with the same.

The first one is difficult to achieve because the nationalist bourgeoisie feel obligated to demand more than proportional power, which the central bourgeoisie will resist. But it is at least stable because no bourgeoisie, central or peripheral, will feel their regional social peace attacked. The second is easier to attain because the central proletariat is normally willing to offer more power to the progressive peripheral nationalists in exchange for its more liberal platform, but it is very unstable because, as shown in Spain in 1936, it threatens the political center bourgeoisie's self-preservation rights.

In the long run, the easier and more efficient solutions to facilitate power transfer from the economic peripheries to the economic centers are likely to be the two latter type of alliances inasmuch as intra-government transfers are the closest substitute for intra-party transfers. In the short run, however, they can be counteracted by nationalistic alliances in the political center, created to oppose or control the transfer. These short run anomalies are, to start with, very difficult to achieve because it is in the center where class antagonism is stronger.

What then is the soundest strategy to normalize an inverted multi-regional state? Once it is verified that the multi-regional structure hinders the creation of country-wide class parties or alliances of the western type which could facilitate a power transfer, and that this structure renders infeasible an attempt to form territorial nationalistic alliances in the center to oppose it, it appears that the only way to have inverted multi-regional states revert smoothly to normalcy is the creation of government alliances of a mixed class and territorial character. Of the two possibilities the only one having a significant chance of longterm success is the post-electoral alliance of the center's bourgeoisie with the peripheral nationalists.

The decentralization of power to the peripheral regions will demand that nationalists not be compensated by an increase in the central state power. The weight of the expanded global government could suffocate whatever slight chances of national economic growth remained. That indeed would be a self-defeating measure, because the object of the whole political operation is to set up a political structure which can raise the national rate of growth through the implantation of the economic policies outlined before, for it is the basic condition to achieve the country's stability. It also needs to be done in accordance with the basic, historic, non-written constitution of the multi-regional states. The multi-regional government has to provide, by public or private means, whichever is more efficient, public goods which cannot be provided by the regional governments and are the guarantee of multi-regional self-preservation. Similarly the regional governments must provide those public goods which are necessary to guarantee regional self-preservation. Regional governments, in their turn, must decentralize to municipal governments the responsibility for public goods which are essential to their self-preservation and which were the basis for their origin.

In the public goods arena, allocative efficiency is not attainable except with constitutional and fiscal institutional structures guaranteeing public decision-making. Productive and distributive efficiency criteria are not unequivocally related to the allocative ones because, by definition, there is not a one-to-one correspondence between production, consumption and distribution of public goods (44). Additionally, allocative, productive and distributive efficiency are even farther removed from assignative efficiency because public goods are the foundations of the states where private and public economic activities take place. Therefore, they cannot be moved around for the convenience of the content (the citizens) without modifying the container (the state). Their allocation must be fundamentally constitutional not economical. Only their production, distribution and financing need to be efficient.

Public goods assignation criteria, therefore, must be territorially coincident with their distribution. If they should be distributed to all the constituent citizens of a state, because that is what justified the state, its provision should also be assigned to that state. Otherwise the state cannot perform its obligation and a dangerous void appears in the system of govenment. Transgression of that second norm, by erroneous efficient criteria reallocation to higher order states is almost as grave an attack on the stability of the system of states (in inverted multi-regional states) as a universal reduction of public goods would be in the normal ones.

254

In short, transforming a conservative and unstable inverted multi-regional state into a progressive and stable one does not require reeducation of its population up to those standards or application of the latest constitutional schemes in fashion, or attempting to industrialize artificially through Western blue-prints. It is purely a policy problem of reallocation of power from the political to the economic centers of that multi-regional state so as to guarantee that its new centralization produces automatically the internal economic growth which is a necessary condition for stable national functioning.

To achieve this it is necessary first to conceive of a structure of government which is big and small enough to facilitate growth. Second, this government should be as integrated as possible with regard to economic decisions in order to maximize growth potential. And, thirdly, it should be decentralized in a manner which guarantees that the various public goods are provided by the government at the level closest to the citizen. Once such a structure is conceived, it has to be implemented by a majority government made up of an alliance of the regions and political forces most affected.

NOTES

1. P. Vilar, Historia de Espana (Madrid, 1975).
2. Carrir, Espana 1808-1939 (Madrid, 1968).
3. See also J. Conelly, La Semana Tragica: Un Estudio de las causas economicas del anticlericalismo en Espana (Barcelona, 1971); G. Brennan, The Spanish Labirynth (London, 1943); R. Herr, Modern Spain (New York, 1971); and E. Macefakis, La Reforma Agraria y la Revolucion – Campesina (Madrid, 1970).
4. R. Herr, ibid.
5. D. J. Elazar, "Federalism" in International Encyclopedia of the Social Sciences (1968).
6. J. Althusius, Politicha Methodice Digesta (Cambridge, MA, 1932).
7. T. Hobbes, Leviathan (New York, 1950).
8. J. J. Rousseau, The Social Contract (New York, 1962).
9. J. Locke, Two Treatises of Government (Cambridge, MA, 1964).
10. Nozich, Anarchy, State and Utopia (New York, 1974).
11. J. M. Buchanan, The Demand and Supply of Public Goods (Washington, 1979).
12. J. M. Buchanan and Tullock, The Calculus of Consent (Ann Arbor, MI, 1962).

255

13. D. J. Elazar, op. cit.

14. Elazar, ibid.

15. J. M. Hillgarth, The Spanish Kingdoms (London, 1976).

16. L. Suarez Feranndez, "Las Raices Historicas de la Pluralided," Espana de las Autonomias (Madrid, 1981).

17. J. Vincens Vives, Historia Social y Economica de Espana y America (Barcelona, 1959).

18. F. Braudel, El Mediterraneo y el Mundo Mediterraneo en la epoca de Felipe II (Madrid, 1976).

19. J. M. Elliot, Imperial Spain (London, 1964).

20. R. B. Merriman, The Rise of a Spanish Empire in the Old World and the New (New York, 1962).

21. J. Linsay, El Mediterraneo Occidental e Italia (Madrid, 1981).

22. J. R. Lasuen and Rubio, "La Evolucion de las Regiones Espanolas, 1860-1969," (Madrid, 1976, mimeo).

23. Vazquez de Prada (1981).

24. Carr, op. cit.

25. J. R. Lasuen, "Spain's Regional Growth" in N. M. Hansen (ed.) Public Policy and Regional Economic Development (Cambridge, MA, 1974).

26. J. Olabarri, "La Cuestion Regional en Espana, 1808-1939," in La Espana de las Autonomias (Madrid, 1981).

27. J. R. Lasuen, La Espana Mediocratica (Madrid, 1979).

28. Lasuen, ibid.

29. P. A. Samuelson, "Aspects of Public Expenditure Theories," The Collected Scientific Papers of Paul A. Samuelson (New York, 1975) p. 1233.

30. E. F. Denison, Accounting for United States Growth, 1929-1969 (Washington, 1974).

31. E. F. Denison, Accounting for Slower Economic Growth (Washington, 1979).

32. D. Usher, The Economic Prerequisite for Democracy (Oxford, 1981).

33. Lasuen (1974), op. cit.

34. J. R. Lasuen and A. Pastor, "Perspectivas Regiona les de Espana," in Espana de las Autonomias (Madrid, 1981).

35. J. R. Lasuen, F. Wasservogel and A. Montserrat, "Quelques Aspects du Processus de Developement du System des Nation: Estabilite Polarisation, Diffusion," in Revue of Economic Politique,No. 2 (1970).

36. J. R. Lasuen, "Multi-regional Economic Development, An Open Systems Approach," in Lund Studies in Geography, Series B , No. 37 (1971).

37. J. R. Lasuen, "Urbanisation and Development. The Temporal Interaction between Geographical and Sectoral Clusters," in Urban Studies, Vol. 10 (1973).

38. J. Galtung, "A Structural Theory of Imperialism," in Journal of Peace Research, Vol. 2 (1971).

39. Galtung, ibid.
40. Lasuen and Pastor, op. cit.
41. J. Rawls, <u>A Theory of Justice</u> (Cambridge, MA, 1971).
42. Nozick, op. cit.
43. A. W. MacMahon, <u>Federalism: Mature and Emergent</u> (New York, 1955).
44. J. M. Buchanan, op. cit.

PART V: SUMMARY AND CONCLUSION

REGIONAL POLICY IN A SLOW-GROWTH ECONOMY

Harry W. Richardson

Introduction
    This chapter develops from some ideas advanced a few
years ago by Bill Miernyk related to the hypothesis that the
slowing down in world economic growth will require drastic
rethinking of our ideas about regional policy (1).   The
starting point of his analysis is that the phase of long-
term growth is over because of growing worldwide scarcities
of energy and other resources.   More specifically, although
world population and energy demand have both increased
exponentially since the middle of the nineteenth century, up
to the 1950s population grew faster than energy demand.   In
the 1950s, however, energy demand began to grow faster than
population and the two curves crossed.   Moreover, from the
late 1960s energy supply increased more slowly than demand,
and prices began to rise (culminating in OPEC's 1973 and
subsequent price boosts).   As a result, there was a sudden
drop in the economic growth rate of industrialized countries
in the 1970s.   Their performance since 1973 has not been the
result of the coincidence of two nasty short-term recessions
but is the beginning of a long-term trend.
    The stagnation of the national economy does not imply
the absence of change in the spatial distribution of
population and economic activity.   Some regions gain while
others lose.   In the United States context, it is not
difficult to guess which regions gain and which regions
lose.   Since 1969 the energy producing states have experienced the most rapidly increasing per capita incomes, while
the states most dependent on imported energy have experienced relative declines in per capita income.   Most of the
interregional income convergence of the last decade and a
half has taken the form of upward shifts by net energy
producers and downward shifts by net energy consumers.
However, this convergence does not represent a steady
movement towards a spatial equilibrium of interregional
income paths.   On the contrary, these income paths will
cross over with the formerly low-income energy and resource-
based regions rising above the national average.   In fact,

258

by the year 2000, according to Miernyk's forcasts, the Rocky Mountain region will be the richest and New England the poorest region in terms of regional per capita income.

Existing and past regional policies, which have focused on promoting economic development in lagging regions and in depressed central cities, are not designed to deal with the zero-sum situation. In this new game, there are two main alternatives: attempt to stop, or slow, the interregional shifts; or accept the shifts, and ameliorate the problems of those affected by them.   The first alternative is inefficient, and probably infeasible.   The second alternative, implying subsidies, may be justified if the interregional shifts are from regions with above-average incomes to those with below-average incomes.

Slow Growth and its Causes

There is no doubt that the world economy and its constituent parts grew more slowly (slow growth is interpreted here as a long-term phenomenon) in the 1970s than in the 1960s.   Table 5.1 displays growth rates for major economic indicators by country group in the 1960s and 1970s using data published by the World Bank.   These data show marked deceleration in gross domestic product, gross domestic investment, consumption, exports and manufacturing output for almost all country groups combined with a sharp increase in the inflation rate.   However, the growth rates do not suggest the emergence of a global stationary state. The industrialized countries fared significantly worse than other country groups, particularly the middle income countries which, with the notable exception of inflation, performed almost as well in the 1970s as in the 1960s. Moreover, using decadal growth rates cuts across cycles, and the picture would be much gloomier if the periods 1960-73 and post-1973 were combined. For example, the growth rate in GNP per employed worker slumped between the periods 1963-73 and 1973-79 from 1.9 percent per annum to 0.1 percent in the United States, 3.0 percent to 0.3 percent in the United Kingdom and from 8.7 percent to 3.4 percent in Japan (2).   Since the deceleration coincided with an approximate doubling of the impact of energy imports on the balance of payments (see the final column of Table 5.1), it is consistent with Miernyk's hypothesis. On the other hand, there were some bright spots. Many countries managed to maintain employment growth rates in spite of rising unemployment.   Another obvious point is that the weighted averages hide a wide spread of performance among countries in each country group, and a few countries succeeded in bucking the deceleration trend.

Some data on growth rates before and after 1973 have been published by UNCTAD (3).   They show that the average growth rate in GDP for developed market economies slumped

Table 5.1: Economic Performance in the 1960s and 1970s (Percent Per Annum Growth)

	GDP 1960s	GDP 1970s	GDI* 60s	GDI* 70s	Manufacturing Output* 60s	Manufacturing Output* 70s	Consumption* 60s	Consumption* 70s	Exports* 60s	Exports* 70s
Low Income Countries	3.9	3.6	4.6	3.6	6.6	4.2	3.9	3.1	5.0	-0.8
Middle Income Countries	6.0	5.7	7.6	7.2	7.6	6.8	5.3	4.9	5.5	5.2
Industrialized Countries	5.1	3.2	5.6	1.5	6.2	3.3	4.3	3.5	8.7	5.7
Capital Surplus Oil Exporters	13.0	6.0	..	..	..	16.1	..	..	9.5	-1.2
Centrally Planned Economies	4.9	5.6	..	..	..	..	..	..	..	..

* Median; other growth rates are weighted averages

.. = Not available

Table 5.1 (cont'd)

	Population		Urban Population		Labor Force		Prices*		Energy Imports As % of Commodity Exports	
	60s	70s	60s	70s	60s	70s	60s	70s	1960	1977
Low Income Countries	2.5	2.2	3.7	4.0	1.7	1.9	3.0	10.6	9	16
Middle Income Countries	2.5	2.4	4.2	3.8	2.4	2.5	3.1	13.1	11	20
Industrialized Countries	1.0	0.7	1.8	1.2	1.2	1.1	4.2	9.4	11	23
Capital Surplus Oil Exporters	2.9	3.2	5.8	5.5	2.6	2.8	1.2	22.2	..	0
Centrally Planned Economies	1.7	1.4	3.0	2.6	1.4	1.7	..	..	..	..

*Median; other growth rates are weighted averages

.. = Not available

Source: World Bank, World Development Report

from 5.2 percent per annum in the period 1963-1973 to 2.6 percent in 1973-80 while the corresponding growth rate for developing countries fell only from 5.6 percent to 5.2 percent (4). The deceleration was somewhat more dramatic for manufacturing output; the average growth rate fell from 5.8 percent, 1963-73, to 1.6 percent, 1973-80, in developed market economies and from 8.1 percent to 3.6 percent in developing countries (5). Although the performance of every developed market economy deteriorated after 1973, this did not happen in every developing country. Several developing countries showed a modest improvement in the growth rate of GDP after 1973 compared with the previous decade; the list includes Nigeria, Egypt, Indonesia, India, Malaysia, the Philippines and Chile (6).

If more up-to-date data were available, they would show a serious decline in growth rates over the period 1973-82 compared with the decade before 1973. This decline would be more dramatic for the industrialized countries than for other parts of the world, and for certain indicators (e.g. investment, in respect to which many countries experienced negative growth rates) it would be calamitous. There is strong evidence for a slowing down in growth; the hypothesis of emerging zero economic growth is more debatable.

It is still unclear, moreover, how far current economic problems may be cyclical, aggravated by some unexpected exogenous shocks, rather than secular. For instance, Otto Eckstein in a book written before the even deeper recession of 1979-82 argued that the recession of 1973-76 was "an episode not a turning point." He suggested that: "Double-digit inflation and the Great Recession were the results of new elements: an unpopular war, the first explosion of food prices in twenty years, and the organization of OPEC," all of them "major surprises (7)."

The contrary argument of secular stagnation associated with energy supply problems and associated price increases (i.e. the Miernyk hypothesis) is probably more popular. For example,

> if inadequate investment is coupled with sporadic oil supply interruptions and repeated sharp prices, such as were experienced in 1974 and 1979, the nation's material living standards could slide in the last twenty years of the century as rapidly as they rose in the twenty years after World War II (8).

There is merit in this point of view. Only a blind optimist would interpret the current lull of easy supplies and price stability as a sign of yet another change in trend.

There are several other explanations of slow growth

that can supplement or reinforce the resource scarcity
hypothesis. These will be mentioned in passing rather than
discussed extensively, since this is not a treatise on the
causes of slow growth however fascinating that topic may be.
Some (e.g. Walt Rostow, Jay Forrester) have argued that the
early 1970s was the beginning of the downswing of a
Kondratieff long-wave characterized by rising food and raw
material prices, higher rates of inflation, interest and
unemployment and slower rates of economic growth and
industrial investment. Yet others have suggested that
economic decline reflects the shrinking investment
opportunities found in advanced capitalist economies. This
is consistent with the increased internationalization of
production that has occurred in the last two decades (see
the next section). A slower rate of growth of world demand
combined with a greater dispersion of world supply implies
severe adjustment problems for the original industrial
producers (i.e. the industrialized countries), and
particularly for their older industrial regions. This
interpretation is supported by the fact that deceleration
tendencies have been stronger in the industrialized than in
the developing countries.

Another hypothesis is that there are built-in
retardation forces at work in mature economies, many of them
connected with the theory of eventual retardation in the
growth rates of individual industries. Mature economies can
maintain their aggregate growth rates only if they succeed
in diversifying their industrial structures with new
products and new industries. If they fail to achieve this,
their growth rates will decline. This hypothesis opens up a
Pandora's Box of explanations why some developed economies,
such as the United States and the United Kingdom, have
become less innovative and growth-minded. These range from
changing values (such as erosion of the work ethic) and
managerial failures (e.g. risk aversion, the use of scarce
capital for mergers rather than investment in process
development) to the cost of government regulations that
adversely affect competitiveness and the lack of incentives
for saving (and investment). The elimination of some of
these pathological symptoms would require only changes in
government policy, but others would require major societal
change. A related hypothesis is that the structural
transformation from an industrial to a post-industrial
economy (i.e. the shift from a production to a service
economy) leads to declining productivity and economic
atrophy (9).

There is clearly no shortage of hypotheses to explain
slow growth. This does not imply that the explanatory
hypotheses are convincing. For example, a United Nations
report concludes that:

The slowdown in growth in the developed market economy countries has, to date, defied satisfactory explanation. A central feature has been the decline in labor productivity. Among the reasons put forward in explanation of this phenomenon are changing attitudes toward work, the proliferation of government regulations, existing tax structures, accelerated inflation, shifts in relative prices, changes in the quality of the labor force, lack of adequate innovation and inadequate research and development. However, attempts to measure empirically the impact of such factors have proved inconclusive, and even the most meticulous statistical investigations into the sources of growth fail to explain why it has been slowing down persistently (10).

To avoid a detour, the rest of this paper will simply assume that slow growth is permanent. The justification for this apparently cavalier step is that if there is a serious probability of slow growth the regional scientist needs to begin to explore what implications this might have for regional policy.

Internationalization of Production, Slow Growth and the Regional Problem

One very specific explanation of slow growth, especially in the mature capitalist economies, is found in radical critiques of capitalism, and more particularly in the role of MNCs (multinational corporations). The problems of slow growth in demand, endemic under late capitalism, are compounded by actions of MNCs on the supply side. They have responded to declining rates of profit in host countries (e.g. the United States, Western Europe and Japan) by building plants in developing countries where the opportunities for exploiting labor (low wages equal high profits) are much greater. By leapfrogging in this way they have bypassed the lagging regions in the host country, because the latter do not offer them the same wage-cutting benefits (11). Thus, the increased internationalization of production has had dramatic effects on the lagging regions of developed countries. The rapid capital shifts by MNCs have resulted in regional and local policymakers having a much lower degree of leverage over them. Also, there are much greater risks that an individual region may lose its markets. Finally, attention to the social costs of capital movements (both in and out) are given less attention than economic efficiency, cost-cutting and profit maximization under conditions of slow growth (12).

The question arises as to whether these problems can be tackled by policy. Pickvance (13) has argued that in

Britain regional policy incentives are no longer intended to change the spatial distribution of industry but are merely a politically palatable means of giving massive subsidies to large-scale industry. The two pieces of evidence supporting this view are that regional policy incentives have favored capital-intensive firms with little pretense at trying to generate employment and that they have been very unselective in the sense that they have been given to firms that would have moved to the assisted regions in any event. Thus, the "British government's strategy is to hold on to a share of . . . internationally mobile investment by offering increasing levels of restructuring aid (14)." Holland (15) suggested an alternative strategy for "harnessing meso-economic power" (16) including the selective use of public enterprise, public-private planning agreements for location decisions, strong location of industry controls and threats of nationalization for MNCs that consider flight abroad.

In developing countries MNCs have tended to choose locations (except for resource industries) close to the primate city in the core region (17). Governments have been reluctant to attempt to control their location decisions on the ground that the MNCs may flex their meso-economic muscles and choose to go elsewhere (18). Thus, the MNCs have made little positive contribution to the attainment of regional policy objectives in developing countries. On the other hand, they have not contributed to slow growth there, since the agglomeration economies of the core region remain strong enough that centralized locations are consistent with economic efficiency and growth maximization.

Zero-Sum Game Implications of Slow Growth

There is widespread agreement that the end of the era of continued economic growth would have dramatic repercussions on society. Kenneth Boulding suggested that it would demand major changes in ways of thinking, habits and standards of decision-making, and in institutions (19). Noam Chomsky argued that continued economic growth was a safety valve for redistribution demands:

> The idea that economic growth will continue without limit has been a very effective device for controlling and limiting demands for redistribution of wealth . . . The notion of limitless growth could be employed to bring about consensus instead of conflict by overcoming the demands for redistribution of wealth, which would certainly be heard if one could not look forward to gaining more of life's benefits by some other method (20).

Similarly, Thurow (21) has argued that distributional issues, being very contentious, are among the most difficult questions for democracies to solve.

In the context of developing countries, the redistribution-with-growth strategy (22) was developed to tackle the problem that <u>trickle down</u> effects from uncontrolled growth were weak and appeared very late. The idea behind redistribution-with-growth was to redistribute the incremental output generated through growth by direct intervention by the government to redistribute productive assets to target groups (both the rural and urban poor). The argument was that the <u>haves</u> in developing countries might be persuaded by the political capital that might be created if at least part of the increment in growth were redistributed. But suppose the developing economies ceased to grow. The question of whether redistribution-<u>without</u>-growth is consistent with political stability is purely rhetorical.

The extension of these arguments to the regional policy sphere is rather obvious. Regional policy analysis has always assumed a growing economy in which redistribution of resources to lagging regions could be supported nationwide because it did not imply zero growth in the prosperous regions, only slower growth. But if the national economy ceases to grow (23) interregional development becomes a zero-sum game in which gains to lagging regions require absolute (as well as relative) losses in the rich regions. In the zero-sum situation, support for regional policies is likely to evaporate.

Escape from the Zero-Sum Dilemma?

Before discussing the regional policy implications of a slow growth economy, it may be worthwhile to explore the question of whether there is any escape from the zero-sum interregional development game. The first point is that even if slow growth is permanent, it does not mean that <u>zero</u> growth is imminent. If slow growth is due to resource scarcity, this constraint is an ultimate boundary not a tight chain. It will be more difficult for regions and nations to grow, but not necessarily impossible. The drive to grow by firms, regions and nations can, and will, continue. The real implication of slow growth is that we can no longer look for automatic, sustained economic growth to solve all our problems, especially the problems of distribution. Furthermore, to the extent that slow growth is the result of factors other than the law of diminishing return such as managerial failures, a declining innovation rate or the substitution of a leisure for a work ethic, then it is possible - though difficult and improbable - that the process could be reversed.

If slow growth is largely the result of energy supply problems, it would be defeatist to accept that <u>nothing</u> could be done about them. There is <u>some</u> scope for further exploration, better recovery methods, the development of alternative fuels, and more conservation (24). Also, to the extent that the problems have been exacerbated by runaway growth in energy demand, slow growth itself is part of the solution via its dampening effect on demand.

Moreover, the energy problem has widely differential effects from country to country. The worst sufferers are, and will be, those industrialized countries with fuel-hungry economies and negligible access to energy resources such as many West European countries and Japan and the low-income countries with zero resources and a limited capacity to pay world energy prices. The major oil producing countries are the major beneficiaries, of course, while several middle-income countries have recently discovered resources and begun to produce energy in sufficient quantities to meet their own needs.

Another argument, common among planners in developing countries, is that slow growth is an opportunity to be grasped rather than a source of regret. Why? As long as growth was guaranteed, policymakers could rely on trickle down hypotheses and redistribution-with-growth models to deliver higher living standards to lagging regions and the poor. That these mechanisms usually failed was casually ignored. But if aggregate growth ceases, these develop-ment-from-above mechanisms have to be abandoned. This creates a hospitable environment for experiments with novel strategies, variously labelled as development-from-below, self-reliance, basic needs development strategies, and selective spatial closure (25). It would be another detour to begin to describe what these approaches mean. However, most of them share common characteristics. These include: an emphasis upon the mobilization of unexploited local resources (e.g. the use of unemployed labor in community projects); the substitution of the benefits of sharing in decision-making for increases in material welfare; a focus on satisfying human needs through the provision of low-cost services rather than via the proliferation of consumer goods; rejection of high GNP growth rates for their own sake on the grounds that they are likely to be associated with an unequal distribution of income; and a variety of policy instruments for the protection of local industries, for guiding the structure of production towards labor-intensive basic goods and for stopping leakages from local development impulses into other parts of the national economic system. Obviously, these strategies have more chance of being adopted in low-income countries not tainted by modernization or in very rich countries with nonconformists jaded by materialism (communes in Oregon or small villages in Maine and Vermont?).

The zero-sum game hypothesis in a regional policy context assumes that the benefits of policies to aid assisted regions will be at the expense of non-assisted

267

regions. As reported by Brian Ashcroft elsewhere in this book (Part III), this need not be the case. First, regional policy incentives have attracted foreign investment which might not otherwise have come to a particular country (e.g. in the United Kindgom, Belgium, Ireland). This is an extension to the world level of the argument that zero national growth is compatible with positive growth in some but not all regions. Zero world growth is equally compatible with positive national growth, especially for countries that are favored in international capital markets. Second, there is evidence that regional policy incentives have induced local assisted-area firms to expand, and only a fraction of this can be explained by substitution for growth elsewhere (e.g. income multiplier effects now retained locally that were formerly transmitted nationally). Third, and possibly most important, the spatial redistribution of national aggregate demand could raise the effective production potential of the economy (for example, by dampening inflation rates in the regions with the tighter labor markets) (26).

The implication of the retardation hypothesis discussed above is that mature economies can combat slow growth only by diversifying their industrial structures by promoting new innovations, new products and processes, and new industries. In the United States in recent years this argument has generated considerable pressure for a national industrial policy to encourage this process. Although it is possible that a national industrial policy could be directed towards shoring up declining industries, most economists would recommend the opposite - that national industrial policy should reinforce the private market by helping it to select and promote the winners. Since the problems of lagging regions are very often the result of specialization in declining industries (national losers), this suggests a direct conflict between the aims of industrial policy and those of regional policy (27). According to this view, policies to fight slow growth in the aggregate economy would make regional problems worse and the implementation of regional policies more difficult (28).

However, there might be two possible escape routes from this dilemma. One is to promote the rapidly growing industries in the lagging regions. This is not as difficult as in, say, developing countries because lagging regions in mature economies usually have the necessary prerequisites in the form of infrastructure, services and labor pools. However, in the United States, regional policy incentives have never had enough teeth to overcome corporate locational preferences, while West European experience suggests that such incentives have a high probability of being effective only when combined with controls on industrial development in the non-assisted regions.

268

The second solution might be to promote the small-scale business sector as a means of reconciling national regional policy and national industrial policy. In the United States, for example, 60 percent of jobs are created in firms of less than twenty workers while perhaps one-half of all jobs are created by independent small entrepreneurs. Also, small firms account for a substantial proportion of all industrial inventions and innovation, and make a dispro-portionate contribution to new technological advances. This raises the possibility that promoting small businesses in lagging regions might stimulate job creation <u>and</u> promote productivity growth and innovations, thereby serving both regional and industrial policy goals. Unfortunately, this prescription has a major snag. The firms and industries that create many jobs are not the same firms and industries that are high-productivity or innovative. As a result, the trade-off between industrial growth policy and regional policy appears unavoidable.

> Recommendations for support of low-productivity industries do not mesh well with the primary aims of industrial policy - national efficiency, export expansion, import substitution, and GNP growth - even when justified by regional concentration of troubled industries. Similarly, recommendations for support of high-productivity activities (often very capital intensive, with limited employment opportunities concentrated in high-paying jobs) do not always support regional-policy objectives of employment growth, particularly among the low-skilled or long-term unemployed (29).

Some years ago, I drew the distinction between <u>competi-tive</u> growth according to which "the growth of one region is always at the expense of another," clearly the zero-sum game case, and <u>generative</u> growth, whereby "the growth performance of an individual region can be raised . . . without neces-sarily adversely affecting the growth rate of its neigh-bors (30)." Generative growth should not be equated with the discredited growth-promoting regional policies of the 1960s and early 1970s. Instead, it is similar to self-reliant regional growth strategies. Even without the stimulus of outside aid, there may be some scope for local and regional policymakers to intervene to improve local prospects for development. True, these actions are not going to be of sufficient magnitude to have enough of a feedback effect on the national growth rate to eliminate slow growth, but they offer some alternative to the defeat-ist alternative of lying down and allowing slow growth to take its toll on lagging regions. Actions might include improvements in intraregional spatial organization, eliminating bottlenecks in the transport or public service systems and creating conditions favorable to local economic development (e.g. policies to provide risk capital for small indigenous entrepreneurs). A striking example of the scope for generative growth approaches is policies to promote small-scale industries in the secondary towns of peripheral regions in developing countries, where the major constraint on expansion is not the lack of effective demand but of credit and technical assistance. These and similar types of intervention are a much preferable strategy to the policy alternative implied by the competitive growth model, namely, interregional competitive bidding to attract the shrinking volume of mobile industry.

Do the considerations discussed in this section add up to the conclusion that slow growth can be controlled and its zero-sum game implications for interregional development avoided? Unfortunately not. They suggest that the situation is not so bleak that recognition of slow growth should be interpreted as approval of inaction but they are, in the end, palliatives rather than solutions. The need for reassessing the appropriateness of regional policies under conditions of slow growth remains as strong as ever.

Regional Policies in Recessions

There have been no observable experiences of how regional policies might work under conditions of slow growth. The only possible period that might qualify as an era of secular stagnation is the 1930s (and even in this case a better description might be a very deep and long depression), but at that time regional policies were either in their infancy or, in some countries, did not exist. However, there are some experiences of the effectiveness of regional policies during cyclical recessions. Since it may be possible to extrapolate from the conditions of short-term recession to those of long-run slow growth, examining regional policies in recession periods is a reasonable starting point.

For a variety of reasons regional policies do not work very well in recessions. There is a shift in the policy-makers' preoccupations; they become much less concerned with the spatial distribution of output and employment than with their overall levels. Also, recessions lead to a sharp fall in government revenues, so that the resources available for regional expenditures, and the willingness to make these expenditures, decline. Firms become unresponsive to whatever incentives are offered, because the willingness to relocate is much stronger in conditions of rapid growth, especially since many firms move because they lack the space for expanding capacity at their existing site. As for individuals, the capacity of migrants to move out of areas with poor employment opportunities is reduced because both the monetary resources to finance a move are reduced and the incentives to move (e.g. expanding job opportunities) are weaker.

A more complex argument is that the rationale for regional policies is eroded during recessions. Particularly in countries where ratios of unemployment compensation to wages are high and where automatic stabilizers are powerful, the gap between recession and boom income levels is narrower in lagging than in prosperous regions. Furthermore, differentials in rates of unemployment between regions narrow because of such influences as the specialization of the more prosperous regions in rapidly growing but cyclically unstable industries. A more ambiguous point is the location of temporarily closed plants in multiplant firms: in some cases closures are spatially concentrated in the lagging regions because transport cost differentials make plants located there the high-cost establishments; in other situations, the peripherally located branch plants are the last to be shut down because, being more recent, they embody a superior (i.e. more efficient) technology. Higher absolute levels of unemployment are found everywhere and localized pockets of severe recession may be almost as frequent in the leading as in the lagging regions. In these circumstances, the government may (as the British government has in recent years) increase spatial selectivity in the distribution of its reduced regional policy expenditures, but over the country as a whole break away from the sole focus on lagging regions. Since the manufacturing sector is the most cyclically sensitive, there may also be a shift of regional policy efforts in recessions periods towards promoting service industries and/or dispersing government employment.

In recessions with high levels of unemployment, the need to create jobs anywhere dominates over the desirability of creating jobs at particular locations. Hence, regional policies have to compete on the same basis with other employment-creating measures. Can they compete? There is a dearth of research on this question, but one study of British experience (31) suggested that per capita job creation costs from regional incentives were "of the same order of magnitude" as from other fiscal measures. If this were generally true, it would imply that there is no justification for deserting regional policies during cyclical recessions.

This brief review suggests that it is much more difficult to implement regional policies during recessions. Also, the most favored strategy of inducing industry to relocate to lagging regions or, as is more common, persuading new firms and additions to capacity to relocate is particularly ineffective. There has not been a serious concern with this problem among policymakers because recessions turn around and the policies begin to work again.

271

Of course, this solution - evaporation of the problem - cannot be expected under conditions of slow growth.

Regional Policy Options Under Slow Growth

Slow growth does not suggest a single unambiguous policy prescription. Instead, it points to a range of different regional policy options, which might be used singly or in combination. However, what is clear is that many of the policy approaches that were followed in the 1960s and 1970s are inappropriate for economies suffering from slow growth. This is because they were almost all aimed at promoting economic growth in lagging regions under the assumptions that aggregate economic growth would continue at a healthy rate and that the policy problem merely consisted of diverting a higher share of this growth to the less developed and/or depressed regions.

These obsolete policy measures include locational fiscal incentives to persuade firms to relocate from leading to lagging regions. Such measures work only when the volume of interregionally mobile industry is substantial, and this volume is a direct function of the rate of industrial growth. As this rate declines towards zero the volume of mobile industry becomes progressively smaller. In these conditions, either locational incentives are too small with no results, or, if large enough to have any effect, they merely induce firms to relocate for the fiscal benefits without increasing growth. In fact, this could lead both to premature abandonment of production facilities in the area of origin and to efficiency losses associated with diversion from an optimal location. Similarly, growth center strategies are even more likely to fail in slow growth economies because their initial stimulus is industrial dynamism and the intersectoral linkages around one or more propulsive industries. The concept of a propulsive industry obviously needs re-examination under conditions of slow growth.

The first policy option is to accept that regional policies, at least of the place-oriented kind, will not work and to find alternative means of dealing with the equity objectives that are traditionally used to justify regional development policies. This option has two variations. The first is to abandon regional policies, to rely on macro and sectoral policies to maximize GNP, to the extent that slow growth constraints permit, and then to redistribute part of the benefits of this growth from richer to poorer regions. A justification for this approach is that the search for greater economic efficiency and higher production becomes more important than ever under slow growth, and efficiency losses are tolerated much less. The strategy clearly accepts the zero-sum game approach. It is concerned with developing a mechanism for the most equitable distribution of a fixed pie, or at best a slowly growing one. An

272

improved revenue sharing program might be such a mechanism. According to this strategy, interregional transfer payments arranged through the taxation system substitute for the regional development expenditures of traditional regional policy programs. The approach has the substantial advantage that it minimizes <u>net</u> national government expenditures which will be perpetually sluggish under slow growth conditions. On the other hand, a serious drawback is that it probably involves <u>absolute</u> income sacrifices by the populations of the richer regions. Thus, interregional conflict may become more serious, even explosive.

The second variant is the substitution of people-oriented policies for place-oriented policies (32). This also means a clear redistribution strategy, except that the redistribution takes the form of transfers to individuals rather than to local and regional governments as implied by revenue sharing approaches. People-oriented approaches in a regional policy context cover a variety of measures. These include income maintenance programs and reform of direct taxation to reduce poverty regardless of location, welfare payments to immobile populations locked in severely depressed regions, and relocation assistance to migrants from areas with an excess supply of labor to areas where labor markets are closer to equilibrium. In general, the balance among income maintenance, welfare payments and relocation assistance (33) will depend upon the political and institutional conditions prevailing in a particular country. However, whatever the mix chosen, by focusing on the needs of individuals this approach implicitly accepts the argument that regional development policies are merely an indirect way of improving their welfare. This argument has merit even under conditions of rapid economic growth when people-oriented and place-oriented policies become <u>feasible</u> alternative means to reach the same end. Its strength is reinforced under slow growth, however, because the alternative strategy of mainstream regional development policies is almost bound to fail.

A second major policy option does not call for the abandonment of regional policy, but instead makes the case for regional policies that are very different from those pursued in the past. Such a change would again reflect a shift from economic development towards more emphasis on equity and individual welfare. For example, a shift of focus from regional economic development policy to regional <u>social</u> policy might be highly appropriate under slow growth. In many countries, especially developing countries, lagging regions suffer severely from deficiencies in social services (health, education and general social services) and in social infrastructure and public facilities (34). The political objections that arise in discussions to transfer income directly from rich to poor regions are much more difficult to mobilize where the policy aims at giving priority to backward regions in social service provision on the ground that the prevailing levels of services lag severely behind accepted national standards. Moreover, the design of social sector policies may imply very different regional impacts even if the content of the policy is superficially devoid of spatial considerations. For instance, a policy emphasizing primary education rather than tertiary education and primary health care rather than high-technology curative medical care will discriminate in favor of rural and against highly urbanized regions. The most important attraction of regional social policies is undoubtedly their political acceptability. A policy goal of equalizing social services per capita among regions will (in most cases) absorb substantial resources and require these to be transferred from rich to poor regions (35), but the goal is probably much more palatable to the residents of prosperous regions than a goal of income equalization.

The potential conflict between industrial and regional policy was discussed above. The negative conclusions of that discussion were based largely on analysis of the situation in the United States so that the topic merits a brief re-examination in the context of slow-growth conditions. There are two approaches to industrial policy in these conditions. One is to concentrate on the stagnating and declining sectors by attempting to slow down the decline of older industries; the other is to foster an environment favorable to the spawning and rapid growth of new industries (e.g. the high-tech strategy). The first is likely to be more consistent with regional policy since the older industries tend to be spatially concentrated in either lagging or potentially lagging regions. The second will probably conflict with regional policy goals, in developing countries by encouraging continued development in the primate city and the core region, in developed countries by favoring the newer regions rather than the older industrial regions. Although the first option may be more attractive from the regional policy prospective, it would be dangerous for the mature industrial economy to adopt since such a course of action would only hasten its decline relative to newly developing economies.

On the other hand, whereas the shoring-up approach is inadvisable as an overall industrial strategy, this does not rule out the possibility of some defensive actions on the regional policy front to help to alleviate the problems of industrial structure in lagging regions. For example, it would not be a good idea to use semi-permanent public subsidies to keep uncompetitive firms in business or to introduce the frequently recommended policy of charging exit taxes to firms that wish to relocate to improve efficiency. On the other hand, there may be reasonably efficient types of public intervention that might be helpful. Interregional differentials in the growth of firms (hence, output and employment) are often primarily explained by differentials in the closure rate of establishments, with starts more evenly distributed. Local governments, in particular, may be able to slow down closures by various actions at critical phases in a firm's history. Even if these actions have a fiscal cost, they may be justified if the aid is temporary rather than permanent. Of course, such actions should be focused on potentially viable firms that run the risk of bankruptcy because of temporary misfortunes not on chronically uncompetitive firms that are bound to go out of business sooner or later.

In the highly unusual situation where economic growth is close to zero and interregional differentials in economic performance are substantial <u>but</u> interregional cost differentials are small, it may be justified for governments to persuade firms to relocate even if no net growth can be expected. However, this special case does not require the retention of a general program of regional locational incentives. Instead, it suggests the desirability of targeting financial assistance to overcome the transaction costs associated with moving, i.e. the relocation costs.

Another <u>nationally</u> justifiable strategy is the deployment of any policies that do not involve heavy public expenditures to attract or retain international industrial investment in lagging regions. Holland's recommendations for "harnessing meso-economic power" mentioned above (36) would not be appealing to market-oriented economies, but they may be able to divise an alternative approach based on incentives that by attracting foreign investment and creating jobs might create more government revenue than their cost.

Historically, most job decentralization efforts have focused on the manufacturing sector. This focus is in current circumstances misdirected. Manufacturing is the most serious victim in slow-growth economies. Moreover, its job-creating potential per unit of investment is much lower than the services sector. In post-industrial society the service sector continues to perform well even under conditions of slow growth. The problem here lies in identifying those components of the service sector that are locationally mobile. A substantial proportion of it consists of personal services, commerce and small-scale business services that are local and remain dependent on the formal manufacturing sector. But in most countries the national government remains a major employer and a considerable proportion of its labor force is engaged in routine functions that can be decentralized. Also, changes in communications technologies provide an unprecedented opportunity for the successful dispersion of quaternary offices.

275

Since government revenues are likely to be sluggish under conditions of slow growth, policies that are economical of government expenditures deserve particular attention. This accounts for the appeal of self-balancing tax-subsidy schemes with which the government, in effect, compulsorily arranges interregional transfer payments through the private sector. For example, cross-subsidy schemes to compensate peripheral regions for specific locational disadvantages (e.g. in transport, energy costs), whereby consumers in rich regions are charged above-cost prices to enable those in the lagging regions to be supplied at less than cost, would fall into this category. The most attractive type of tax-subsidy scheme, however, would apply to the industrial sector, either as a whole or in part. Firms in prosperous regions would be taxed in order to subsidize those in lagging regions. This would change interregional production costs, stimulating industrial growth in the latter while discouraging it in the former. Although a more powerful tool under robust growth conditions, the policy could also work under slow growth. From the point of view of the national economy, the only requirement would be that the growth induced in the lagging regions should be at least equal to the growth deterred in the more prosperous regions. As suggested above, there are reasons for believing that this condition may frequently be satisfied.

Given the importance of job creation goals in regional policy, a wage subsidy would seem to be the most appropriate form of subsidy. Glickman (37) lists several advantages of wage subsidies: they are good substitutes for income-maintenance programs in terms of their impact; they promote the substitution of labor for capital; they can easily be targeted to specific groups; they can attract workers, including discouraged workers, into the labor force; and they may even have a marginal impact in reducing the inflationary rate via their favorable effect on wage costs. Financing a wage subsidy in peripheral regions by a tax on capital in core regions might be the optimal strategy from the point of view of regional policy and employment goals (38).

Since some of the above arguments imply that the national government is much less effective as the source of regional policy intervention when the aggregate economic growth rate falls, local governments, community organizations and private sector initiative may step in to fill the void. If it is much more difficult to attract or divert resources from elsewhere, the local development process must be <u>endogenized</u>. This implies the mobilization of local resources and their more efficient reallocation to ensure a pattern of development that is less dependent on external economic conditions. This suggests, as discussed above, the

relevance of <u>generative</u> <u>growth</u>, <u>self-reliant</u> <u>development</u> and
<u>selective</u> <u>spatial</u> <u>closure</u> concepts. The underlying assump-
tions of these strategies are: lagging regions currently
operate <u>inside</u> rather than on their production possibility
frontiers; and, under slow growth conditions, the impulses
from other regions and abroad are, more likely than not,
negative so that the costs of regional closure are much
lower than in conditions of rapid growth. Unfortunately,
while these self-reliant strategies have a substantial <u>a</u>
<u>priori</u> plausibility, there is little practical experience of
how they work in practice, and what their operational
content would be. But they do underline the point that
while slow growth is a constraint it does not have to be a
noose.

Finally, if slow growth is closely associated with
resource scarcities, especially of energy resources, this
offers a new challenge to regional policy. Since these
resources are not uniformly distributed but are spatially
concentrated in a few regions, their development creates new
kinds of inter-area equity problems, such as the recent
debate in the United States about whether or not State
severance taxes should be federalized. Also, resource
exploitation creates serious intertemporal problems of
development, namely the familiar boom-bust pattern of
growth. There is considerable scope for designing regional
development policies for resource-rich regions based on
optimal rates of exploitation (i.e. orderly development
paths that maximize long-run rents and avoid the boom-bust
cycle) and promoting high social rates of return (particularly from the perspective of improving local income
distribution; resource exploitation is a notoriously
regressive form of economic activity).

Conclusion

This paper was initially inspired by Bill Miernyk's
argument that energy and other resource constraints were
bringing the era of rapid economic growth to an end, and as
a result interregional growth in the United States would
become a zero-sum game in which the energy-rich regions
would continue to grow at the expense of the others. This
new situation required dramatic changes in attitudes to
regional policy, shifting the emphasis from the promotion of
economic development to mechanisms for redistributing income
from rich to poor regions and for aiding individuals (e.g.
relocation assistance).

These arguments were partially accepted in this study.
The hypothesis of slow growth was examined in a world-wide
context and complementary explanations in addition to
resource scarcity were suggested. These included the
effects of internationalization of production, built-in
retardation forces in mature economies, and the possibility

of a Kondratieff downswing.

Also discussed was the possibility of escape routes from the zero-sum game dilemma. These include the feasibility of relief from energy resource constraints (and slow growth constraints in general), the potential for self-reliant and generative growth strategies, the possible reconciliation of industrial policy and regional policy, and the arguments in favor of the hypothesis that the spatial redistribution of economic activity might raise aggregate output even in a slow growth economy. However, these possibilities are merely palliatives, not solutions.

Although there is little experience of regional policy under slow growth conditions, there is considerable evidence regarding what happens to regional policies in cyclical recessions. The volume of interregionally mobile industry dries up, regional development expenditures decline, and migration rates fall off. The attention of policymakers turns from regional to macroeconomic and sectoral concerns. On the other hand, interregional unemployment rates and income gaps narrow, in part because of the specialization of prosperous regions in cyclically unstable industries. However, if regional policies can create jobs at a cost comparable to other job-creation measures, the desertion of regional policies in recessions may not be justified.

Slow growth conditions suggest the need to abandon traditional regional development policies such as locational fiscal incentives to firms and growth center policies. However, other regional policy options may be more relevant: a focus on macro and sectoral policies to maximize GNP combined with improved revenue sharing programs to redistribute income to lagging regions; the substitution of people-oriented strategies, such as income maintenance policies and relocation assistance, for place-oriented strategies; the substitution of regional social policy, stressing elimination of lags in health, educational and social service provision in poorer regions, for regional economic development policy; the search for industrial policies that might help the older industrial regions without resorting to permanent subsidies (helping to avoid plant closures especially by local efforts, targeting fiscal assistance to cover relocation costs, measures to attract or retain international investment, and focusing relocation efforts on the government and service sectors rather than the manufacturing sector); the development of self balancing tax-subsidy schemes to minimize public expenditures; the mobilization of local resources in self-reliant development strategies; and the implementation of policies to smooth out the development paths in resource-rich regions.

278

NOTES

1.   W. H. Miernyk, <u>Regional Analysis and Regional Policy</u> (Oelgeschlager, Gunn and Hain, Cambridge, MA, 1982).
2.   See U. S. President, <u>The Economic Report of the President</u> (U.S. Government Printing Office, Washington, D.C., 1980). Of all industrialized countries, only West Germany maintained a respectable performance, with a decline from 4.6 percent to 3.2 percent. But conditions in West Germany have deteriorated sharply since 1979.
3.   United Nations Conference on Trade and Development (UNCTAD), <u>Trade and Development Report 1982</u> (United Nations, New York, 1982) 3 volumes.
4.   Ibid, Volume II, p. 88.
5.   Ibid, Volume II, p. 117.
6.   Ibid, Volume II, p. 118.
7.   O. Eckstein, <u>The Great Recession</u> (North Holland, New York, 1978), p. 151.
8.   W. F. Thompson, J. F. Karagonis and K. D. Wilson, <u>Choice over Chance: Economic and Energy Options for the Future</u> (Praeger, New York, 1981), pp. 165-166.
9.   See K. Hughes, <u>Corporate Response to Declining Rates of Growth</u> (Lexington Books, Lexington, MA, 1982), pp. 3-48 and E. F. Renshaw, <u>The End of Progress: Adjusting to a No-Growth Economy</u> (Duxbury Press, North Scitvate, MA, 1976) for an elaboration of some of these arguements.
10. UNCTAD, op. cit., Volume II, p. 3.
11. S. Holland, <u>Capital Versus the Regions</u> (Macmillan, London, 1976).
12. N. J. Glickman and E. M. Petras, "International Capital and International Labor Flows: Implications for Public Policy," Working Paper No. 53 in Regional Science and Transportation, University of Pennsylvania, Philadelphia, August, 1981.
13. C. G. Pickvance, "Policies as Chameleons: An Interpretation of Regional Policy and Office Policy in Britain," in M. Dear and A. J. Scott (eds.), <u>Urbanization and Urban Planning in Capitalist Society</u> (Methver, London, 1981).
14. Ibid, p. 260.
15. Holland, op. cit.
16. The meso-economic sector represents a middle layer between the macro level of national economic policy and the micro level of the small competitive firm. It consists of MNCs and other large-scale firms that wield almost independent power and are difficult to control by national governments.
17. However, domestic firms are even more reluctant to decentralize.
18. This argument may not be very strong. MNCs frequently operate plants in a particular developing country

279

to supply the expanding domestic market behind high tariff walls rather than to export (H. W. Richardson, "Industrial Policy and Regional Development in Less-Developed Countries," in M. E. Bell and P. S. Lande (eds.), Regional Dimensions of Industrial Policy (Lexington Books, Lexington, MA, 1982) pp 93-120).

19. This suggestion was made in a speech in May 1978 quoted by Hughes, op. cit., p. 3.

20. W. L. Oltmans (ed.), On Growth (Capricom Books, New York, 1974), p. 285.

21. L. C. Thurow, The Zero-Sum Society: Distribution and the Possibilities for Economic Change (Basic Books, New York, 1980).

22. H. Chenery, et al, Redistribution with Growth (Oxford University Press, London, 1974).

23. Note that although zero economic growth is a fairly extreme case it is not the limiting case since national economies can decline.

24. W. F. Thompson, et al, op. cit.; D. Yergin and M. Hillenbrand (eds.), Global Insecurity: A Strategy for Energy and Economic Revival (Houghton and Mifflin, New York, 1982).

25. W. B. Stohr and D. R. F. Taylor, Development from Above or Below? The Dialectics of Regional Planning in Developing Countries (Wiley, New York, 1981).

26. See B. Higgins, "Trade-off Curves and Regional Gaps," in J. Bhagwati and R. S. Eckaus (eds.), Development and Planning: Essays in Honour of Paul Rosenstein Rodan (Allen and Unwin, London, 1973).

27. G. C. Cameron, "The National Industrial Strategy and Regional Policy," in D. Maclennan and J. B. Parr (eds.), Regional Policy: Past Experiences and New Directions (Martin Robertston, Oxford, 1979), pp. 279-322.

28. M. E. Bell and P. S. Lande (eds.), Regional Dimensions of Industrial Policy (Lexington Books, Lexington, MA, 1982).

29. H. A. Garn and L. C. Ledebur, "Congruencies and Conflicts in Regional and Industrial Policies," in Bell and Lande, op. cit., p. 49.

30. H. W. Richardson, Regional Growth Theory (Macmillan, London, 1973), pp. 86-88.

31. J. Marquand, "Measuring the Effects and Costs of Regional Incentives," (Department of Industry, Her Majesty's Government, Government Economic Service Workshop Paper No. 32, London, 1980).

32. The main rationale for place-oriented policies in the past is that they would be efficient in the long run by promoting sustained economic development. However, if economic development opportunities are very limited and may become more rather than less so in the future, it makes more sense to help people directly.

280

33. Relocation assistance is merely one example of measures to increase the income-earning potential of individuals. Education and training programs and other forms of human resource investments are another example. However, their record has been generally poor because of the neglect of demand for labor considerations. In the absence of complementary measures to increase labor demand, they operate largely as an indirect form of relocation assistance (if the trainees subsequently move) or as a more palatable form of welfare payment (if the trainees remain immobile and unemployed).

34. This generalization is not univerally valid. For instance, O. J. Firestone ("Regional Economic and Social Disparity," in O. J. Firestone (ed.), <u>Regional Economic Development</u> (University of Ottawa Press, Ottawa, 1974), pp. 205-267) found that regional disparities in social indicators in Canada are much narrower than regional income disparities.

35. The two main exceptions to this conclusion are where the richer regions have lower per capita services (perhaps because of differential population pressure) and where governments require full cost recovery from users for all services supplied.

36. Holland, op. cit.

37. N. J. Glickman, "Emerging Urban Policies in a Slow-Growth Economy: Conservative Initiatives and Progressive Responses," Working Paper No. 49 in Regional Science and Transportation, University of Pennsylvania, Philadelphia, May, 1981.

38. Taxing one factor in some locations to subsidize another factor in other locations may result in complex production distrotions that are difficult to measure. Intuitively, these distortions are probably quite small.

SOME PERSPECTIVES ON THE FUTURE OF REGIONAL DEVELOPMENT POLICY

George J. Demko

There can be little doubt that the issue of regional development is an important and universal problem. Every nation with only rare exceptions is, has been, or will be confronted with guilt, unrest, and even violence related to problems of regional inequity. The Brazilian Northeast, Appalachia of the U.S., Catalonia, Normandy, Slovakia, the Hungarian Plain, the Mezzogiorno, and many, many more examples the world over represent deprived regions from either real or perceived causes in economic, political or other terms. In some nations these are urgent issues, in others old nagging problems, and in yet others, potential powder-kegs. Despite such persistence and visibility regional problems rarely occupy a pre-eminent place in the minds of national leaders. The issues of economic efficiency, national defense, public health and others dominate most national agendas. Regional problems consequently are left all too often to smolder and are subjected to temporary palliatives when they come to the point of national attention or erupt.

The argument for such disregard is that efficiency policies in economic development will trickle down economic benefits to all regions eventually. It is also argued that development is a zero-sum issue and thus resources are better spent in highly productive regions. This may not be the case for all regions, however, and, indeed, less efficient short-term investments may lead to long-term efficiency in lagging regions and significantly affect overall national productivity. This is clearly an issue which merits much more research attention.

In the arena of regional development theory it is also apparent that greater attention must be paid to variables other than economic. Cultural, ethnic, environmental, psychic and many other elusive dimensions must be added to our concepts and models if true notions of regional equity are to be achieved. Obviously our measurement of regional differences and levels suffers drastically from standard

282

economic determinism. Preference structures of regional populations are rarely ever investigated in constructing our classification schemes.

Given the present state of affairs, even if regional development theory were fully developed, its result or offspring, regional policy would appear to be subsidiary and secondary to national aggregate economic policy. Thus, attitudes of planners and politicians must also be altered.

In terms of regional policy measures and programs there exists a similar myopia. Decision-making regarding "cures" rests usually in the economic center with little attention to the population of the lagging regions and their needs or their perception of their needs. Most policy measures are applied with little regard to monitoring mechanisms, cost-benefit analysis, or predicted time-horizons for success. Indeed, even regional policy goals or definitions for success are rarely obvious.

There can be little doubt that regional problems will not go away. Given their relative permanence it is important to study their many dimensions. Eastern and Western Europe are particularly important in this regard in that a) there is a long record of experience in dealing with regional development problems and applying regional policies, b) there is a wide variety of types of states - socialist, mixed, large, small, c) and there exists the longest and best record of commitment to solving regional problems. Although the latter has been insufficient to bring about solutions at this point in time, there has been much learned and thus some mistakes may be avoided in other areas. The most important task, however, is to continue our work to understand regional processes, to share our knowledge and, once sure of our ground, transform this knowledge into effective policy.

Printed in the United States
by Baker & Taylor Publisher Services